A Time We Remember

Celebrating a Century in Our Quad-Cities

by Bill Wundram and the Quad-City Times

published by the Quad-City Times

To Mert & Joanie —
Happy Holidays
and Best Wishes for
3000 and Beyond

Bill Wundram
1999

Acknowledgments

The *A Time We Remember* book team: Bill Wundram, author; Deborah Brasier, editor/production coordinator; Peggy Dykes, Rebecca Heidgerken, Thomas Heidgerken, Jeanne S. Ketelaar, Pat Lee, Whitney L. Smith, Shari Tisinger, production; Roy Booker, research; Craig Brown, quality control; Craig Chandler, photo director; Greg Boll, Jeff Cook, Larry Fisher, Geoff Krieger, John Schultz, photography.

Compiling a book of the size and scope of *A Time We Remember* would not have been possible without the advice, assistance and generosity of many individuals. When the call went out for photographs, memorabilia and remembrances from a century in our Quad-Cities, the response was overwhelming. In all, more than 200 *Quad-City Times* readers rooted through scrapbooks, shoe boxes, trunks — every place where pieces of the past are kept — to offer contributions. Those "loans" are what give this book its unique personality. And so, we are eternally grateful to:

Allyn Adams, Kenneth Ahrens, Bob Anderson, Alice Andresen, William Baltzer, Bob Balzer, Bernice Bell, Willard Bevins, Rita Blanchard, Michael Blaser, Donald Bohms, Harry Boll, Blaine Bolte, Bill Boots, Mrs. Russell Bowers, Dale Brooks, Dolores Bultinck, Phil Caldwell, Ardean Carlson, Ellie Carlson, John Carver, Gordon Cavanaugh, Gloria Cesar, Don Challed, William Cleaver, E.L. Conard, Boyd Conklin, Raymond "Choo Choo" Conwell, Linda Cook, Rose Cowley, Hazel Cox, Robert Cramer, Judy Creen, Kenneth Criger, Louise Curry, Ralph Curtis, Jerri Daebelliehn, Marie and Tony DeKezel, Joan DePaepe, Barbara Dockery, Herb Doden, Nancy Dopler, Jack Downing, Rev. Cliff Egert, Helen Elmergreen, Bj Elsner, Carol Erickson, Jane Ernst, Jane Erps, Delores Esbaum, Walter Fitchner, J. Fladlein, Vicki Forlini, Jean Franck, Vera Frank, Ed Froehlich, Dick Froeschle, Judith A. Colgan Fuller, Louis Gaeta, Tom Getz, William Getz, D.E. Gano Hansell, Mike Gawrysiak, Jane Gibson, James Godke, Vicki Gray, Charley Grayson, Lynn Cutler Gronke, Marlon Groy, Opal Gruemmer, Marjorie Gustafson, Greg Gutgsell, E.L. Hamann, G.R. Hamann, Dr. Alan Hathaway, Mary Laing Haynes, Shirley Hazen, Harold Heath, Tom Heidgerken, Ed Heisterman, Karl Hellman, Elmer Henning, Ralph Heuer, Arn Hilbert, Leon Hoffmann, Mildred Hofmann, Lois Holzinger, Bill Homrighausen, Harold Huggins, Clarissa Hunt, Gladys Ihlefeld, Clemma Isenberg, Harriet Jackson, Alan Jansen, Arlene Jens, Lois and Wayne Johnson, Pat Johnson, Margo Jones, Wil Juckem, Janet Kademan, Dale Keeler, Lois Kempton, Jean Keppy, Ruth Killinger, Forrest Kilmer, Joseph Kimmel, Dorothy Kingsbury, Sally Klemme, Harold Krause, Frances Kruse, Jane Laedke, Dorothy Lage, Tom Lagomarcino, Sr., Joe Larson, John Lavelle, Julie Leabo, Dwight Leckington, Mary M. Legler, E.J. Leonard, Michael Liebbe, Joan Lindle, Bob Lindquist, Bob Lofgren, Tim Long, Margaret Loter, Joyce Luckritz, Mary MacKenzie, Dick McGrady, Merlin Madsen, Kit Mayer, Ron Medd, Del Menke, Janet Meyer, Douglas Miller, Janet Miller, Norman Miller, Penelope Miller, Barbara Mohr, Connie Mohr-Wright, Max Molleston, Kay Mongiat, Charles and Elda Marie Morgan, Clara Mortiboy, Donna Muilenberg, Robert Mulvihill, Clara Myers, Doris Nelson, Glenn Nelson, Jeanette Nelson, Phyllis Neville, Vivian Niehaus, Thelma Nopolous, Don Ockleman, C.W. O'Hare, Dolores Orr, John Page, Lou Parker, Ray Pasvogel, William Perry, Mrs. C.E. Pfitzmaier, Dick Pianca, Harvey Prinz, Elsie Quick, Larry Radetzki, Mrs. Orlo Rahn, Franciska Rasmussen, Frances Rathbun, Wanda Rathje, Carol Reynolds, Betty Richter, Del Riefe, Kathie Robertson, Mary Ann Robinson, L.R. Roeder, Fran Roederer, Bob Ross, Shirley Glynn Rucker, Dwain Ruser, Bob Sass, Imogene Brown Saunders, June Schindler, Nancy Schmidt, John Schnekloth, Mildred Schnekloth, Lois Schoene, Ernest Schroeder, D. Schwener, Weir Sears, Jr., Larry Shannon, Lloyd Shelangoski, Yvonne Mumford Simpson, Margaret Sinkhorn, Whitney Smith, Ila B. Smock, Cindy Soltau, Lloyd Speak, Dick Stahl, Bob Stewart, Ben Stoneking, Don Stormer, Dr. John Sunderbruch, Dorothy Efflandt Swanson, Les Swanson, Sally Switchboard, Nancy Tabor, Elsie Teas, Joe Terronez, Glen Thede, Barbara Tiemeyer, Roald Tweet, Boyd VanLandegan, John VanSpeybroeck, Marjorie VanWinkle, Henry Vargas, Don Verschoore, John Vize, Ed Voss, Don Wachal, Don Wall, Carolyn Walters, Ken Warren, Arretta Wetzel, Kay Whan, Janet Willetts, Karen Williams, Beverly Witmer, Theresa Witt, Robert Worman, Dorothy Wulf, William Wulf, Dr. Albert Zimmer, Eileen Zost.

Also, Alcoa Davenport Works, Tim Wilkinson and Cindy McDermott; The Associated Press; AT&T Museum, Telephone Pioneers, Charlene Poffenberger; Augustana College Alumni Magazine, Augustana College Art Gallery and Collection, Sherry Mauer; Augustana College Library, Judy Belan; Bettendorf Public Library, Hedy Hustedde, Paul Odell, Barbara Reardon, Rita Rosauer, Judi Sarafin, Maria Wegscheid; Bishop Hill (Illinois) Heritage Association; Bishop Hill (Illinois) State Historic Site, Cheryl Dowell; Centennial Bridge Commission, Sue Nelson; Center for Belgian Culture; Circus World Museum, Baraboo, Wisconsin; Cumberland County Historical Society, Carlisle, Pennsylvania; Davenport Public Library, Mary Herr and Amy Grosskopf; City of East Moline, Richard VanRies; Family Museum of Arts and Science, Bettendorf, Carolyn Anderson; The Figge Collection, Filling Station restaurant; Friendship Manor, Marjean O'Brien; Harlan's Fine Foods, Jeff Hagberg; Herbert Hoover Presidential Library, West Branch, Iowa; The Mark of the Quad-Cities, Steve Hyman; McDonald's Restaurants, Jim Freyberger; MidAmerican Energy, Palmer College of Chiropractic Archives; Putnam Museum of Science and Natural History, Eunice Schlichting; Quad-City Development Group, John C. Gardner; Quad-City Symphony Orchestra, Lance Willett; Rock Island County Historical Society; Silver Oaks Communications, Julie McHard; Smithsonian Institution; U.S. Army Corps of Engineers, Rock Island District, Ron Dies; University of Notre Dame, Von Maur, Jennifer Sauter; Whitey's Ice Cream, Jeff and Jon Tunberg.

Other sources: *A-Rafting on the Mississipp'*, *Alcoa Davenport Works: The First Fifty*, *Davenport: A Pictorial History*, *A History of the Quad-City Symphony*, *How It Was To Be Young Then*, *Joined By A River*, *Lee's Legacy of Leadership*, *Moments With Mark Twain*, *The Murrow Boys*, *The Quad-Cities: An American Mosaic*, *Rock Island: Yesterday, Today and Tomorrow*, *The Town Crier*, *Treadmill to Oblivion*, *The Verse By the Side of the Road*, *Voices on the River*, *We Americans*, *Where's the Rest of Me?* Files of the Davenport *Daily Times*, *Democrat & Leader* and *Quad-City Times*; photo archives, ABC, CBS and NBC.

Artists in *A Time We Remember*

John Bald, best known as a wildlife artist, began his career as a sign painter and is now taking a partial leave from that field to concentrate on regionalism. His winter scene of Davenport's Vander Veer Botanical Park lagoon is representative of his newest venue. He did the eagle format used as an illustration in this book not so much for the eagle, but for a try at architectural work. He graduated from St. Ambrose University and lives in Blue Grass, Iowa. John Bald Gallery is in the Village of East Davenport.

Michael Blaser, Bettendorf, is one of the most highly regarded of America's regional artists. His works hang in many corporate and private collections, and his specialty is maritime art. He has done city-scapes of riverfronts and waterfronts of cities from Savannah, Georgia, to San Francisco, California. Blaser, former art director for Deere & Co., is illustrator for *Cruising World*, *Boating* magazine and *Sail* magazine. He attended St. Ambrose University and the American Academy of Art in Chicago. Michael Blaser Gallery is in the Village of East Davenport.

John Bloom, Davenport, was a colleague of Grant Wood at the renowned Stone City Art Colony. He is considered one of the most noted American regionalists. His work is hailed internationally. He has won many awards for his paintings, drawings and wood carvings. He attended St. Ambrose University and enrolled at the Art Institute of Chicago. In his third year there, he was teaching. Bloom is represented by Mississippi Fine Art Ltd. in the Village of East Davenport.

Byron Burford is an internationally recognized American artist who has had 71 shows in major art galleries. He has received a Guggenheim Fellowship and has been represented at the Venice Biennale, one of the world's significant art exhibitions. Burford has had four Ford Foundation purchase awards, and grants from the National Institute of Arts and Letters. He is a resident of Iowa City and graduated from the University of Iowa where he was a full professor of art. His hobby is being a drummer with circuses throughout the Midwest. ("Victory Celebration," a gift of Mr. and Mrs. Isadore and Ruth Evelyn Katz, acquired with support from Arts Midwest's Members and Friends in Partnership with the National Endowment for the Arts, 1989, Augustana College art collection.)

Paul Norton, Moline-born, went to work as an artist for an engraving firm the day after graduating from high school. In later years, he was art director of L.W. Ramsey Co., Davenport, one of the major advertising agencies in America. Norton's work is exhibited through the world, including in the White House, Art in American Embassies collections and Discover America Art. His work also has appeared in major magazines. After his death, a Bettendorf elementary school was named for him.

Kenneth L. Prestley, Rock Island, initially was a commercial artist for national magazines and has illustrated, he says, most everything from cookbooks with millions of circulation to publications for Deere & Co. He has settled down to serious art with his own gallery, Odd Little Gallery, in LeClaire, Iowa. He studied in Paris, France, and at Marymount College, Terrytown, New York. He graduated from Southern Illinois University. Prestley is a partner in Blue Sky Communications of the Quad-Cities. His hobby is circus lore.

Ellen Wagener has a love affair with Iowa and its flat plains, and describes herself as "a landscape artist." Her work is in many corporate collections with paintings in headquarters of companies such as Maytag Corp. and Pioneer Hybrids. In 1997, she won "best of show" at the Bi-State Competitive Art Exhibition at the Davenport Museum of Art. She is represented by Sherry French Gallery in New York City, Olson-Larsen Gallery, West Des Moines and Hudson River Gallery, Iowa City. She is a graduate of the Corcoran School of Art, Washington, D.C. She is a native Iowan by choice, and a lifelong resident of DeWitt, where she shares her studio with her border collie, Sadie.

To Peter, who will
always be in our memories.

Scott County Corn

Ellen Wagener
In the collection of Valley State Bank, Eldridge, Iowa

Remembrance II: St. Paul on the Mississippi

Michael Blaser

"In the early years, a pilot had only knowledge and instinct to steer by; there was not a single navigation mark to help him.
Steamboats ran day and night, in high water and low water, calling at scores of cities and towns, and at rural landings to wood-up with fuel,
and the only map was in the pilot's mind 'Below Dubuque to towhead 62. Coming up when all the bar is covered there. Hold open
to right of high trees on towhead and then close enough by the big cottonwood to safe water.' Piloting was an exacting art."

— From the memoirs of Capt. Walter Blair, Davenport, pilot and owner
of the Morning Star, Helen Blair and Columbia

Our Magnificent Mississippi

"A pilot cannot see enough mornings on the river. In starry nights and when heavy waves can break up a chain of barges, it is always a magic, wonderful, mystic place ... the river."

— Capt. Larry Williams, Davenport,
on his last trip, retiring after 42 years as a river pilot

chapter one

Always, the River...

One day, while traveling in a van with a bunch of tourists, we neared the I-74 bridge between Moline and Bettendorf. The day was gray until the Germans saw the mile-wide Mississippi River.

"Ah! Der Fluss. Der Mississippi," they cried. We had to circle around and park on the Iowa shore while they reached for their cameras. "Wunderbahr," the Germans repeated with glee as the sun broke the clouds.

The Mississippi River, by any account, is magic.

Once, in Vietnam, our tour guide was curtly proper. He earlier had advised us that during "the war," he was not on our side. He spoke flawless English, and at one point asked where we were from, as if he cared a hoot. I told him Davenport, Iowa, which meant nothing until I added that we lived on the Mississippi River. He beamed, shook my hand, and said, "Mark Twain." There was instant rapport, and he rattled off the names of Huck Finn and Tom Sawyer, and told of his admiration for Twain's masterpiece, *Life on the Mississippi*. He said that while being taught English, he learned about America, and came to love the Mississippi River, which he likely will never see.

No other river in the world is steeped in tales that are so swift and deep, flowing through willow marshes and metropolitan cities. And always, in the Quad-City region, it is THE RIVER that is our premier ray to fame.

It is characters, too, like Catfish Bob, who lived in a shantyboat near Nahant,

On a sunny Sunday afternoon in the late 1930s, the Streckfus excursion steamer J.S. upriver of Lock and Dam 15. The Government Bridge is in the background.

An Arabian Nights mood for the forward deck of the excursion boat J.S.

The Thunderbird, actually a barge, was operated as a pleasure/passenger boat by the Williams family through the 1960s. It carried riders between Rock Island and Davenport, and was a summertime favorite of young children and harried mothers looking for a way to amuse them.

At the top, the President in the 1930s as an excursion boat on the Davenport levee. Lower photo, the President making the full circle, returning to the levee in 1991 to anchor the Quad-City riverboat gambling industry.

Symbols of the river: A running light and Mark Twain's *Life on the Mississippi*.

Iowa, and said, "A man can't afford an overcoat, the price of whiskey the way it is."

It is Fred Kahlke, the cynical, growly boat builder of Rock Island's Mill Street, and "Ma" Greene, the pilot whose ghost still haunts the gee-gawed passenger packet, the Delta Queen.

So many recall, with memories fond, the Streckfus excursion boats — the President and the Capitol and the J.S. — that hooted into our towns in the warm of summer and wintered in Davenport's Credit Island harbor. On summery days, their calliopes screamed from a dozen miles away, a clarion that a steamboat was 'round the bend and would be waiting for passengers on the shores of Davenport and Rock Island.

It would not be uncommon for three excursion boats or packets to be tied with thick ropes side by side on the levee, sternwheeler and paddlewheelers like the Avalon and the Gordon C. Greene and the J.S., named for John Streckfus, a farmer boy from Edgington, Illinois, who had a hankering for steamboats and built a mighty excursion empire. He brought jazz up the river, and Louis "Satchmo" Armstrong joined the Streckfus boats when they headed out from Davenport each springtime.

So much has changed, so little has changed. The President, a favorite excursion steamer, is back on the Davenport levee, now a gambling casino. The Casino Rock Island is a duplicate of the type of trim packet that once sat in that place.

Many still rhapsodize at mention of the W.J. Quinlan ferry. It crossed between the shores of Davenport and Rock Island, a nickel a ride, or a dime at night when a jazzy band played "Tea for Two" and the sports with brilliantine-slicked hair dance-dipped their lady loves on the upper deck dance floor.

Always, the river. It was that way, in the long-ago mists of morning and twilight, echoing with the loggers' horn as the great rafts floated downstream from the pineries of the north. Few today can comprehend the days when the Mississippi River would be choked with rafts of logs, herded by steamboats, every log involving the acumen of Rock Island's nationally known lumber king, Frederick Weyerhaeuser.

It was a dangerous river then, of snags and sandbars and boat-eating rapids, awaiting the rush and rumble of paddlewheels. Pilots once named chains of the Rock Island rapids for the steamboats whose wooden hulls were pierced — sending them to the bottom where their bones likely remain. Still — notwithstanding locks and dams — the river is not without peril. A few autumns ago, the Delta Queen tore the bejesus out of its red paddlewheel on a wing dam not far from LeClaire, Iowa.

Capt. John Streckfus, in a rare photo, framed by the giant stacks of one of his excursion boats that wintered at Credit Island harbor, Davenport.

The arrival of excursion boats such as the Sidney was an occasion that brought hundreds to the levee.

Despite today's skilled, tricky demands of handling strings of barges — the length of football fields — piloting is a romantic trade. I stood in the wheelhouse with braided Capt. Larry Williams on his last trip after 42 years on the Mississippi. He wept without shame, staring into the breaking dawn and said: "A pilot cannot see enough mornings on the river. In starry nights and when heavy waves can break up a chain of barges, it is always a magic, wonderful, mystic place ... the river."

Though outward appearances have changed, the river remains basically the same: turbulent, untamable, unpredictable. On the Smithsonian's "River of Song" TV series, pilot-singer-composer-folk artist John Hartford sang:

"Always, the pilots. Always, the river. Where do the souls of dead pilots go ... they fly like birds over the river in summer skies."

Always, in Quad-City Land, the river ...

'You could ride all day for a nickel'

She had a rambunctious career. Raucous, fun, easy on the pocketbook — everyman's quick ride across the Mississippi River: "Five cents. Have your fare ready. No bills over $5 cashed," announced placards at the docks in Davenport and Rock Island.

Of all the storied boats in the Quad-Cities, the chunky W.J. Quinlan ferry rode the top wave for a half-century. She (all boats out of courtesy must be called "she") was built in 1904 at the Kahlke Boatyards on Mill Street in Rock Island. In all those years of chunk-chunk-chunking across the river in high and low water, she never strayed more than two miles from where she was built.

She was a ferry by day, a bingo parlor in the afternoons, a casino by night and at most any hour, a place to slake an alcohol thirst.

Everyone loved the Quinlan. During World War II bond drives, Davenport High's band cruised back and forth playing the doughboys' song, "Over there,

Paul Norton

The W.J. Quinlan

send the word to beware, over there." A regular free-riding passenger was Bozo, a Rock Island dog.

Passengers patiently waited at the docks in Davenport and Rock Island on summery days, cooling their faces with funeral home fans until the Quinlan — usually on time — arrived for the 10- or 12-minute crossing.

On balmy afternoons, families picnicked on the lower deck, traveling all day for a nickel. In later years, owner Fred Kahlke lifted the price to a dime, then 15 cents, always claiming he was losing money. By way of mention, he died a millionaire.

By night, the Quinlan's decks were rimmed in ruby lights, a crimson firefly slowly plodding the river, while the bands of Tony Catalino and Lee Johnston serenaded upper-deck dancers.

The rivers of memory are filled with tales of the W.J. Quinlan, so-named for its original owner. One day, when the boat was filled with kids from the Iowa Soldiers' Orphans Home, Capt. Hannas White died of a heart attack at the wheel. The boat twisted in midstream, steaming toward piers of the Centennial Bridge until the frantic engineer climbed into the pilot house to right it.

Kahlke, an irascible cigar-chewing curmudgeon, never looked the part of the wealthy bank director he was. His claptrap office housed a round dining room table, heaped three-feet-high with

Fred Kahlke, in his crumbling Rock Island boatyard, always dreamed of rebuilding the Quinlan.

Passengers alighting from the Quinlan in Rock Island.

"Judge now whether another such river can be found on the globe ... which combines so many wonders with such great utility ... and to which futurity promises such brilliant destinies."

— Giacomo Beltrami, Italian explorer, dreamer and romanticist, aboard the Virginia, first steamboat to navigate the upper Mississippi in 1823

"It was always the custom for the boats to leave New Orleans between four and five o'clock in the afternoon ... steamer after steamer falls into line, and the stately procession goes winging its flight up the river."

— Mark Twain

The best fuelwood for steamboats came from the upper forests of the Mississippi River. Many farmers, or island squatters, made a living from their wood racks:

NOTIC
to all persons takin wood from
this landin, please to leav a ticket
payable to the suscriber at $1.75
a cord as heretofore
— Amos Sikes

"Man don't need to go to church if he lives on the river. River is a holy thing."

— Ben Lucien Burman, quoting a shantyboat man in "Look Down That Winding River"

unopened envelopes. But Moline's Bill Getz — a boater and a longtime Kahlke pal — insisted that "Fred never failed to spot an envelope with a dividend check."

The wood-hulled Quinlan, after all those years with so few repairs and thick with four inches of paint, finally was condemned by the U.S. Coast Guard in 1946. She moldered in the Kahlke boatyards where vandals crashed out windows and pigeons roosted to smother its once-shiny dance floor with dung. Always, though, Fred Kahlke insisted that he was going to rebuild her. His dream never came true. The Quinlan slowly rotted away until torched by vandals on a spring night in 1967. Her owner died in 1975, at the age of 93, taking with him memories of the grandest of riverboating days.

The excursion boat President and the ferry Quinlan were lively companions on the Davenport levee. Placards like this were posted around the Tri-Cities boosting the President.

Timber-r-r-r!

One of the most prosperous river industries the Quad-Cities has known in this century was history by 1905.

The timber industry had been on the "boom" from the mid-1800s, and the Mississippi was awash with logs cut up north, then carried by rushing tributaries into the big river to sweep downstream to the Rock Island sawmills of Frederick Weyerhaeuser and F.C.A. Denkmann. "Boom" was a loggers' term for fenced areas nestled by the mills where workers would corral the timber until it could be cut into lumber. Logging companies branded their logs to be sure of receiving proper credit at the mills; at the heyday before the northern timber was depleted, there were 2,000 different brands.

A more orderly process was conjured up by Sam R. Van Sant, another Rock Islander, who invented the sternwheel steamer for pushing "rafts" that were formed up north. A raft was made by lashing together logs lengthwise into narrow strips called brails. The average raft had six brails; it was a city block wide and two city blocks long, although some rafts were up to five blocks long.

Weyerhaeuser became a timber titan by doing what no one had attempted before; bring a sense of order to the logging and lumber industries. He formed associations of mill owners to pool resources and profits, and he developed a reputation for fairness and equity. His business sense also brought early prosperity to the communities that became the Quad-Cities; lumberyards and mills and millwork factories all grew from the sawmills of Weyerhaeuser and Denkmann.

Still, by 1905, the northern timber was played out, and the firm of Weyerhaeuser and Denkmann shifted operations to the northwest and south. In time, it became the largest timber holder in the United States.

For years after, a ghostly reminder of the logging industry remained. Along the Mississippi shore near the viaduct connecting Rock Island and the Arsenal, underground fires smoldered, until the 1940s, fueled by the sawdust that had seeped into the soil when the mills furiously ran to keep up with the flow of logs.

Weyerhaueser-Denkmann mill near the Mississippi River, Rock Island.

Rafting on the Mississippi near Davenport, Iowa.

Rafts of logs from the northland were floated to mills in the Tri-Cities, Clinton and Muscatine. The bowboat, Gypsy, keeps this raft in the center of the stream. The raft is powered downstream by a pusher boat in the background.

A Moment in Time   John Bald

Taming the Father of Waters

Of all the construction projects in the long history of our Quad-Cities, one of the most awesome was Locks and Dam 15. It cost $6 million, an astounding amount when the contract was let in the Depression year of 1931.

It created great excitement, clogging traffic on the Government Bridge as drivers — gawking for a better look — stopped their cars. Street car passengers took regular trips on the Bridge Line to watch the immense project which, at times, completely closed the river.

The world watched because the locks and dam between Davenport and Arsenal Island were the first to be built on the upper Mississippi. The purpose was to make the river navigable by creating a series of pools and safekeeping the 9-foot channel (safe water depth for towboats).

Though strictly a skilled-labor project, many WPA workers were hired. It was, indeed, a major lift for the Tri-Cities during the depths of the Depression. Similar projects were undertaken up and down the river; Lock and Dam 13, Clinton, was completed in 1939; Lock and Dam 14, LeClaire, Iowa, was completed in 1940; Lock and Dam 16, near Muscatine, Iowa, was completed in 1937; and Lock and Dam 17, New Boston, Illinois, was completed in 1939.

The vast system was not operable until 1934, and by the end of the 1930s, 26 locks and dams stretched up and down the Mississippi River to create "stair-steps" for river traffic.

The bed of the Mississippi River was a jumbled mass of men, machines and material in this September 1933 photograph of work on Locks and Dam 15.

U.S. ENGINEERS
Miss. River Lock & Dam #15

By February 1934, workers had begun assembling the locomotive crane that runs along the top of the service bridge.

U.S. ENGINEERS
Mississippi River Dam #15

U.S. ENGINEERS
Mississippi River Dam #15

General view of completed dam, view from top of Clock Tower building.
604-121.43   March 20, 1934.

Above, construction of Locks and Dam 15, the first on the upper Mississippi, was completed in 1934. At left, more than 30 years after construction was completed, the locks and dam continue to fascinate. When a roller gate had to be raised in 1966, spectators lined the upper walkway.

When America came calling to Davenport on U.S. 6, the neon-glow of the Tall Corn Motel sign beckoned the travelers to a good night's rest. The motel at what now is the intersection of Kimberly Road and Harrison Street gained a modicum of fame for its giant ear of corn sign, and it became such a landmark that it was shown in a *Reader's Digest* spread about disappearing icons of the motoring world. The motel and sign were demolished in 1986 to make way for another icon of the car crowd — a drive-through restaurant. Shucks!

Kenneth L. Prestley

From Tin Lizzies to Tail Fins

"Why on earth do you need to study what's changing this country?" asked a life-long resident and shrewd observer of the Middle West. "I can tell you what's happening in just four letters — A-U-T-O."

— From "Middletown," by Robert and Helen Lynd, published in the 1930s and 1940s

chapter two

Down the Road

In 1954, when he was 16, Ed Voss of Durant, Iowa, bought a sweet 1950 Chevy. Reluctantly, he sold it when he went into the service. He never forgot that car. Four decades later, at a Minnesota car show, he spotted a 1950 black Chevrolet, a duplicate of his first car.

Before long, it was in his garage with a new license plate: "1ST CAR."

When people ask him, "Is that really your first car?" Voss smiles and answers, "No, but it's close enough."

Voss and his license plate and memories of his sweet 1950 Chevy are a phenomenon that is impossible to explain satisfactorily. It is the Quad-City love affair with cars. We've come to a pretty pass when a fellow will stay home from church on a sunny Sunday in order to polish his car, but that is our way of life. Why, wheels are a downright spiritual thing.

Freedom: Wheels gave us our first independence from mom and dad, and it has been that way from the time of the Tin Lizzy to the Plymouth swept-wing tail fins of the '50s and what I like to call the "Cruise-O-Matic" age of the 1960s and the 'Vettes. And on to the wheels that are tailing out the 20th century — those vans and Jeep Cherokees and the likes of the Chevy S-10 pickups. Better than half the sales of Quad-City wheels in 1999 were vans, pickups and SUVs.

Oh, there are all kinds of statistics like the preceding. It's figured there are 514 cars for every 1,000 people in the Quad-City region. Roll that one around; half the people around our towns have cars!

Cars have brought a culture: Interstates — we call them by their nicknames,

Ruth Schabilion and Harvey Prinz with the new car he bought in 1951. It was the first Nash Rambler sold in Davenport, and this photo commemorates his first date with Ruth, who he later married.

This isn't the 1950 Chevy that Ed Voss bought four decades ago. Instead, it's a duplicate of that first car. He found it in Minnesota a few years ago, and now it occupies a place of honor in his garage. The license plate: 1ST CAR.

"My Champion is tops in quality and *how it saves on gas!*"

Lowest priced Six in America

BIG, ROOMY, NEW 1942 **STUDEBAKER CHAMPION**

Many special Studebaker features at no extra cost!

➡ Finest materials and craftsmanship!
➡ Remarkable gas and oil mileage!
➡ Low repair cost! Top trade-in value!

FACTORY DELIVERED PRICES BEGIN AT
$810*
FOR A CHAMPION BUSINESS COUPE
FEDERAL TAX INCLUDED

COMMANDER ...... $1108 and up
PRESIDENT 8 ...... $1242 and up

*These are delivered prices at factory, South Bend, Indiana, as of November 26, 1941. Federal tax included. Prices and specifications subject to change without notice—but Studebaker quality will remain constant. C.I.T. terms.

GOEDEN MOTORS
1509 9th St., East Moline
Phone East Moline 493

H. & H. MOTORS
609 Sixteenth Street, Moline
Phone Moline 863

Otto E. Schroder with May, his pacer, in 1912. When the automobile came along, Otto — like countless other farmers — faced the wrenching decision: keep the horse, or sell it to buy a Model T. He sold the horse.

I-74, I-80 — began breaking up the countryside in the 1950s; and bumper stickers; and motels, the on-the-go descendants of tourist cabins. Roadside diners gave way to fast-food drive-throughs. All that hustle to get anywhere spawned road rage, an unnatural appendage to the cult of the car. Cars also have given birth to shopping malls and, of course, parking meters, the first of which cropped up on our landscape in 1943.

Parking meters? Bridge tie-ups? Never-the-mind. Quad-City drivers simply have a neverending love affair with cars, and cars generate love. Listen to the story of Harvey Prinz, retired pastor of Davenport's St. Mark Lutheran Church: "In 1951, I bought the first Nash Rambler sold in Davenport, and the first date I had in the car was with a pretty girl named Ruth Schabilion. This was the first time a date helped me polish a car. I was so impressed with her willingness to help me that two years later we were married."

The love affair with cars beeps back to the first Tin Lizzies in Tri-City Land. In the early 1900s, it was a wrenching decision for folks to give up their horses in exchange for Model T Fords. Otto E. Schroder, who lived west of Blue Grass, Iowa, was proud of May, an ex-pacer race horse that could do a mile in 2 minutes, 20 seconds. It was tough and tearful, but in 1912, Otto sold May so he could buy a Model T.

Graying gearheads look upon the early 1950s as the chrome-bedecked pinnacle of the automobile. The cars of the early '50s symbolized the glory of the automobile.

Cars were excitement — real excitement — in those years, remembers Vinje Dahl, Davenport, the latest in a long family line of Ford dealers.

"We would paper the windows of our showrooms so people wouldn't look in," Dahl says. "We'd announce that the new models would be unveiled on a certain date. People would actually get up early and stand in line for a first look at a year's new model."

No wonder. Dinah Shore was singing, "See the U-S-A-y-y in your Chevrolet-y-y" and the enticing ads in newspapers and magazines were poetry. A 1953 Cadillac advertisement in the *Saturday Evening Post* reads:

"The Cadillac is, in essence, an education in all good things in motordom. If you are looking for an extraordinary experience, we urge you to visit your Cadillac dealer soon. The car is waiting for you — waiting to give you the most revealing ride and experience of your life."

The rushing thrill of the American lock on the automotive market would inevitably hit the brakes. By 1957, the No. 1 import (though sales were slow) in the Quad-Cities was the Volkswagen, fondly called the Beetle. The Beetle was such an attraction in 1953 that — when the first one was parked on Second Street in Davenport — a reporter from the *Daily Times* was assigned to write a feature story about why the owner would buy such an outlandish car.

Rock Island motorists paid $3 for wheel tax stickers like this for years until the tax ended in 1987.

The day the bridge opened

On July 12, 1940, the Centennial Bridge opened between Rock Island and Davenport. The toll was a dime. It went to 15 cents in 1979; to a quarter in 1981 and 50 cents in 1991.

The honor of being the first motorist to have a flat tire on the bridge went to Bill Montgomery of Davenport. "Other drivers couldn't believe it; here it was a brand-new bridge, just opened, and already a guy was changing a tire."

Earlier that day, Norma Burke, Davenport, was the first person to walk across the bridge. "It was going to open that day — July 12 — and I beat the ribbon-cutting. I was going to make my own record. Instead of taking the ferryboat from Davenport to my job at Royal Neighbors, I walked across. A real thrill, a really fun first."

Eldorado BY CADILLAC

"In their beauty ... in their luxury ... in their performance ... and in their unique acceptance — they are, without question, the leading representatives of the great Cadillac name," read this 1956 Cadillac Eldorado advertisement.

19

Old gearheads never change

Today, low-rider pickups have neon lamps on their bottom-sides; or speed-sports have aerodynamic wings on the trunk lids — more stability. Street rodders inject nitrous oxide for fast spurts.

But even great-grandpa went gaga over gadgets. Gadgets? The Bosco Co. in Davenport sold a collapsible rubber driver, deflated when not in use. It would be blown up with a tire pump, and was supposed to look life-like to discourage thieves.

Long-distance sirens were sold to clear the way.

Craziest gadget was a radiator ornament that stretched back over the hood and looked like a snake. The honk came out of the snake's mouth.

Cruising the Lincoln Highway

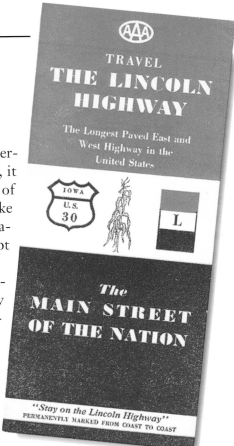

If ever there was an idealized icon of motoring America's past, it is the Lincoln Highway. Still today, it is a Mother Lode of the motor car, and caravans of those cranked-up in nostalgia — vintage car buffs like Dr. Al Hathaway of Davenport — lead summer caravans along its sometimes shady, sometimes windswept paving. Sometimes, grass even grows in its cracks.

As near as anyone can recollect, the first trans-continental concrete ribbon across America was firmly tied through the Quad-City region in the promising year of 1915 — 85 summers before the year 2000. Now, it's called U.S. 30, but it began as Lincoln Highway, christened in red, white and blue. Posts and tree trunks along the way were painted the tri-colors to direct bewildered motorists that, "This is the American way to go."

On a sentimental journey, I followed — as best I could — in the past and present route of our region's Lincoln Highway, U.S. 30. It led me from Morrison, Illinois, across the wide Mississippi, past bright red Midwest Gothic barns, through cornfields and small towns like Lowden, Iowa, that still proclaim "Opera House" in bold letters on a few rooftops.

It is the ultimate Sunday drive. Today, most sections of the roadway are new. But some stretches of the original "Old 30" malinger as in a Grant Wood painting. There is so little traffic that grass grows like a long green serpent through center cracks of some paving. Old 30 is so hushed between Wheatland and Lowden that I met not one car, though I passed a farmer on a tractor.

We began our slow sojourn in soft, shady Morrison, a long-time traveled byway on the Lincoln Highway. Familiar Morrison landmarks pass our windshield — the Parkview Motel, "Key to a Perfect Rest" — and Mike and Barbara Winandy's Hillendale bed and breakfast. She's a fountainhead of truth about the Lincoln Highway, as chairman of the Illinois Lincoln Highway Association. She tells how four communities, including the Quad-Cities, wanted the Lincoln Highway, but the route through Morrison was the most direct on the way west.

"There was a lot of debate. Albany, Illinois, wanted it to go through there, too."

She suggests we look for the remnants of two tourist cabins on Rock Creek at the edge of town. The place once was a stopover for motorists, anxious for the adventure of riding the Lincoln Highway,

Bright and shiny Coca-Cola delivery trucks took up curb space in downtown Davenport in 1918.

perhaps all the way to pick oranges in the sunny land of California. Sure enough, we spot the cabins, all that remains of the Log Cabin Tourist Spot. Not far away, at Pioneer Cemetery, the bleached white tombstones are stark against the pale blue of the wild chicory plants. Were it not so plentiful, chicory would be beautiful.

We cross the Mississippi on U.S. 30 to Clinton. The river runs wide and deep, and through here the log rafts once floated from the pineries of the north. Here, the Lincoln Highway likely always passed alongside the

It wasn't long before every family had to have an automobile — and few resisted the temptation to make it the centerpiece of a family portrait. This mud-splattered Model T center door sedan was photographed in 1924.

Martin Milner and George Maharis of television's "Route 66."

Getting your kicks on the Restless Ribbon

Everybody had a car by the 1930s — or at least wanted one — and the newest dream for those early gearheads was to cruise the Mother Road, Route 66.

It was an odyssey to reach California on Route 66. Get your kicks, on Route 66 ... Winona, Flagstaff, Ari-zo-na.

Drivers needed courage. Tires were so thin and innertubes so patched that motorists would say grace over them before heading out every morning.

One old postcard along the way speaks of hamburgers so juicy that it took a dozen napkins to soak up the grease. Another tells of staying at the Wagon Wheel Motel. It was one of the first in the country to take on that new-fangled word combining motoring and hotel. The postcard for Wagon Wheel beckons a safety slogan: "Fall asleep at our wheel, not yours."

"Get Your Kicks On Route 66" — 30 singers recorded that tune ... Nat "King" Cole and Bing Crosby and even the Rolling Stones. But it was Bobby Troup who first made the tune famous.

Route 66 was fun, the home of the first frozen custard and landmark places like Honeymoon Roost, the Cozy Dog and Big Texan. It was a restless ribbon, always unashamed that it was out to make a buck. Commerce, Oklahoma, named Route 66 "Mickey Mantle Boulevard" because it was a stickball playground for the Yankee slugger.

But the world stopped for Route 66 in the late 1970s. The interstates were here! The interstates were here! Shucks, it took five interstates to replace Route 66.

The Route 66 drive-ins and the tourist cabins and the greasy spoons closed. Tumbleweeds rolled down the highways where cars and semis once were paced a dozen feet apart.

Then, a humble but aggressive Arizona barber named Angel Delgadillo pushed for a national movement to save Route 66. Much of it had been barricaded shut, but thanks to Delgadillo, Route 66 is alive and well ... right down to the greasy spoons and the Honeymoon Roost.

In the shaky year of 1937, a dozen Tri-Citizens in three cars headed with hesitation to Chicago, and then westward on Route 66, a great lark of motoring. Joe Wagner, a Davenport real estate man of hope who pushed the campaign to get Iowa out of the mud, was one of those Route 66 motoring pioneers.

He loved cars, and Joe wrote home: "Lots of places to eat. Stopped at a new idea of a place called Steak and Shake at Normal, Illinois. Maybe we should invest. Looking forward to Barney's Beanery on the coast. They say there is a place called Tee Pee where we can stay in concrete wigwams."

That was the dawn of what John Steinbeck called the Mother Road in his masterpiece, "The Grapes of Wrath." Route 66 did not head through the Quad-City region, as did U.S. 30, the Lincoln Highway. Old 66 struck out from Chicago, down through Illinois and to the Southwest. At first, only 800 miles of the route was paved. It took until 1937 to pave the rest, and by then, Route 66 was the Main Street of America.

celebrated Smith Bros. store, with wagon wheels and garbage cans side by side at the front door.

Dick Herrity, who spent a lifetime with the Clinton County Engineering Department, says the "Original 30, or Lincoln Highway," once was routed along Clinton's Bluff Boulevard and down Fifth Avenue.

"There are still sections of the original Lincoln Highway behind Clinton's Target," he says. (The original Lincoln Highway began in New York City and ended at Lincoln Park, San Francisco.)

Outside Clinton, U.S. 30 takes on the temporary look of an interstate, two bee-busy lanes in each direction. Beyond DeWitt, the old Lincoln Highway reverts to a more acceptable two lanes, through small Iowa towns like Grand Mound, where the welcome sign says, "There's No Place Like Home." Unmistakably, in Wheatland, I spot a turn that veers to the right off new U.S. 30. It unquestionably routes me to the old original Lincoln Highway. This narrow section rolls on for dreamy green miles.

A concrete bridge — not recommended for travel — is so tight that two cars can barely meet, side by side, without scraping fenders. Signs in Wheatland note this as the Lincolnway. Citizens are not going to forget the old roadway that brought them a modicum of fame.

It becomes 235th Street at the edge of Wheatland, with more grass growing in the cracks. There is no traffic. It is so quiet that I hear a windmill squeaking beside a fence. All the way to Lowden, I meet no cars.

Travel off the interstate, if you please. Meet the real MidAmerica.

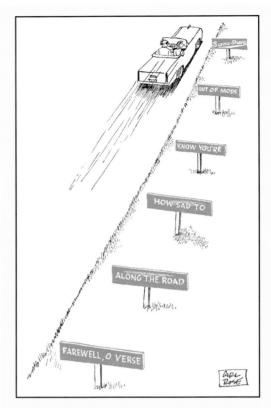

Burma Shave — the verse by the side of the road

So much was changing, and so were the cars. By 1927, the spidery Model T Fords had been pulled from Henry Ford's production lines and the sporty Model A's, with a gen-u-ine stick shift on the floor, were available in natty colors like auburn, ocean green and seaside sandy tan. We were in the dawning years of America's love affair with cars.

Into this scene, along the Lincoln Highway through Clinton and Morrison, and on Route 66, and all roads in between, burst the most enterprising roadside advertising scheme of all time. Even today, Madison Avenue calls it a stroke of genius — the Burma Shave sign jingles. Allan Odell conceived the idea of using the consecutive merry signs along roads, beginning in Iowa, Wisconsin and Minnesota.

The essential spirit of Burma Shave signs that made America first notice and later cherish was, of course, their

The name "Velie" is more associated with airplanes and the white mansion on the bluff in Moline, but for a few years, the company also made automobiles. This is a 1923 Velie coach.

light-heartedness, explained Frank Rowesome Jr. in his definitive little paperback, *The Verse by the Side of the Road* (Penguin Press). Humor had been so infrequent in the Depression years that it was about as scarce as a trace element.

Into this stepped Odell, an enterprising fellow who had bought the rights to a shaving cream called Burma Shave. Sales languished until he hit upon the jingles that were planted along America's coast-to-coast roadsides. Burma Shave signs became an instant hit, along with knock-knock jokes. Sales soared, and the product became America's most popular shaving cream. The company was so busy it never knew there was a Depression.

Odell was a foxy fellow who knew the times, the motorists and the highways were ripe for his jingles. He arranged for four or five small messages to be planted on orange (later red) wooden placards, 100 paces apart. At 35 miles per, it took about three seconds to proceed from sign to sign, or 18 seconds to cruise through the entire series. This was far more time than any magazine or newspaper ad could dream of holding the eyes of casual viewers. Alexander Woolcott, the journalist and tale-teller, wrote that it was as difficult to read just one Burma Shave sign as it was to eat just one salted peanut.

They were sprinkled all through the Tri-City region, and one day Grover Meyer, who ran the general store in rural Maysville, Iowa, came to town beaming that Davenport finally had been named in a Burma Shave sign near the Donahue turnoff:

If hugging
On highways
Is your sport
Trade in your car
for a davenport.
— Burma Shave

How it happened was a carefully conceived plan. First, an advance man cruised highways, looking for straight and level spots free of any other signs. Once a likely spot was found, the advance man approached the farmer and handed him a free jar of Burma Shave. The advance men were good ol' boys, true back-slappers. When the farmer asked how much it was going to cost him to put up a string of signs, the answer was swift: Nothing. The farmer would be paid. A year's lease would be drawn up on the spot, bringing a farmer $5 to $25. If he balked after a year, the signs would be quickly pulled.

The company had an intricate D-Day-like scheme to track the location of every one of its 10,000 sets of signs. Sign planters worked in crews from trucks. The Odell family called the installers PhDs — Posthole Diggers. Regional warehouses subdivided the country, to make new signs readily available to installers. Husky diggers, mostly hired from the Midwest, were expected to dig 36 postholes a day, no less than three feet deep.

Allan Odell wrote most of the jingles himself, and his brother, Leonard, took over the company in later years. In 1964, a reporter for the *Washington Star* interviewed Leonard in what would be the waning year for Burma Shave signs. He described Leonard as a "genial, talkative man with a highly suspect hayseed air."

The signs made us smile in bad times and war times, but nothing could last. Cars were faster, the interstates made Burma Shave signs impractical. They were designed for 35-mph speeds. The last signs came down in 1963 and 1964.

In a cartoon by Carl Rose, "The Verse by the Side of the Road," is a mournful epitaph:

Farewell, oh verse
Along the road
How sad to
Know you're
Out of mode

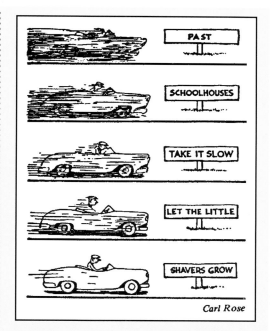

Carl Rose

There were 600 registered Burma Shave jingles

They did not shriek, but were pleasant ditties that never failed to bring a smile:

His face was smooth
And cool as ice
And oh, Louise
He smelled so nice
Burma Shave

No advertiser had spoken in such a manner, and the absurdity caught America's fancy:

Does your husband misbehave
Grunt and grumble
Rant and rave
Shoot the brute some
Burma Shave

Many of the jingles were aimed at the young, hoping to capture beginning shavers for life:

He had the ring
He had the flat
But she felt his chin
And that was that
— Burma Shave

My First Car ...

You may forget your mate's birthday, or your wedding anniversary, but you'll never forget your first car. Was it that Chevy Bel-Air with spinner hubcaps? Smooth. Or a Model A Ford with running boards? Maybe it was that Chrysler Airflow? It came out in the mid-1930s, a strange-looking car that looked the same coming or going. Some people have such an insatiable passion for cars that their lives are dated B.C. and A.C. — before car and after car.

Most Quad-City drivers remember every detail of their first car, the exact color, the year and the precise price paid. For young drivers, it was their first taste of freedom. Reminiscing is a favorite pastime of car owners ...

"**THIS 1937** Ford was purchased from Sexton Ford of Moline in November 1945. I had just been discharged on points from the Navy. Of course, I had to have a car so I hitchhiked to the Tri-Cities as there was none (cars) at all in my area. This Ford was the only one I found in the Tri-Cities, so I shelled out $400 in cold cash for it as I did not want to hitchhike back to Fairfield, Iowa. In 1948 I hired on at John Deere Harvester, East Moline, and moved to an apartment. Retired from there in 1980. I drove the 1937 Ford for five years. A lot of fond memories. Wish I still had it."

— **Lloyd Shelangoski, Davenport**

"**WHEN WE FIRST** married in 1951, my husband and I bought a 1935 perfect-condition Buick light blue convertible roadster, a block-and-a-half long and really sexy. Midwest winters were too much for it and we traded for a more practical car. How often we wished we could have kept it. The dog on the running board was Bob. It belonged to my father-in-law. Every dog he ever owned was named Bob."

— **Ruth Killinger, Port Byron, Illinois**

"**SHE WAS SUCH A LOVELY CAR**, my first car, a 1965 Chevy Chevelle Malibu Super Sport convertible. How's that for a mouthful? She was white with a turquoise blue interior. My parents bought her for me at the end of my junior year in high school. I thought she was the most beautiful car in the world. In fact, I still look at models of her at classic car shows. That car and I went through a lot. She and I led the homecoming parade at L&M (Louisa-Muscatine High School) in my senior year. We drove back and forth from Letts, Iowa, to St. Luke's Hospital in Davenport where I was in nurses' training. If it was 50 degrees and the sun was shining, her top was down and the wind was blowing through my hair."

— **Leslie Rizzo, Bettendorf**

"**WHAT A FINE CAR** for those days. Wow! This is a snapshot of my 1928 Packard Straight Six wire-wheel roadster. It bragged an in-line 8-cylinder engine and a rumble seat and golf club compartment. Four wire wheels to run on, and two wire wheel side-mounts. Class. It had a one-shot oil lubrication system that oiled all four springs at once. I bought it in 1932 for $115. Wish I still owned it today. It would be worth $50,000."

— **Walter G. Fichtner, Davenport**

"**THIS CAR HAD QUAD-CITY ROOTS.** It is a Stephens Salient Six, a car manufactured in Freeport, Illinois, and was named after the founder of the Moline Plow Co. The cars were first in production in 1917 and began using overhead valve units from R&V Engineering in East Moline in 1918. Moline Plow Co. bought out R&V in 1920, reorganizing in 1922 as Stephens Motor Car Co. Production stopped in 1924, with the company producing about 25,000 cars during its seven years of existence."

— **E.L. Conard, Davenport**

"WHAT A SUPER PRESENT. Here is my 1971 super Beetle, a high school graduation gift from my parents. Great color, Volkswagen red. I graduated from West High, and dad had promised me that if I behaved myself, he would buy me a new car when I got my diploma. He made the promise when I was a sophomore. I'll never forget the first Sunday that I drove it to church, Westside Assembly of God in Davenport. Some guys picked it up and carried it to the church lawn. That was a real shock. Rev. Tommy Barnett was the new pastor, and he was the type who really got a kick out of that prank. I had the car for seven years and had a lot of fun with it. I married in 1974, and when we had two kids, needed a bigger car. It had 100,000 miles on it."

— **Jane Ernst, Davenport**

"MY FIRST CAR was a hand-painted bargain that took us everywhere, without much trouble. My husband, Kenneth, was in the army and I was back home, needing a car. In 1943, my dad arranged for me to buy a 1930 Chevrolet coupe for $65 from one of his employees at Rock Island Arsenal. The owner was going to the service, so I had to drive it off Arsenal Island — it hadn't been greased for years, and I could hardly steer it home. I remember buying a 25-cent can of black paint at Grant's and doing the fenders. It looked so good I bought another 25-cent can and painted the entire car and named it Mathilda. We were lucky that it held together. My husband and I (in the snapshot) made several long trips in it to Fort Leonard Wood, Missouri, where he was stationed. He always said to pack tightly, so we could mail our belongings home or get everything on a bus in case we broke down. Once, we did break down near Mediapolis, Iowa, but the mechanic was able to fix Mathilda — he used a condenser from a tractor."

— **Eileen Zost, Davenport**

"I WISH I STILL OWNED all the cars I've bought. I would be rich. One of those cars was the envy of guys everywhere — this '67 Chevy Corvette 427, 435 HP, if you're wondering. I bought it new from Mills Chevrolet, Moline. My first new car was a '55 Chevy Bel Air that I bought for $2,700."

— **Don Stormer, Davenport**

"WE WERE REGULAR CRUISERS on the one-ways in Ol' Blue, our 1957 Chevy. Ol' Blue is still owned by us, and looks just like it did back then in this photo, taken in July of 1963. Good times. Good memories."

— **Bill and Joan Lindle, Princeton, Iowa**

"THIS 1963 FORD FALCON was one of our first cars. It was a year old when I bought it in Rock Island from one of those 'little old ladies' who kept it immaculate. I still have it; it looks just about the same as when I bought it; even the leather is still good. I take it for spins in the summer; one recent year, I drove it all summer long. She's still a beauty, with only 65,000 miles after 36 years."

— **Larry Shannon, Geneseo, Illinois**

"THE PRIDE in your first car is that it usually had to be either a 2-door hardtop or a convertible. This was a way of telling girls, 'This is my car, and not my folks' 4-door sedan grocery-getter.' My first car was a 1955 Chevy 2-door Bel-Air hardtop. It was hunter green and ivory. I bought it after graduating from Davenport High in 1960. I remember gas wars were common, five gallons for a dollar. I remember, too, how it was almost a sin to drive a dirty car. Dinah Shore was singing 'See the U.S.A. in your Chevrolet.' Songs like that bring back memories, like '409' by the Beach Boys. I'll always have a love for the memory of my first car."

— **Dick Bockenfeld, Davenport**

Bumper snickers

It's said that we are bombarded by information everywhere we go, so it is only natural that bumpers have become message boards. What better way to pass the idling time on the slowed-down I-74 bridge than to read about the hopes, dreams, fantasies and political opinions of the drivers around you. But don't get too close!

Do you remember riding the ones?

Cars and drivers change, but one thing remains the same: the first words that come tumbling out of the mouth of a just-licensed-to-drive 16-year-old. "Hey, dad (or mom), can I borrow the car?" echoes as loudly as a bad muffler.

And, as every parent knows — at least every parent who used to be a kid — the claim that a teen child wants to borrow the car to a) return an overdue library book; b) go to choir practice; or c) run back to school to fetch a geometry book, is a bunch of ozone. Sure, that errand may be on the itinerary. But so is the urge to go cruising.

The Beach Boys nailed it — "Well, she got her daddy's car and she cruised through the hamburger stand now. Seems she forgot all about the library like she told her old man now. And with the radio blasting, goes cruising as fast as she can now. And she'll have fun, fun, fun 'til her daddy takes the T-Bird away."

Cruising a la "American Graffiti" is as old as the Model T and as new as the '98 Beetle. On a spring night when the air smells sweet and the end of the school year is in sight, teen drivers go cruising, around the town square or up and down the main drag or along the four-lanes that connect city to city or — and this is a uniquely Quad-City experience — on the one-ways that tie our towns together.

Riding the ones is as all-American as it gets. Homecoming queens and football stars ride the ones. Future priests and high school principals and accountants and Chamber of Commerce presidents ride the ones. There may be a few bad kids, gang-banger types, out there, but overwhelmingly, they're good kids doing what kids have done for generations.

In Moline, back in 1993, the police and city council put their heads together and devised a ban on "repetitive, unnecessary driving" on Twenty-third Avenue, a major four-lane that just happens to pass the high school, a bushel-basket of strip malls with big parking lots, and just about every fast-food franchise ever opened.

The reason for the discretionary ban on cruising was a chorus of complaints by merchants that cruising and idling teens scared away legitimate business. The ordinance prohibited drivers from passing designated areas on the avenue more than three times in one hour between 7 p.m. and 2 a.m. Even the police chief admitted that enforcement would be difficult, and although signs are posted at regular intervals warning drivers to keep their cruising to a minimum, it still goes on.

And it will, as long as there are 16-year-olds with new driver's licenses and moms and dads who haven't forgotten what it is like to be young and carefree on a summer night.

— **Deb Brasier**

Fill 'er up

"Check your oil? Sure, we'll wash your windshield. Check the tires, too."

Not so long ago, every hamlet had its own service station — not a combination pizza parlor and convenience store with some pumps outside. But real service stations, with free air for your tires and a place for the hangers-on to sit around and gab. Gas was in vertical pumps, and you could see the liquid fuel. You'd watch as it was pumped into your gas tank, inching down the big glass tube. Muscular attendants filled that glass reservoir after every customer. Only gasoline, oil, tires and tubes were sold.

In the 1930s, the ultimate in service stations could be found in crossroad communities like Mendon, Illinois, just north of Quincy. Service station "architecture" called for a canopy — a feature returning today to stations that are veritable grocery stores, selling bread, milk and Twinkies, along with gas. Illinois Oil Products, which still is home-based in Rock Island, had 200 of these service stations/bulk distribution centers within a 250-mile circle of the Tri-Cities in the late 1920s and early 1930s. Stations always flew an American flag.

There were no big tanker trucks on the roads until well into the second half of this century. Gasoline was delivered to service stations in trucks like this. Illinois Oil Products assigned tank trucks to serve each of its stations, and this made a formidable fleet crossing paved highways and gravel roads.

In 1974, the Arab oil embargo hit service stations where it hurt the most — no gasoline to sell. Charles Treadway, Davenport, stands disconsolately beside one of his pumps.

Barely visible by the front door is an NRA sign, which stood for President Franklin Roosevelt's National Recovery Act. This Illinois Oil Co. station was in Monmouth, Illinois, in the late 1930s.

Rainy night, downtown Davenport's Third Street, recreated in this painting as it sparkled in 1940. Honking cars, people, a glittery melodrama ... theater row, a tunnel of neon and nightlife beaming upon a shining street ... a time remembered, never to return.

Kenneth L. Prestley

Once the storefronts along the streets of our downtowns sparkled with reflections of the neon signs identifying businesses. As the biggest of the Tri-City downtowns, Davenport drew folks from miles around, often in for a day of shopping and dining out.

Downtowns dressed up for the holidays, too, and long-time Rock Island residents recall when evergreen ropes were draped across intersections.

Where it all began

"When you're alone and life is making you lonely, you can always go…downtown."
— A 1964 song, made popular by Petula Clark
(Welbeck Music, Ltd., a division of MCA)

chapter three

You Could Always Go… Downtown

Downtowns were a faith. Downtowns in the Quad-Cities were the good stuff of downtowns everywhere — the polished apple of our versions of what life should be.

Downtowns were the gleaming Cadillac parallel-parked by M.L. Parker or the old Essex snugged to the curb by Petersen Harned Von Maur in Davenport; or, the sporty Packard sidled alongside Al Klass' Gay '90s in Rock Island, where the piano player couldn't keep up with the bouncing ball of the sing-alongs; or the rosy-cheeked traffic cop, tooting his shrill whistle, barely escaping cars on Moline's Fifth Avenue department store row.

Downtowns were our excitement, our great white way, our Broadway — the glistening movie marquees on rain-wet streets — "double features and newsreels at all showings, folks" — and Bank Night every Wednesday.

Downtowns were gaudy, wooden-floored dime stores, open until 9:30 on Saturday nights, and 8 to 5 daily — but never on Sunday — peddling goldfish and piano music. Downtowns were the elegant Davenport eateries of Johnny Hartman and Sonny Fisher, and the everyman's cafes, like Harold's Coney Island and Best Ever in Rock Island, and Glen Moore's in Moline.

Downtowns were people, people, people.

Shoppers dressed up to go downtown ... no slacks, no jeans. Men usually in neckties. Photo near Second and Main streets, Davenport, 1950s.

Our railway stations were wonders ... the hulking monster of the Rock Island Lines, lording over Davenport like the Elsinore of *Hamlet*; the brown-brick, tile-roofed depot in Rock Island, alongside steel rails stretching like spaghetti. Trains brought visitors to downtown. Downtowns were our Mecca.

Now, all is so quiet, and in our loss of downtowns perhaps there is a moral which none can quite define. Everyone loved downtowns; they grasped and embraced them. Downtowns were a trust of confidence, and citizens are now bereft. But those same citizens had run away to the malls.

Realistically we face — no matter what the great minds may scheme — that down-

When we lost the whistle

Mert Hartsock, one of a half-dozen traffic officers assigned to downtown corners.

"We lost our metropolitan presence when our downtown Davenport traffic policemen were assigned to other duties. Their whistle-tweeting likely didn't mean more than a change of lights from red to green, but it gave Davenport a big-city, metropolitan air. They stood at the corner or often in the center of an intersection, whistling traffic and guiding people across the street before we had 'walk' and 'don't walk' on the traffic lights. Bobby Meyers, the friendly traffic cop at Third and Brady, was once voted Davenport's outstanding citizen. Who can forget rosy-cheeked Ray Musselman, guiding the traffic and people in and out of Davenport Bank. When we lost traffic cops, Davenport lost a lot of class."

— Frank Folwell Sr., long-time downtown Davenport merchant

towns will never be the same, no matter how hard the planners and the talkers may design. Now, we have the memories, and as Ziggy once cartooned:

"No matter how old they get, memories never spoil."

We are left with memories and old photographs of stores and streets and cars filled with people, traveling down memory lane ...

Shopping for shoes at Thom McAn, the place with the X-ray machine, where you'd put on a new pair and wiggle your toes to see if the shoes fit, and see your bones jiggle, and then going next door to Martin's to knock off a hot roast beef sandwich, 35 cents.

Third Street in Davenport was magic, with six movie houses, the mammoth Orpheum and Capitol, and the smaller Esquire (before that, the Columbia) and also the State and Garden and Star. Third Street was the place to be, with nearly a half-dozen eateries in every block, places like Brooks 130 Grill, and beside it the Louisiana Barbecue, where George and Mary reigned and no panhandler ever left hungry. Siegel's and Ziffren's pawn shops were side-by-side neighbors, greeted across the street by Brud's. Brud Cawley promised an insult with every drink, and next to the RKO Orpheum, Larry Lux played the Hammond organ at Leo Kautz's Sportsman's Grill. It was elegant, then, to call every place a grill.

No, you never went hungry or thirsty on Third Street. Junger's had a squeezed orange juice palace across the street from the great-domed Capitol movie house, with a Spudnuts nearby, and there were three — count 'em — cafeterias within sight of each other. One was a Bishop's; another was the Times, also served by Bishop's, but with cheaper prices; and the storied Shannon's.

Roy Shannon called his place a dairy lunch, with little marble-top elbow stools where you'd dine by yourself if you chose. Shannon's began on Main Street, and enlarged to bustling Third Street where he was still serving meat pies for 39 cents when the place was sold in 1979.

"I was reluctant to raise the price to a quarter, but we finally had to end up at 39 cents," Roy said. The last meat pie under Shannon ownership went over the glass-topped counter on September 30 of that year. Shannon's was one of those downtown institutions, where the faithful still savor the thought of their chicken a la king and biscuits. Dr. Don Allard

Shoppers could buy a dress for 49 cents; shoes for $1.88; wash pants, 98 cents. In 1936, this Fourth of July sale was held by J.C. Penney.

The last of the downtown Davenport street sweepers was Herman Muhs, who worked all night with his wide broom and cleaning cart. He was killed in 1947, struck by a motorist on an icy morning. Herman was a beloved downtown fixture and 700 mourners — many of them merchants — were at his funeral.

Second Avenue, Rock Island, in the late 1940s.

The crossroads of the Quad-Cities

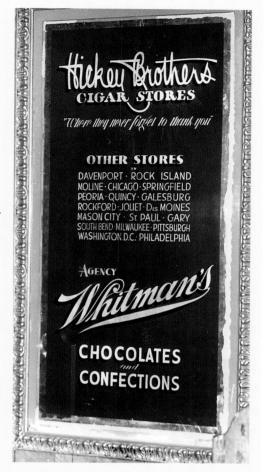

says: "I would come downtown on Mondays, just to get Shannon's creole lima beans with a pork chop on top."

Always, downtowns hustle-bustled with eateries and food-eries. In Rock Island, the memories linger of the hungry dining at the Toastie Shop or, for a bagel and lox, Orwitz's.

Grocery stores, too, with catchy names like Brady Street Basket and Feeney's and the White Market and Geifman's, and Prinz's Fruitland in Davenport; and Tenebaum's and Vesole's in Rock Island. And butcher shops, with sawdust floors, places like the Chicago Butcher's in Moline and the Crescent Market in Davenport and the place in Rock Island where you could pick out your chicken — live — and only minutes later, walk out the door with a dressed fryer.

"Mom and dad took pride in polishing the red delicious apples and pyramiding oranges in their downtown window. It was a class act," remembers Harvey Prinz, a retired Lutheran minister from Davenport.

But always, it was the stores, the big department stores, that lured the multitudes to the Quad-Cities from half-a-hundred miles.

The names of those long-lost downtown stores rattle like the forgotten slams of ghostly cash register drawers: Petersen's and Parker's and Hill's in Davenport; McCabe's and Younkers in Rock Island; the New York Store and Block & Kuhl in Moline. McCabe's claimed it inaugurated the "White Sale" concept copied by merchants all over America. Petersen's was the consummate department store, with its storied Christmas windows making us an envied rival to Marshall Field's in Chicago.

"To me, the ultimate was Petersen's," says Dr. Peter Ryan, a Davenporter now living in Anchorage, Alaska. "The excitement of standing outside in the cold, waiting until Petersen's unveiled the Christmas display windows with the moving elves. Wow! And who can forget the mezzanine of M.L. Parker, where you could play 45s before you bought them."

Hickey Brothers No. 8 at Second and Brady, Davenport, was the cross-roads of the Quad-Cities. Bill Hickey would arrive at the store in his green Cadillac by noon every day. He was a dignified, cigar-smoking fellow who had the world wrapped around his finger like a cigar band until his empire went up in smoke. Once, Bill Hickey had 130 cigar stores in the United States and Cuba, 68 of them with lunch counters. No. 8 had a big water tank; lobsters, anyone?

Bill Hickey was one of those inimitable personalities who wore a Kelly green suit on St. Patrick's Day to match the gaudy outfit of a local creature named Jonesy. Jonesy, a banty rooster of an ex-jockey, had a dozen different-colored suits to match his mood of the day. To complete the ensemble, he painted a circle of color on each cheek to blend with the color of his suit.

All sorts of characters crossed paths at one time or another at Hickey's No. 8. There was Chandra, a mystic in a turban, reeking of incense and draped in dime-store jewelry. He offered to read palms or minds. Most avoided him, but it was said he was quite a ladies' man.

The swells and the would-be swells dined elbow-to-elbow at the half-block-long lunch counter of Hickey's No. 8. Food was good and cheap. Bennie Seguhn lorded over a U-shaped section of the lunch counter where a baritone named Murph liked to serenade customers. Bill Hickey tolerated Murph, as kindly as he paid homage to E.P. Adler, the *Daily Times* publisher, banker and general do-gooder who daily bought three Admiral Bering cigars for $1.

"I remember Murph so well," says John Carver, who all but ran the Hickey empire. "Mr. Hickey enjoyed Murph because he had such a good singing voice." Murph, though, would get his seasons mixed and would likely sing "Silent Night" on St. Patrick's Day when he should have been crooning "Mother Machree."

Petersen's Olive Nut Spread

Olive nut spread was one of the choice sandwiches in the downstairs tea room of Petersen Harned Von Maur, downtown Davenport. There are many versions, but this is the most authentic — it is from Helen Stoefen, who made it for years for the tea room:

3/4 cup softened cream cheese
1/2 cup mayonnaise
1/2 cup chopped pecans
1 cup stuffed green olives, chopped
2 tablespoons liquid from olives, to moisten as needed
Dash of black pepper.
Mix well.

When I was 6 or 7, my mom gave me $2 to spend on Christmas gifts for my family, so I went to downtown Davenport and spent $1.50 on my dad and three brothers. I had 50 cents left to buy a gift for my mom and went to Folwell's. I saw this nice linen set of a tablecloth and four napkins, but I knew it was awfully expensive. I went to Mr. Folwell (Frank) and asked the price. He asked how much I had to spend, and I told him 50 cents. He could see how much I wanted that set for my mom. He said: "You're in luck. It just went on sale for 50 cents." My mom was thrilled. It was Irish linen!

— Donald Murphy, Davenport

Hill's, now an empty lot in downtown Davenport, was a favorite of the farmers. "I did everything at Hill's, from lugging around bolts of cloth to running the roll-handle elevator," says Bill Jasper, Davenport. "The building had no air conditioning, I remember when John Orr, the manager, would march onto the elevator blowing giant clouds of cigar smoke. When I'd see him coming, I'd groan, 'Oh, God.' After that, I never smoked cigars in my life. There was nothing I didn't do at Hill's; at Christmas, I even ran the electric trains in the basement."

Downtowns had something for everyone, like Teft Rubber Stamp Co. in Davenport or Phil and Charley's Army Store in Rock Island. No one quite figured out what "army store" meant because there were no Army surplus goods. John Norton, the silvery-haired manager of Harry's Army Store in Davenport, once winked, "It's just sort of a gimmick to get people in," as he sold a pair of four-buckle galoshes. Kistenmacher's Drugs, a vintage pharmacy, sold the best hard licorice drops in the Quad-Cities, and in the back room, Naomi fitted trusses.

You could get anything in our downtowns — Oriental rugs at Rashid's or fine suitcases and purses at Wirtels, with its rich essence of leather as soon as you stepped inside the store in Davenport. Temple's Sporting Goods in Moline — a class act. Rock Island's finest young citizens were clothed at McGarry's and shod at Gersick's Junior Boot Shop. Downtown Davenport alone had 12 men's and women's shoe stores, with names like Baker's and Kinney's. Richter's menswear had a giant bear in a glass case at his entrance. No one knew

It never was too cold or too snowy to stand in front of the big windows, as generations of holiday shoppers once did, and marvel at the whimsical Christmas displays in the windows of Petersen Harned Von Maur's flagship store in Davenport.

Welcome, please

"In the late 1920s, Davenport merchants had a program to encourage people from nearby towns to shop downtown. For several years, they issued a circular 'Davenport Guest' sticker to be placed on the inside windshield of a Model T Ford, or whatever. This enabled shoppers to park for unlimited time anywhere downtown. Police would not mark white chalk on the tires on these cars. This was long before parking meters, and putting chalk on tires was the only way police could tell which car had parked too long in the same space."

— Ernest R. Schroder, Davenport

Kenneth L. Prestley

The Garden Shop, at the corner of Third Avenue and Seventeenth Street, Rock Island. In the background, the marquee of the Fort Theater, now Circa '21 Dinner Playhouse.

the significance, but it scared the gotta-go-shopping jitters out of the kids.

Where has it all gone, to that heaven in the skies for great downtowns? Downtowns with a Mosenfelder's menswear, or Simon and Landauer, where Alan Landauer told jokes about having the slowest elevator in Davenport, maybe the world.

"It was so slow, we could play a round of bridge between the first and second floors," says Tom Otting.

Downtowns with the prim ladies at the LaRose in Moline or Miss Pinkus at Abraham's in Davenport; she knew a thousand Quad-City women by their first names. Stanley Simmons, who ran the show at M.L. Parker's ... soft-spoken Stanley, who a couple times daily adjusted the carnation on the lapel of his natty floor walker who stood, nodding and bowing at the Brady Street entrance, or Robert Millett, dapper in his bowtie, who seemed to be everywhere at once at McCabe's.

Places and names, always names, because downtown merchants were personalities unto themselves. Morris Citron would stand outside his Davenport store and scold the people passing by:

"Those shoes on your feet have cardboard soles. Come in. I sell you real leather soles, cheap."

"A trip downtown was a major celebration," remembered Dick Hengl of DeWitt, Iowa. "I

Lock your brakes!

Paved with bricks the size of a loaf of bread, the Davenport levee was a sloping wonder on the riverfront. It was, at times, even a seaplane base.

Cars parked there for free. It was downtown's first municipal parking lot. Several times a week, when a motorist would forget to tighten the emergency brake, a car would coast down the ramp into the river, soaked to its rooftop. On warm weekends, motorists would carefully park close to the river and wash their cars — the Quad-Cities' first free car wash.

Heavy iron rings were sunk into the bricks so excursion boats like the President and J.S. could tie up. The W.J. Quinlan ferry docked on the levee, not far from the Pipe Dream, a trim passenger vessel made by Harry Godley in his back yard. The Pipe Dream offered pleasure cruises and could serve as a party boat, aided by deckhands Bill Gress (later of radio and TV fame) and Dick Karwath.

For thrills, Godley had speedboat rides, $1 to the Centennial Bridge, or $2.50 to Credit Island and back.

The oddest use of the levee was as a seaplane base. George Duvall, who flew to fame as a senior pilot for TWA, once offered plane rides in a pontoon plane with the name of Voss Washing Machine Co. on the side. As an enticement, the purchase of a Voss washer entitled the buyer to a free airplane ride, Duvall once said.

Skid row

Downtowns had their rough edges, and the roughest was Skid Row, the 400 block of Davenport's West Second Street. The corner was anchored by the respectable St. Louis House, but it was all downhill for the watering holes along the street. The places had enticing names, like the Silver Moon and the Silver Dollar. The Silver Moon had a unique "appliance" just outside the front door — a vertical pipe, not unlike a firepole. It was there for blotto patrons to grab on to when they left the place, so they wouldn't fall on their faces on the sidewalk.

walked from home on West Eighth, stopping at Seventh and Harrison for a cool drink from a pump, and then buy some licorice whips at Sitrick's grocery store. Mom gave me a quarter, and it lasted all day. I would go to the Star Theater, where it cost a kid only a nickel, and then to the Famous Cafe for a dime hot dog. If it was getting dark, and the movie was spooky, I'd walk up the middle of Harrison Street. But no one ever bothered me."

The safety of downtown Davenport always impressed John Carlin. "I worked at my dad's gas station at Front and Ripley from when I was a kid until going into the service. I sold gas for 20 cents a gallon. We were right in the middle of a pretty tough district, sort of a Barbary Coast. A bar called the Bowery, with a bartender called Maddie, was a hangout. It was a tough area, but I always felt safe."

Well, one can suppose, nothing can last forever. The Quad-City downtowns were showing their age, and malls were a new lure. Rock Island's New York Store closed in 1962, to be followed by chain-store-names like Montgomery Ward, Sears and J.C. Penney, and then Carson's in Moline and McCabe's in Rock Island. Petersen's hung on in downtown Davenport. Certainly, Petersen's never would leave downtown. But it did, and now the familiar, swishing, revolving front door is dusty and locked.

In 1973, Davenport council member Greg Cusack made a prophecy: "If we're going to save downtown Davenport, we're going to have to do it in the next 20 years."

It didn't happen the way he must have foreseen. But the gambling boats and microbreweries and big-deals like The Mark have brought a different vigor to our downtowns. Still, it is the stores that count, and retailers have rushed to SouthPark and NorthPark and Elmore Avenue in the exodus from downtown — save for a few like Schneff's and the Gentry Shop in Davenport, and Barkan's in Rock Island. In downtown Kewanee, Illinois, Good's grows more immense each year.

Still, shoppers must miss the dime stores and their goldfish, three for a dime.

The Main Street annex of Petersen Harned Von Maur's flagship store in Davenport. The photo dates to the late 1950s; the building later housed The Loft, which catered to teen-age shoppers.

By 1920 the Kahl Building — going up here — was completed at West Third and Ripley streets, Davenport. At left, the old Columbia Theater. The car is a 1915 Buick roadster.

Smile, you're in downtown Davenport!

Every face tells a story, and this unique photo gallery is a study of faces in downtown Davenport, in the late 1930s and early 1940s ... faces that wear smiles, faces that are serious, faces that are worried. They were "captured" by a roving photographer who snapped "Candid-Camera" type photos and handed the subject(s) a numbered coupon for ordering the picture from Jewel Photo Service, Davenport. The price: 50 cents.

On a downtown shopping excursion, grandma holding her granddaughter's hand. Ella Seaman Boeh is the grandma; Mildred Blunk Schnekloth is the granddaughter, both of Eldridge, Iowa. The name on the box is the Bee Hive.

The Rucker family of Bettendorf: Shirley, Sally, Dottie and Angie.

Elmer Bolte and his grandfather, Rudolph Korthaus, Walcott, Iowa, on Second Street, near Main.

In straw hat and white shoes, Lee Turnbull, publisher of the Davenport *Democrat & Leader* newspaper, chats with an unidentified listener.

Reflecting in this photo is Hickey No. 8 store; likely, it was taken on Brady Street. Rose Cale is holding the sack; Gertrude Cale is pushing Beverly Cale in the stroller. The toddler grew up to become Beverly Witmer of Durant, Iowa.

A shopping trip meant dressing up — no slacks or casual clothing allowed. On the left, Margaret Dawartz, now Margaret Sinkhorn, East Moline, and her mother, Anna Beguhn Dawartz, Davenport.

Getting from here to there...

"Clang, clang, clang went the trolley. Ding, ding, ding went the bell. Zing, zing, zing went my heartstrings."

— *Judy Garland in the movie*
"Meet Me in St. Louis" (Decca Records)

Standing and hanging onto the straps or perched upright on the straight wicker double seats, Tri-Citians found the trolley and the interurban speedy, efficient ways of getting from here to there.

Trolleys swayed across miles of spider-webbing tracks and overhead wires, the motorman up front in his square-topped hat, a commanding and envied figure. The Tri-Cities held on to its trolleys until 1940, when square-nosed buses took over.

As warmly remembered as trolleys are the interurban cars, which whisked passengers and freight (such as cartons of peeping chicks or Muscatine melons) on the old CD&M (Clinton, Davenport and Muscatine) at speeds up to 60 mph.

Trolleys and interurbans quit at nearly the same time. When buses took over, Tri-City Railway was faced with what to do with 150 street cars. They were sold as scrap to A.D. Harris Company, Rock Island. The salvage company hauled one trolley around town on the back of a double-length truck, with an advertising sign offering old street cars for sale as summer homes or diners. There were few takers. The trolley was forever dead.

The year, 1906. A trolley crossed the narrow trestle to Campbell's Island, East Moline.

In the days before two-car families — or when even a single car was a luxury — mothers and children rode the street cars.

The conductor, in his square-topped cap, leans from an interurban car on the Davenport-Clinton run in the 1920s. Passengers were carried across the Mississippi via the Government Bridge.

Interurban cars were the prime means of transportation between Muscatine and the Tri-Cities. This pickup stop is the 200 block of Brady Street, Davenport.

The first bus to cross the new Centennial Bridge on July 12, 1940, carried a full load of passengers.

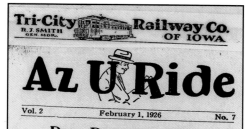

Snub-nosed buses replaced Tri-City trolleys in 1940.

Tri-City Railway Co.

R. J. SMITH GEN. MGR.

OF IOWA

Az U Ride

Vol. 2   February 1, 1926   No. 7

Does Davenport Need Street Car Service?

THERE are a lot of interesting things in the Annual Report this year. Among other things it shows that the Davenport car lines and the Bridge Line carried 8,450,000 passengers during the year 1925. This figure, of course, includes all passengers—those who paid fares in cash or tickets, those who paid half fares, those who rode on transfers, and those who rode on pass privileges, such as city employees and employees of the Tri-City Railway Company.

Practically speaking, 8,450,000 passengers make quite a crowd. If every person living in North Dakota, South Dakota, Montana, Wyoming, Colorado, and New Mexico, Idaho, Utah, Arizona, Nevada, Washington, Oregon, and Californi had ridden on the Davenport and Bridge Line cars once during the year, it would still require 1,256,609 people (or about the population of Maine and New Hampshire besides) to equal the number of passengers carried.

The astounding magnitude of figures such as these will perhaps help to convey to your mind the important significance of street car transportation to the community.

The street car system as a means of urban mass transportation stands second to none in the world. The commercial importance of having such a service consistently and dependently available for the residents of this community would make a mighty interesting subject for a 3000 word essay. Anyone want to write it?

The figures are improbable, but this 1926 pamphlet claimed that Davenport trolley car lines and the inter-city Bridge Line carried 8,450,000 passengers in 1925. That would have been about four times the population of all of Iowa.

The 5 and 10s have gone the way of the buffalo nickel and the Mercury dime

Fred Keller, the Kresge manager in Davenport, is flanked by Peg Dolan, left, and Esther Posios during a store meeting. Peg was a piano player in the sheet music department.

"Oh, if the world could be like it was then, and downtown was the same today."

— LuAnn Brabant,
Eldridge, Iowa

For shoppers, the dime store was the anchor of downtowns. It was where generations went for a spool of thread, a goldfish or a canary, a broom, a bite to eat.

Now, the Kresges and the Woolworths and the Newberrys have cashed it in. The empire of retailing necessities at working man's prices has gone to five-and-dime heaven.

Throughout the Quad-City region, the dime stores folded many summers ago. In Rock Island, they faded away and The District eventually emerged. Moline's dime stores were boarded up long ago, as were those in East Moline and Milan and Clinton and Muscatine. Clinton's five-and-dimes were among the last to go.

In Davenport, Second Street west of Main is described in old city directories as "dime store block," with Woolworth's, Kresge's and Grant's in a sprawling wonder of hairnets and hat pins and Howdy-Doody billfolds. Now, the block is a parking lot.

Leaning back to the years of dime stores in Davenport, Annette Rickeberg of Davenport misses the doughnut machine at the front counter of Woolworth's, buying thread and needles and Rit dye in the shade of ecru. Evelyn Buddin, Davenport, misses going into a little curtained booth and having a dozen pictures of herself snapped for the princely sum of a dime.

Barbara Lawton, Davenport, misses her every-Saturday treat — a toasted ham sandwich with lettuce and mayonnaise along with a chocolate malt, all for 35 cents. Gayle Randolph Sr., Bettendorf, will never forget the time he spent 15 cents for an incense burner to give his mom on Mother's Day.

From turtles to tools to oilcloth for the kitchen table, the dime stores had something for everyone.

"Where else could you get envelopes, a pound of coffee and a sack of orange slices?" asks Cliff Reisenbigler of Morrison, Illinois. "Along with orange slices, I remember marshmallows covered with toasted coconut. Hard for a kid to resist."

The wide array of merchandise is one of Reisenbigler's favorite memories: "I was 12, in about 1921, when the country was aroused by radio. I went to Woolworth's, which had a wide array of radio parts. I made a crystal set, got the 'cat's whisker' adjusted and at 6 every night would listen to B.J. Palmer and his chimes concert on WOC."

There may not be a baby boomer today who didn't once own a parakeet, turtle, goldfish, hamster or baby Easter chick from the dime store. The chicks, often dyed in neon colors, frantically cheeped in their paper bags as they were toted home.

The aisles were a magic bazaar. Children prowled the toy department (nothing more expensive than a dime or quarter) while mom slipped away to buy Wildroot Wave Powder. For kids, it was a Disneyland of its day, with nickel toys in the lower bins.

Jo Vandecar, Davenport, remembers seeing life through the dime stores, "First getting paper dolls, and then thinking I was hot stuff when I was allowed to buy

Tangee lipstick," she says. She particularly remembers a dime store essence, Evening in Paris perfume.

"It came in a blue bottle with a little tassel at the top and I thought it was the best-smelling stuff I had ever known. I saved my pennies for a long time so I could buy a bottle. It conjured up all kinds of romantic images to a pre-adolescent girl."

For the hungry, there was no place finer for a good, cheap meal than the dime store.

"If I didn't have enough money for lunch, I'd buy a sack of broken gingersnaps for a nickel," remembers Joe Winckler, Davenport.

"We would walk down Harrison Street hill for lunch on special occasions. I can still taste that hot turkey sandwich with cranberry sauce for 39 cents," says Jo Vandecar.

"My favorite was the Woolworth specialty of the house," says Barbara Hansen Tiemeyer, Davenport. "It was called the Catalina Club, a three-decker of tuna and egg salad, with potato salad and a Cherry Coke. That was big-time expensive — 75 cents."

Woolworth stores, the original five-and-dimes, were founded by Frank Woolworth in 1879 in Lancaster, Pennsylvania. He loved music and frequently had a piano player in his stores. This led to the sale of 35-cent sheet music from a piano pounder who played requests. In Davenport, Peg Dolan was a piano pounder in the Kresge store on Main Street; her punishing of the keys could be heard all the way to Second and Third streets.

If you worked in a Tri-City area dime store, you worked hard and long hours. "Six days a week for $17 a week tops, and open until 9:30 on Saturday nights, but they were happy times," says Flora Hahn Snyder, Bettendorf. "They kept the candy storage room locked, because the help liked to snitch malted milk balls. Nylon hose were such precious items they were locked up, too. Oh, how I miss the dime stores. They were the heart of downtown Davenport."

Young women were the stalwarts of the dime store personnel, and they gave rise to the popular ditty, "I met my million-dollar baby at the 5 and 10 cent store."

"I remember fibbing about my age to get a job at the Davenport Kresge's. I was only 17," says Mary Yegge, DeWitt, Iowa. "Kresge's was on the south side of Second Street in 1924, before we moved across the street to a big, swell store. Imagine this, I was only 17, but they put me in charge of the hardware department — 2,500 items. Kresge's always boasted that it carried 2,500 things in the hardware department."

Floor walkers wore out their soles, remembers Erma Wallenge, Davenport. "There were usually two girls to a counter, and if a customer was seen waiting too long, the floor walker would let out a shrill whistle for the clerk to hurry up. Those were the days of real service."

You were special if you worked in a dime store. One Quad-Citian, mourning the loss of Woolworth's, said she lived in rural Scott County in the 1930s and when saying her prayers at night would recite, "God bless the dime store lady."

THIS IS YOUR RECEIPT — DO NOT DESTROY

Employee ___Zost___

Date of Payment _____

Total Wages: $ ___2.15___

Am't of Tax: F.O.A.P. $___02___ State $_____

F. W. WOOLWORTH CO — EMPLOYER
FORM SL15-200M

Eileen Zost's pay slip for one Saturday at the downtown Davenport Woolworth store — $2.15.

In the early summer of 1947, plastic turtles were slow sellers at Kresge's in downtown Davenport until Dolores Voss (Orr) took over the counter. Says Dolores, "I demonstrated in the aisle telling customers to 'just pull the string and watch them go.' The Davenport store sold more turtles than any other in the United States, and this picture of me appeared in the national Kresge's newsletter. My moment of fame."

"Going downtown Rock Island could fill up an entire day. We'd catch the Eleventh Street bus and get off by the Dutch Inn. Then we'd stroll through McCabe's, where the manager seemed to keep a close eye on us as if we were up to no good. McCabe's had an alley entrance and the dime stores were just steps away. Out the front doors there, and we'd scoot across Second Avenue to VanGoor's, where we'd pick up the new KSTT Good Guys survey and buy the latest 45 for a dollar. By then it was time for lunch at Swan and Bahnsen's or the Toastie. Hopefully, there would be a new movie at the Fort or the Rocket."

— Mary Jo Williams

Moron's Ecstasy

Ingredients:
Six flavors of ice cream,
approximately one pint.
Six fruit and cashew and peanut
toppings, which includes:
bananas, two halves of Melba peach, raspberry
syrup, mixed flavors, Maraschino cherries, tutti-
frutti syrups, pineapple syrup, strawberries,
whipped cream. Chocolate syrup if desired.
Price: $1

NOTICE: The management assumes
no responsibility of any kind, shape or manner.
Any person moron enough to finish a Moron's
Ecstasy is eligible for membership in "Crawford's
Royal Order of Morons."
— From 1942 menu card, Crawford's
Sugar Bowl, Davenport

Satisfying the soul

"What really distinguishes ice cream parlors is their atmosphere and therein lies the difference between a sundae that satisfies the palate and one that satisfies the soul."

— New York Times,
"The Romance of the Ice Cream Parlor"

chapter four

Fizz, Fun & Phosphates

"It's 9 o'clock in the morning, a little early for ice cream. But with the Iowa sun already well into the sky, few places offer better escape from the summer heat than the Wilton, Iowa, Candy Kitchen, a turn-of-the-century ice cream parlor and soda fountain. Here, you'll find walnut booths, stained glass fixtures and ice-cold phosphates the color of Christmas lights."

A roaming reporter for the *Washington Post* made that report while searching America for soda fountains. He found they were alive and well and actually staging a comeback: Item, the booming success of Lagomarcino's authentic new soda fountain in the Village of East Davenport, and the born-again old-time soda fountains in malls and arcades.

For the young, the soda fountain always has been a place to improve social graces through conversation.

For the seniors, it was a place to prop elbows on the marble counter and solve the problems of the world.

In the fizz of strawberry sodas are memories of drug store soda fountains in places like Swan & Bahnsen and Larson's in Rock Island, or the original Lagomarcino's in Moline (in business for 91 years now). In Davenport, there was Burt's Pharmacy, Emeis-Hansen, Swan's and Bill Day's, and the half-block-long soda fountain at the downtown Walgreens.

Too, there were the authentic no-nonsense all-soda fountains like Iowana, Gosselin's, Crawford's Sugar Bowl and Superior Dairy.

At the peak of whipped cream with a cherry on top, America had 100,000 soda fountains. City directories for the Tri-Cities in 1928 list 32.

It's not only to the malls and arcades that soda fountains are returning. They actually are an interior design option: The owners of one Davenport condo are having an authentic soda fountain built for their basement.

Most certainly, Whitey's — in all its gleam and sparkle — can be considered a soda fountain of sorts. Some of the old-

Orange-flavored syrup came from Orange Crush dispensers, to be mixed with carbonated water.

It's questionable whether the Green River soda drink originated in the little western Illinois town — no longer in existence — that gave it its name.

One of the most traditional of soda fountains in America is the Candy Kitchen in Wilton, Iowa, operated by Thelma and George Nopoulos. The Candy Kitchen was opened in 1910 by Gus Nopoulos, George's father, with a $35 inventory of cigars, ice cream and candy.

timers never left. Lago's and Wilton's Candy Kitchen will fizz through eternity. Jim Dreibelhaus has a four-booth, five-stool soda fountain in his pharmacy in West Liberty, Iowa.

"Class reunions always return, en masse, for cherry Cokes," he says.

May Drugs in Columbus Junction, Iowa, hangs on to its century-old fountain with 20 feet of uncut marble.

American Soda Fountain Co., Chicago, which repairs, collects and deals in all things related to soda fountains, has a steady business selling old fountains and those little round fountain stools. "I've picked up a couple hundred fountain stools from closed Woolworths," says Bob Schy, owner of the company.

Virl Banowitz of Maquoketa, Iowa, the king-guru of antique dealers in MidAmerica, always has an eye out for old soda fountains which are in top demand for new installations in new locations. Back bars sell for $8,900 to $65,000. Front bars (counters) run $200 a foot, twice that much for marble.

Obviously, we are doing more than creating memories. Maybe the day will come when we'll sit down and relax with a Happy Thought (banana split) instead of hurrying through the drive-up for a Super-Size in a paper cup.

From a tiny white frame building on Moline's Sixteenth Street, Whitey's Ice Cream has grown into a MidAmerican dynasty. Chester "Whitey" Lindgren sold his business to employee Bob Tunberg in 1953; today, Bob's sons Jon and Jeff, above, run the company and have expanded the many, many ways that fans can get their Whitey's fix. Turtle malt, anyone?

Old Mill is remembered for trying square instead of round scoops in special-made square-top cones. The idea never took off, so Tri-City ice cream parlors reverted to the traditional style.

Little has changed at Lagomarcino's soda fountain in downtown Moline since this photo was taken in 1967. Behind the counter is Tom Lagomarcino, Sr., who called his apron "my working robe." Also behind the counter, Aunt Mary Lagomarcino and Joe Schenone, a family cousin. The fountain/candy store was opened in 1908 by Angelo Lagomarcino, Tom's dad, an immigrant from northern Italy.

Tom Lagomarcino Jr. in the family's Village of East Davenport soda fountain and restaurant. The walnut back bar, built in the 1880s, came from Snow White pharmacy and soda fountain in Maquoketa, Iowa.

Shh! The great hot fudge secret

One of the most guarded secrets in the Quad-Cities is the recipe for Lagomarcino's hot fudge.

The Lagomarcino family will not reveal any of the ingredients that make it so deliciously famous.

In 1918, Angelo Lagomarcino purchased the hot fudge recipe from a traveling salesman. He paid $25 for it, which appalled his wife, Luigia. He was scolded for spending that much money.

The sauce still is made one small batch at a time, a new batch each day. Angelo intended it to be served in a little pitcher, so it could be drizzled as preferred over ice cream.

It still is served Angelo's way.

Downing's Dairy, on Twenty-fourth Street at Stadium Drive in Rock Island, was but a bicycle ride away for youngsters in need of a Popsicle, a cold drink or a chocolate chip cone on a summer afternoon.

Magazines like McClure's asked questions such as "Does jazz put the 'sin' in syncopation?" This was the cover on one of the last issues — the magazine folded in 1929.

Singing the blues ...

"Once I built a railroad and made it run, made it race against time. Once I built a railroad, now it's done. Brother, can you spare a dime?"

— E.Y. Harburg, 1932, Harms Inc.

chapter five

From Good to Bad to Worse

What a slap-happy time to live, in the late 1920s. Charleston ... Charleston ... the Tri-Cities was on a big toot ... A cabaret in the basement level of the Kahl Building where Marj Velie, of the grandiose Velie family of Moline, slid fingers across a long, slender cigarette holder elegantly fashioned from mother-of-pearl.

It was a time of crossword puzzles and chain letters and mah-jongg and that new craze called miniature golf played on cutesy courses out on Blackhawk Road in Rock Island and down on Rockingham Road and over on Harrison Street in Davenport. A fellow named Oscar had a snappy course and a rustic log cabin-like root beer stand out there.

Happy times are here again, we'll sing a song of cheer.

Norman Baker, the charlatan of charlatans, had Muscatine on its ear, chanting out the window of his purple Cord limo that cancer could be cured. President Hoover was so impressed by this fellow Iowa-boy that he pressed a telegraph key in the White House to start the press for the first edition of Baker's newspaper in a building that still stands, not far from the Mississippi in Muscatine.

The vast army of the Depression unemployed is summed up in this picture of a rag picker, photographed on West Second Street, Davenport. Notice the dog in his cart.

Life was a revel of sons and daughters "petting" in rumble seats at Prospect Park, Moline. Life was riding high, and that included the Graf Zeppelin lazing slowly over Davenport. Billy Klinck, "My Pal" Billy, was urging every Tri-City "pal" he knew to buy Cities Service stock, to the later misery of all who did.

Happy days are here again, we'll sing a song of cheer.

Giddy gaudy days — but the Great Crash of the stock market, bank closings and the Great Depression that followed would burn deeply into the local conscience.

Families lived in shanty boats such as this along the Mississippi River below Rock Island.

The Grapes of Wrath, John Steinbeck's 1939 novel, told the grim story of the migration to California of displaced Oklahoma farmers. Steinbeck won the Pulitzer Prize for literature; an Academy Award-winning film starring Henry Fonda followed.

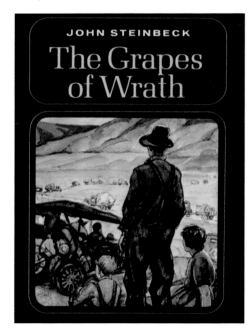

In 1933, this family trekked by handcart from Seattle, Washington, to Davenport so father could enroll at Palmer School of Chiropractic.

Happy days are not here again, we'll not sing a song of cheer.

One September night in 1931, Jim Stopulos, a downtown Davenport kid, was walking home.

"I remember so distinctly," he says. "I saw the office part of the 'unsinkable' Davenport Union Savings Bank at Third and Brady all lit up. I had never seen it so bright. The next day, I knew why. The bank was out of money."

With frightening swiftness, businesses locked up. But in 1933, the Bettendorf Co. — a vast bulwark that surely never would fall — was on the teetering edge of bankruptcy. Davenport Locomotive Works closed its factory, but still tooted its whistle every morning at 6, as it had done to wake its workers, as a benign gesture of hope for better days. Fifty Tri-City companies folded in 1933.

It was a bitter time of fear, fright. No unemployment checks, no Social Security, no medical protection — and no jobs. Employment at the six Deere plants in Illinois fell to 716, but the company stood by the farmer. Its reputation of today was fortified because it never foreclosed on a single piece of farm equipment.

It was a bare-bones struggle for survival in the land that then was called the Tri-Cities. Curtis Ford of Davenport remembers wandering to a sandy pocket beneath the Government Bridge on the Davenport side of the river.

"This guy was a great sculptor, but he was broke," Ford recalls. "No one was buying statues during the Depression, so he was carving sand figures, some of them crucifixes, really big things. People would come by to admire, and drop a nickel — maybe just a few pennies — into a Karo syrup can that was at his feet."

One man was mining coal in his back yard at the edge of Coal Valley, Illinois, and selling it by the bucket from a stand on his front lawn. Farmers found it cheaper to burn corn, which was selling for a dime a bushel, than to buy coal. By 1932, one out of every four people in this region was without work. Within a year, it would be one out of three. The workless scrambled to make a few dollars a week. Clamming took off, with 12 clam shops punching buttons in Andalusia, Illinois. Few of the young had money for college. At the University of Iowa, one student paid a semester's tuition by bringing in a wagonload of potatoes and smoked hams for Kellogg House on the campus.

An enterprising Bettendorf artist-type named Lester Voorhees had a steady hand and a palette of paint. He would make the rounds of used car lots, striping (deco-

Cahill's Grocery & Meat Market
3643 ROCKINGHAM ROAD
PHONE 2-6565
Davenport, Ia., _____ 194_

Mr. _____

No. _____

ACCOUNT FORWARDED

Reg. No. _____ Clerk _____

Your account stated to date. If error is found return at once.
Wagner's Printery, Davenport, Iowa

A week's supply of groceries cost $4.90 into the early 1940s. Butter came in three-pound slabs; cream was in pints; two pounds of pork chops cost 52 cents; bread, 16 cents.

rating) old cars to spiff them up, from one side of the hood all the way around to the other. He charged 50 cents. "In a good day," he remembered, "I would stripe 10 cars. Five dollars was a lot to earn in a day." In later days he would harrumph: "Kids make that much in an hour flipping burgers."

The hard-scrabble irony of those years — impossible to imagine as this century turns — is told by Mary Yegge, of DeWitt, Iowa. "I worked in the shoe department at Petersen's in Davenport for $14.80 a week in early 1930. When business got worse, my pay was cut to $8.90 a week. But it was a job and we were glad to have it. We were buying a house at 513 East Tenth Street in Davenport, and how can I ever forget, but we had nine people eating at our table — aunts and parents. And the income from all of us was only $18 a week.

"We made it," she says. "We must have been made of the right stuff. No one had anything, but we were all in it together."

The butt of all the misery was President Hoover, who once was hailed as an almost-hometown boy. He was held in disdain as a scapegoat for all the problems of the region and the nation. On the stage of the Columbia The-

American Rescue Mission, Rock Island, was a savior during the Great Depression. Family baskets are ready for Christmas distribution.

A Depression widow's battle to save farm and family

"I was 10 years old when my father died in 1927. He had a stroke while fixing a fence, and was only 40. It was a struggle for my mother, Annie Badtram, to rear a family of eight children, the youngest age 1, in the Great Depression years on a farm in Lincoln Township of Scott County.

"Mother was so lucky to be on the farm and keep us together. We raised everything on our 80 acres — corn, hogs, we milked cows and raised chickens and ducks. We butchered four hogs in the winter and canned meat for summer. My brother trapped rabbits. He didn't use a gun. Mother would even pickle some rabbit meat when we had plenty.

"We canned more than 100 jars of vegetables and fruit, all from our garden and fruit trees. Mother baked four to six loaves of bread at a time. All our clothes were hand-me-downs. We didn't go anyplace much. No 4-H or church. Just a grade school education in a one-room schoolhouse.

"Mother had help from neighbors the first year, because in the beginning she didn't know much about farming. After that, with the help of my brothers, we were able to do all the work ourselves.

"We were all happy to have a home and plenty to eat during the Depression. Mother taught us how to do everything, and to save for a future day. She passed away in 1965, a very remarkable woman."

— Dorothy Badtram Dammann, Eldridge, Iowa

Troubled faces in the summer of 1938. Edwin Prinz, standing, returned to Davenport to open a grocery store after bank failures in South Dakota closed his business there. Seated is his father, Charles Prinz, who grew vegetables in Bettendorf to make a living.

ater in Davenport, a stand-up wiseguy comedy jasper worked a trained dog into his act.

"Sit up," he commanded the dog.

The dog flopped over, as if faint, its feet in the air.

The comedian cracked, "I said to sit up, not act like President Hoover."

I know this to be true. I was a kid, laughing from one of the box seats in the grand old theater.

The cities of Davenport and Rock Island and Clinton and Muscatine and Moline wore expressions of defeat, despair, guilt, fear, bitterness. Without jobs, unemployed men shifted from one town to another. Vast armies of men were labeled as tramps or hoboes, though they once held respectable jobs. American Rescue Mission in Rock Island was a mecca of salvation. H.F. Donaway, a self-styled major, daily fed 150 men (never women) bowls of potato soup filled with big hunks of bacon ends, which he was given by the old Kohrs Packing Co., now Oscar Mayer, in Davenport. The men were a worn army of unemployed, part of the long defeat. They were hungry, homeless and had been drifting long enough for all hope to be lost.

These were railroad towns, and the workless rode the rails, hopping off boxcars in Silvis or Nahant, a railroad yard on the western edge of Davenport, or in Clinton. Some marked an "X" on the sidewalk or fence in front of a place with a friendly dog and, usually, a free handout.

My dad, a stern man, nonetheless had a soft heart for any hobo who came into his grocery store wearing a hat and necktie. He figured they once were reputable people, down on their luck. He would feed them bologna or cheap cheese sandwiches, and on cold nights they were allowed to sleep by the furnace in the store basement. I was always scared to death to go to the basement, for fear of finding a hobo down there!

Life went from bad to worse. In 1932, Charles Carpentier, mayor of East Moline, issued a statement: "The year found us in the depth of despair."

WPA crews, sometimes called the Wheelbarrow Brigade, worked on Tri-City roads, dug a lagoon in Credit Island Park, tore up trolley tracks, and helped with projects ranging from building the first stage of the new locks and dam system on the Mississippi to construction of Rock Island High School.

A WPA worker sloshes tar on a brick street in Davenport.

Depression's phantom rider

This ghostly tale has its origins in the Great Depression, likely because people would believe anything to take minds off their misery.

The tale was told and retold in locales from Rock Island to Rock Falls, from Blue Grass to Buffalo. It is still told today, the account of the vanishing hitchhiker.

The story has been vaguely tracked to the 1930s, and those who tell it claim it is true.

The traditional version goes something like this:

"While I was in high school, the students began telling the story of the ghost ... seen by a man a few nights before. It was a very foggy night. It seems that it was in the wee hours of the morning [and] the man was driving home from a business meeting.

"As he started under a certain underpass, he was flagged by a young girl dressed in a white formal. He stopped and asked if he could help her. She answered that he could take her home. She gave him her home address. It was on a dimly lighted street that the home was finally located.

"The man drew the car to the curb and got out to open the car door for his passenger. When he reached the other side ... he found no one there. Thinking that she may have gone in, he rang the doorbell to make sure she was safe. After a time an aged woman answered the door.

"He told her he had brought her daughter home and wanted to make sure that she had made it inside safely. The woman began to cry and told him, 'My daughter was killed ... in a terrible car accident just outside of town 20 years ago tonight on her way home from the high school prom. Tonight is not the first time that she has since tried to get home.' "

Still, President Hoover was saying, "I am convinced we have passed the worst and with continued effort we will rapidly recover. Happy days are around the corner."

To forecast the end of the Depression was as much of a cliche as the "light at the end of the tunnel" was in forecasting an end to the Vietnam War in the 1960s.

Hoover went down in a tumble of defeat; hope was the handout given by Franklin D. Roosevelt, who was saying, " ... The only thing we have to fear is fear itself." President Roosevelt was recommending that everyone go to the movies and see Shirley Temple. "Cheer up. For 15 cents, you can watch this little princess and forget all your problems." At the Fort in Rock Island and the Capitol in Davenport, the dimpled dolly was singing, "On the good ship Lollypop."

The Works Progress Administration, or WPA, or Wheelbarrow Brigade, as it was called, came along to dig a lagoon at Credit Island Park and to help build the high school that still stands in Rock Island. The biggest WPA project of all was the locks and dam system on the upper Mississippi, beginning with the one in Davenport.

But any promised cheer was years to come. The Tri-Cities did not recover until the astounding boom years of World War II. The fear, the defeat and despair, hung on until the Arsenal was peaking out with nearly 18,000 workers and Bettendorf Co. was making prime movers and Deere was turning out implements of war.

Those who lived through the Great Depression never will forget. They are the frugal ones who try to pass on to their grandchildren a warning more precious than gold: Waste not, want not.

Says Jim Stopulos, who saw those lights burning in the windows of Union Savings Bank:

"The kids of today will never know what it was like when everyone was poor. But then I wonder, do they really care? Happy days are here again."

Join the march ... to OLD AGE SECURITY

Return YOUR APPLICATION FOR A SOCIAL SECURITY ACCOUNT NUMBER *through the post office* NOT LATER THAN DEC. 5TH 1936

WHO IS ELIGIBLE

HOW TO RETURN APPLICATION

— *Social Security Board*

Social Security was one of President Roosevelt's reforms.

Panic at Third and Brady streets in Davenport, a 1931 run on the Union Savings Bank. A string quartet inside was of little effect in calming depositors who demanded their cash.

I want my money!

The panic cry was like a thunderclap when the run began on Tri-City banks during the Great Depression. It was the most frantic time for finances in the long life of these communities. It was grimly happening, too, all over the nation.

What happened here was a microcosm of nearly every city, town and hamlet.

The Great Depression had struck with frightening vengeance. Jobs were gone. Factories had closed, and the thrifty, skeptical folks of our communities felt it safer to stuff their hardearned money into the mattress or bury it in an empty Karo syrup can in the back yard than to keep it in a bank.

Quintessential stories:

Davenport had two sturdy banks, among the strongest in the Midwest. American Savings Bank & Trust was easily the largest bank in Iowa. Union Savings Bank was next in line. But by the autumn of 1931, depositors were

hounding the banks for their money.

The run was most fierce on American, which borrowed $100,000 from the Union on a frantic day in '31. By noon it was gone, and the bank closed with depositors pounding on the doors.

Union would always be solvent, the thrifty Germans convinced themselves. They made up the bulk of the depositors, but most of the bank's resources were tied up in farmland, and the bottom was falling out of farm prices and land.

Logic was not on anyone's mind. Depositors lined up, four abreast. Many were at Union's doors all night to be first in line. Some brought market baskets, insisting they be paid off in small denominations. The baskets were for carrying off their cash.

To soothe the panicky mass, a string quartet was hurriedly booked from the Tri-City Symphony. They played from the bank's balcony level, while a sopra-

no, Ethel Baker Waterman, sang "Ah, Sweet Mystery of Life." It was a portent of times to come.

E.P. Adler, publisher of the *Daily Times* (predecessor of the *Quad-City Times*) and a director of the Union Bank, rushed up and down the lines of the anxious depositors with his own passbook in hand. To encourage confidence in the bank, he wrote his personal guarantee of the amount on deposit — with the amount the individual sought to withdraw.

But Union was at death's door, and it, too, ultimately closed. A moratorium was to come in 1933, temporarily closing all American banks.

But before, Adler was making things happen, a hero of that day and many others. He was drafted to reorganize Davenport's American Bank. Across the Midwest, all eyes were on him, for this could be a pattern for other reorganizations. On a chilly November night in 1931, 5,000 people jammed

Headlines from Tri-City newspapers.

Davenport's Masonic Temple auditorium. There was not enough room, so they filled lodge rooms. Others sat on the long marble corridor floors. Loudspeakers broadcast the hopeful message of reorganizing the bank.

Adler called for subscription of $1,500,000 in new capital stock, enabling the return of some cash to strapped depositors.

The crowd was enthusiastic. They would be happy about anything that offered hope. One man questioned, "If we have a new bank, what'll be it called?"

Adler, a shrewd and witty business-man, replied: "Don't you think we should have the baby before we name it?"

A $25 prize was offered in a naming contest, and C.F. Simmermaker of Tipton, Iowa, won. It would be Davenport Bank & Trust Co.

The goal for money was oversubscribed in 1932, and the city was so thrilled that factory whistles hooted and church bells rang. On the Davenport levee, Battery B of the National Guard set up field pieces and let go with a salute of 100 rounds.

The new Davenport Bank opened in July of '32 amid apprehension of another bank run. It didn't happen. Citizens

had trust. One customer brought a flower for each teller window.

By the time of the national moratorium in 1933, Davenport's new bank already had more than $12 million in assets.

The success of an Iowa town in getting a bank back on its feet claimed national attention. *Time* magazine even told of "Davenport's success story."

A bank, yes. But the end of the Great Depression was a decade away.

Grim men walked our streets, many of them in neckties and clean-shaven. Their only shame was that they had no work to do.

Tuning In

"Good evening, Mr. and Mrs. America and all the ships at sea. Let's go to press."
— Walter Winchell, staccato-voiced radio commentator and newspaper columnist published in the 1930s and 1940s

chapter six

In Everybody's Living Room

If you were a Tri-City child of the Radio Age, how could you hold up your head among your peers if you hadn't sent in your Ovaltine label for a Orphan Annie secret decoder ring?

And if you are a child of the TV Age you must be asking: "Why would anyone just sit and listen in front of the radio? What was there to see?"

Your keeper of memories of "Lux Radio Theatre," Jack Armstrong the Wheaties-devouring All-American Boy; the "Green Hornet," "Stella Dallas," and Oxydol's "Ma Perkins," Jell-O's Jack Benny and the stereotypical "Amos 'n' Andy" will try to explain.

Can the mavens of "M*A*S*H" and MTV understand the wondrous creations radio listeners "saw" in their imagination, images forever engraved deeper and sharper on the memory than almost any TV pictures?

And so who, from that magic time of the mind, cannot still "see" Fibber McGee's crammed closet; the miserable tenements near "Grand Central Station,"

George Burns and Gracie Allen, one of radio's brightest comedy teams.

"Radio was a god-like presence ... into lives and homes."
— E.B. White, American writer

RADIO STARS

THE LARGEST CIRCULATION OF ANY RADIO MAGAZINE

OCTOBER
10 CENTS

THE DANGERS OF STARDOM
See page 14

Bing Crosby

THE HEADACHES AND HEARTACHES OF CAPT'N HENRY, FRANK PARKER, JOE COOK, DICK LIEBERT, GRAHAM McNAMEE

Bing Crosby, on the 1934 cover of one of the dozen radio star magazines on the market.

All of the Tri-Cities came to a halt when "Amos 'n' Andy" came on the air nightly at 6 p.m. It was repeated at 10.

the footlights going up as "Mr. First Nighter" took his seat in the theater?

That was, of course, radio's golden age of drama, humor and adventure, classical music by great artists, serials and soap operas, star performers, writers, sound effects experts and all who gave the imagination free rein to see and fashion what it would.

The radio listener, as opposed to the passive TV watcher, was a key part of the creative process, instantly "watching" a personal mind's eye production.

If you are of an age when radio was far more than talk shows, music and news, recall these programs and see what memories they stir:

"Mr. Keene, Tracer of Lost Persons," "The Shadow," "I Love a Mystery," "One Man's Family," "Vic and Sade," "John's Other Wife," "Stella Dallas," Fred Allen and his "Allen's Alley" with Senator Claghorn and Mrs. Nussbaum, Ed Wynn, Groucho Marx, "The Lone Ranger," "Easy Aces," "Bob and Ray" and "The Bell Telephone Hour."

Remember radio's "Dragnet," "Dick Tracy," "Louella Parson's Hollywood Hotel," "Our Gal Sunday," "Myrt and Marge," "The Goldbergs," "Your Hit Parade" with Snooky Lanson, and the cornfed comedy of "Lum 'n' Abner"?

Try your facile memory on "Silver Theatre," "Sergeant Preston of the Royal Mounted Police," "The Adventures of Sam Spade," "Suspense," "Mercury Theatre" and "The Rudy Vallee Show."

How about "The Whistler" with its haunting theme song of a lone whistler; the tromp-tromp-tromp of convicts marching in prison on "Gang Busters," and, for certain, "Duffy's Tavern." (The intro: "This is Duffy's Tavern, where the elite meet to eat, Duffy speaking.")

And who can forget how FDR's fireside chats warmed the hearts of Americans chilled by years of economic depression and the spectre of war on the horizon?

When "Amos 'n' Andy" was on in the evening, everything in the country halted. Tri-City movies theaters such as the Capitol in Davenport, the Fort in Rock Island and the LeClaire in Moline stopped the films at 6 p.m., "Amos 'n' Andy" time. They piped the show through their speaker systems, knowing that was the only way they could keep patrons who would stay home rather than miss an episode.

The character of Andy was a hometown boy, Charles Correll, a bricklayer who once played piano for silent films at the old Majestic movie

"Holy mackerel, Andy."
—"Amos 'n' Andy," 1929

house in Rock Island.

There were plenty of kids' shows, aired at about the time school let out, and the characters in them led incredibly exciting lives. Jack Armstrong and his buddies were straight-arrow students at Hudson High. Jack and his friends, Billy and Betty, were rarely there, though. They kept turning up all over the world dodging dangerous criminals and solving crimes that baffled the authorities. So how'd they keep up their grades?

Then there was Little Orphan Annie and her faithful dog, Sandy. This orphan gallivanted around the globe with billionaire Daddy Warbucks, who somehow never adopted her. She always had an odd-ball crew of protectors that included a turbaned giant named Punjab and an ominous little fellow known as "Asp."

Soon there will be no one left who remembers radio's finest hours. Today they might seem naive and overly sentimental. Perhaps they were. But not to the Ovaltine-sipping, boxtop-clipping, decoder-ring wearers who shared their joys and sorrows and loved them.

—Jim Arpy

"Little Orphan Annie" aired
five nights a week from WGN, Chicago.

Home plate, and Reagan on the radio

"The two most testing jobs in America are president and radio broadcaster for the Chicago Cubs," columnist and TV political pundit George Will has written. "Reagan has now held both."

Baseball, by radio, was a ritual of the good old summertime. In barbershops throughout the Tri-Cities, a game was played on the radio every afternoon, while the gents loafed or had a clipper on the sides and some Lucky Tiger tonic. Every bar, every cigar store, had a game tuned to the Cubs, the Sox or the Cards.

Men took Sunday afternoon naps, lulled by the chatter of Chicago Cubs games called by announcers such as Bob Elson of WGN and Hal Totten of WMAQ ... "Lon Warnecke, the Arkansas hummingbird, is on the mound today for the Cubs; Gabby Hartnett's behind the plate and Stan Hack on third."

On summery weekend afternoons, one could walk the shady streets and nearly every home emitted, through the screen door, the sounds of a ballgame.

"One of my favorite memories of childhood was my dad, Al Kohn, stretched out on the floor every Sunday afternoon listening to the Cubs," says Dorothy Wulf, Davenport.

One of those who announced was an upstart named Ronald Reagan, who launched a radio career at WOC in Davenport calling Chicago Cubs games in absentia.

Recalled Reagan:

"In Chicago, in the press box, a telegraph operator would tap out each play. Sitting on the opposite side of a glass window from me in our studios in Davenport, another telegraph operator, hearing the dot and dash code, would type out the message and I would translate it into the audible sounds of baseball ... one day I found myself faced with a terse note: 'The wire has gone dead.'

"I had a ball on the way to the plate and there was no way to call it back. I knew of only one thing that wouldn't get in the score column and betray me — a foul ball. So I had the batter foul the pitch down the left field line ... he fouled for six minutes and 45 seconds."

Rock 'n' Roll on the go

A hundred years from now, nobody will be singing "Puppy Love." But in the early 1960s, Paul Anka's lament over his romance with Annette Funicello was one of the first tunes heard by a legion of Quad-City teens for whom the most important invention of the century was the simple $10 transistor radio.

Suddenly, radio's range was unlimited. With a transistor radio, you could sit under the maple trees in the back yard and listen to Roy Orbison growl his way through "Pretty Woman" or gaze into a star-filled summer sky as the Tornadoes bopped through "Telstar." A transistor radio kept you company as you Dippity-Do'ed your hair and when you washed the dinner dishes. At camps like Archie Allen in Port Byron, Illinois, transistor radios were as necessary as flashlights and mosquito repellent.

In partnership, the transistor radio and rock 'n' roll created a new group of consumers, the sons and daughters of the World War II generation — children whose Depression-bruised parents were loath to deprive them of anything. Advertisers quickly learned to appeal to the transistor-radio market.

Transistor radios took their young owners far beyond the confines of Milan or Davenport or Moline. When an eighth-grade science class at Franklin Junior High in Rock Island was assigned to monitor weather changes — temperatures and winds and the like — over the span of a week, as many reports were based on what was heard over radio station WLS in Chicago as over KSTT in Davenport.

It wasn't all rock 'n' roll: Quad-City teens were introduced to activism early on with events like the United Cerebral Palsy walk-a-thon.

But adolescent memory cells also absorbed, sometimes unwittingly, the news of the world. There were radio owners like Carol Hayes of Sheffield, Illinois, who, to the consternation of her brother, turned off her transistor radio ("to save the batteries") every time a news broadcast came on. But more listened — and heard about events such as the erection of the Berlin Wall and the deadly bombing of a black church in Birmingham, Alabama, and the growing turmoil in Vietnam.

Even the music that came through the tinny, tiny transistor radio speaker changed over the years. The silliness of "Splish Splash" and the bubblegum yearning of "Johnny Angel" mixed it up with the dark-

You weren't part of the "in" crowd in the '60s unless you had your weekly KSTT survey to keep track of the tops in tunes.

ness of "Eve of Destruction" and hard-edged rhythm of "Touch Me." Transistors gave way to boom boxes.

Still, even today, one of the signals of teen-hood in bloom is that summer afternoon when the skinny little kid next door settles in on her front step with a can of pop and a portable radio. Another listener is born.

— **Deb Brasier**

"This ... is London."

The words, dramatically deep-throated, were from Edward R. Murrow. His CBS radio broadcasts from England during World War II brought the horror of war, for the first time, into our living rooms.

Murrow, who began each broadcast with his famous, "This ... is London," assembled a team of young reporters, many of whom would, like their boss, reluctantly make the transition to television news less than a decade later.

Murrow and Co. took listeners to the rooftops as Nazi bombs rained down on London. They took listeners into the streets, the homes, the nightspots of a city struggling to hold its head high against the relentless German assault.

The book *The Murrow Boys* (Stanley Cloud and Lynne Olson, Houghton Mifflin) recounts Murrow's take on the Blitz:

"'Good Lord, they just rained from heaven,' an air raid warden, his face black with soot, told [Larry] LeSueur and [Eric] Sevareid [two of Murrow's fellow broadcasters]. 'I'm just glad to be alive.'

"Hundreds were killed in that first raid, thousands injured or driven from their homes. From a basement window, two wardens carefully lifted a man's body out of the rubble. Under a blood-red moon, women, their faces vacant and dazed, pushed prams piled high with their salvaged belongings over the glass powder in the streets.

"Beginning that evening, London endured 57 straight nights of relentless bombing. As darkness fell, sirens all over the city would issue their quavering alarms, and for the next eight hours or more, Londoners would endure the hum of the bombers, the scream and roar of the bombs, the crash and thunder of the anti-aircraft guns. Sometimes, great landmarks like St. Paul's and the Houses of Parliament and Buckingham Palace were hit. Much more often the targets were flats and shops. When dawn broke, the city's residents would creep wearily from their foul-smelling underground shelters to see if they still had homes and neighbors."

For the first time, Edward R. Murrow brought the horrors of war to the folks back home by way of radio.

"The originator of an overseas reporting program unequaled anywhere, Ed Murrow set standards of excellence that remain unsurpassed."
— William S. Paley, Chairman, Columbia Broadcasting System, 1965

In on the ground floor

"Bill Stern, the Brylcreme shaving man is on the air." The terse sports announcer once spoke at a sports banquet in Davenport.

In all the millions of years the Earth had existed, the airwaves had been eerily silent.

Then abruptly, a decade or so into the 20th century, began a faint and fading, patchy, scratchy caterwauling that would swell to a history-changing crescendo — radio!

Now human voices and sounds would travel instantly through the air, linking people everywhere, and beginning the shrinking of the world that continues into the 21st century.

The Tri-Cities had a big foot in the radio door almost from the beginning. Its infancy was crude and inefficient, but enraptured listeners did not care.

In 1914, R. Karlowa had established what he called Radio-Telegraph 9-Bc in Rock Island. With limited range, it broadcast, on an amateur wave, music, weather reports and news flashes — the format for most radio stations today.

Ever the visionary, Dr. B.J. Palmer, of Palmer School of Chiropractic, bought the Karlowa station in 1922, as the airwaves were coming under federal control. He saw it as a great way to publicize the virtues of chiropractic, as well as a potential advertising money-maker.

The second commercial radio license issued anywhere in the United States went to Palmer's radio station WOC, said to stand for "World of Chiropractic." The first was to KDKA in Pittsburgh.

On the very first WOC program, Davenport Mayor Arthur Mueller played a cello solo. Listeners must have liked it, because he was invited back often. Otherwise, programming was simple. For the sports-minded, WOC managed to broadcast a few University of Iowa football games. And people crowded around their sets when Palmer wove hour-long tales of his travels abroad.

In time, "Radio Rex," pioneered by a man whose last name was Willets, began a program housewives enjoyed. It included the reading of recipes over the air, slowly enough that anyone could write them down.

There was even a radio exercise show, the "Daily Dozen," hosted by Pat Flanagan.

Little Jack Little, a talented musician, had WOC's most popular show, and he used it as a springboard for a successful musical career.

On February 16, 1925, WHBF signed on in Rock Island. Soon, numerous stations were competing for space on the dial. The critics who had called radio a flash in the pan were silenced. Entertainment had come into the home. Radio, for better or worse, was here to stay.

— **Jim Arpy**

"Radio in the 1930s was a calm and tranquil medium. Oleaginous-voiced announcers smoothly purred their commercial copy into the microphones, enunciating each lubricated syllable. Tony Wons was cooing his soothing poems. Bedtime stories were popular. Radio was one unruffled day from 'Cheerio' in the early morning through to 'Music to Read By' at midnight. Radio was fraught with politeness."

— Fred Allen, radio wit, "Treadmill to Oblivion"

Stay tuned ... A log of one day's programming in 1938

6:00	Top of the Morning.
6:30	6:30 Roundup.
6:45	News.
8:30	Peoples Mail Bag.
8:45	News.
9:00	Pretty Kitty Kelly, CBS.
9:15	The Party Line.
9:30	Dave Bacal and His Hi Hatters, CBS.
9:45	Ma Perkins, CBS.
10:00	Mary Lee Taylor, CBS.
10:15	Weekly Shopper.
10:30	Melodic Serenade.
11:00	Mary Margaret McBride, CBS.
11:15	Your News Parade, CBS.
11:30	Hymns of All Churches.
11:45	Betty and Bob.
12:00	Farm Bureau.
12:05	Stock Market.
12:10	Studio Swingapators.
12:20	Inquiring Mike.
12:30	News.
12:45	Eddie Duchin Orchestra.
1:00	Lyric Serenade, CBS.
1:15	Afternoon Recess.
1:30	American School of the Air, CBS.
2:00	Theater Matinee, CBS.
3:00	Tea Time Tunes.
3:15	Between the Bookends, CBS.
3:30	Linger Awhile.
4:00	News.
4:15	Pat at the Piano.
4:30	Dear Teacher, CBS.
	Children's Corner, CBS.
4:45	Man on the Street.
5:00	Del Casino, CBS.
	America's Schools, NBC.
	Junior Nurses, NBC.
	Kitty Keene, WBBM.
	Jolly Joe, WGN.
5:15	Four Clubmen, CBS.
	Buddy and Ginger, WGN.
	The Top Hatters, NBC.
	Marek Weber, NBC.
	John D. M. Hamilton, chairman of the Republican National Committee, will present his party's answer to President Roosevelt's message to Congress in an address, CBS.
5:30	Jack Armstrong.
	Charlie Chan, WGN.

Young listeners mailed in box tops to get Junior G-Man badges.

5:45	Song Time, CBS.
	Tom Mix, NBC.
	Don Winslow, NBC.
	Little Orphan Annie, WGN.
	Lowell Thomas, NBC.
5:55	Tri States Theaters.
6:00	Sport Summary.
	Jack Westaway, WGN.
	Amos and Andy, NBC.
	Hal Totten Sports, NBC.
	Easy Aces, Comedy Skit, NBC.
6:15	Hollywood Screenscoops by George McCall, CBS.
	Uncle Ezra, NBC.
	Mr. Keen, Tracer of Lost Persons, NBC.
	Blackstone Concert Trio, WGN.
	Edna O'Dell, WBB.
6:30	We The People, CBS.
	Lum and Abner, NBC.
	Alistaire Cooke, News Comments, NBC.
6:45	Jimmy O'Dette from Blackhawk Hotel, Davenport, Iowa.
7:00	Kate Smith, CBS.
7:30	Eddie Cantor, CBS.
8:00	Major Bowes Amateur Hour, CBS.
	Kay Kyser Orchestra, WGN.
8:30	Ben Bernie and All the Lads, CBS.
9:00	Tish, CBS.
	The ingenious exploits of Buffalo's so called "Holiday Bandit," George Best, who staged one man holdups in Buffalo stores during the holidays will be heard on Gang Busters. Col. H. Norman Schwarzkopf, former head of the new Jersey State Police, will join the cast as a permanent member tonight, CBS.
9:15	The Madison Square Garden featherweight bout between Henry Armstrong and Eurico Venturi will be presented by Clem McCarthy and George Hicks, NBC.
9:30	Hollywood Showcase, CBS.
10:00	News.
	Amos and Andy, NBC.
10:15	Cab Calloway Orchestra, CBS.
10:30	Leighton Noble Orchestra, CBS.
11:00	Orrin Tucker Orchestra, CBS.
	Tommy Dorsey, CBS.
	Guy Lombardo, WGN.
11:30	Buddy Rogers Orchestra, CBS.
	Lights Out Mystery Drama, NBC.

In the mind's eye

True story: Radio carried the "Adventures of Sherlock Holmes." One story was "The Hound of the Baskervilles," a chilling tale of the Scottish moors and the great killer hound that lurked there. Two small boys in upstairs beds on a cold winter night in rural Iowa. Nothing to be seen but the dim yellow light on the old upright radio.

Then out of the night comes the mournful echoing howl of the great hound lurking somewhere on the dark moors. How they shiver and almost feel the hound's hot breath on their cheeks. More than a half century later they still see that awful moor — and remember.

" ... Able to leap tall buildings at a single bound! It's a bird, it's a plane, it's Superman."
— Announcer, "Superman," 1940

Jack Benny, "Jello-O again," every Sunday night at 6.

"You're a hard man, McGee."
— "Fibber McGee and Molly," 1935

Radio buttons such as this one offered to Dick Tracy fans were badges of courage.

"Britt Reid, daring young publisher, matches wits with the underworld ... He hunts the biggest ... of all game. Public enemies who try to destroy our America."
— Announcer, "The Green Hornet"

"The wheel of fortune goes 'round and 'round and where she stops, nobody knows."
— Major Bowes, "Major Bowes and His Original Amateur Hour," 1934

"So long, until tomorrow."
— News announcer Lowell Thomas, 1930

" ... The story of a woman who sets out to prove ... that romance can live ... at 35."
— Announcer, "The Romance of Helen Trent," 1933 soap opera

It's time to close the door of the Inner Sanctum. Pleasant dreams, hm-m-m-m?"
— The hollow, deathly voice of Raymond on the late-night "Inner Sanctum," 1941

"Who's the little chatterbox?
The one with pretty auburn locks?
Who can it be? It's Little Orphan Annie."
— Announcer, "Little Orphan Annie," 1931, a five-day-a-week serial for kids

"If I dood it, I gets a whipping."
— Red Skelton, "The Red Skelton Show," 1941

"I'm speaking from the roof of the Broadcasting Building, New York City. The bells you hear are ringing to warn people to evacuate the city as the Martians approach."
— Announcer, Orson Welles' "The War of the Worlds," Mercury Radio Theatre, 1938

Clicquot Club Eskimos, in furry out-fits. The band offered radio concerts for Clicquot Club ginger ale.

"Can this girl from a mining town in the West find happiness as the wife of a wealthy and titled Englishman?"
— Announcer for the soap opera, "Our Gal Sunday," 1937

"Hey, Abbott. I'm a ba-a-a-ad boy."
— Lou Costello, "Abbott and Costello," 1942

"Wake up, America! It's time to stump the experts."
— Announcer, "Information Please"

" ... The story of ... what it means to be the wife of a famous Broadway star — dream sweetheart of a million other women."
— Announcer, "Backstage Wife," soap opera

Live on WOC-TV, it was "If You Asked Me," starring an all-Quad-City cast. The early 1950s weekly quiz show was along the lines of "What's My Line?" It preceded John Daly's Sunday night "What's My Line?" network show and WOC claimed the net copied the local program. This was a quizzed-panel, with some questions from the show's announcer, Warren "Buzz" Vasen, at far right, and other questions phoned in by viewers. The panelist with the most correct answers won points, and the prize for the night usually was a box of chocolates, remembers Elly Carlson, one of the regulars on the show. The panel, front row from left, Glen Herman, Elly Carlson and Sy Raben. Back row, Elaine Evans, Joe Brandmeyer and Lois Britton. Note the front of the tables: Venetian blinds.

Warren Vasen

Take sound, add pictures and you have – television!

"Television is a pervasive part of our modern lives."
— Norm Goldstein, author of
"The History of Television"

Today it can be said, without compromise, that every Quad-City household has a TV set. How and when did this all begin, an epochal era that turned us into couch potatoes?

The answer: At 6 p.m. on Halloween 1949, when WOC-TV, Davenport, shook up radio's future by airing a kinescope of the puppet show "Kukla, Fran and Ollie" and became Iowa's first commercial television station.

WOC-TV didn't have the Tri-City TV spectrum to itself very long. WHBF-TV, Rock Island, quickly followed, and a decade or so later, Moline got WQAD-TV. Then along came WQPT in 1983, and Davenport welcomed its second station, KLJB-TV, in 1985.

It was no surprise that this area had been targeted for early invasion by TV. Pioneers in radio broadcasting long since had blazed the trail to this frontier. Then came two reports.

The first was that 400 TV sets had been spotted in the Tri-City area in 1947, their owners presumably pulling in signals from far afield.

The second was that the Palmer family had applied for a permit to add a TV station to its operations. On October 11, 1949, it was learned the number of receivers had grown to 1,750. The video invasion was on.

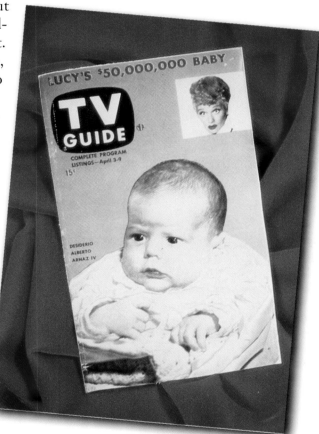

The birth of Lucille Ball's television baby, Ricky Ricardo Jr., was one of TV's memorable events. Lucy was on the cover of *TV Guide* more than any other star.

Milton Berle, "Uncle Miltie," reigned for a decade as TV's "Mr. Television." His 1965 show was "Hollywood Palace."

Video memories? Local viewers may have forgotten the national stir caused by the low-cut gowns Faye Emerson wore on TV fashion shows in the 1940s but not the talents other performers unveiled when network TV came to the Tri-City area in the 1950s.

By way of reminder: In 1950, Emmys were awarded to Alan Young, Gertrude Berg and Groucho Marx; in 1951 to Red Skelton, Sid Caesar and Imogene Coca; and in 1952 to Robert Montgomery, Jimmy Durante, Lucille Ball and Bishop Fulton J. Sheen.

Award-winning shows of 1950 included: "The Alan Young Show," "Pulitzer Prize Playhouse" and "Truth and Consequences." In 1951, winners were "Studio One," "The Red Skelton Show" and "Your Show of Shows." In 1952, the gold statuettes went to "See It Now," "Dragnet," "I Love Lucy" and "What's My Line?"

News was a staple of network TV long before it became the cornerstone of local broadcasting. Back in 1940, Lowell Thomas was simulcasting "Sonoco News" in New York City on radio and in 1948 Douglas Edwards anchored the first nightly TV news on CBS. So when Paul Liggitt, a local radio news reporter who joined WHBF in 1948, was assigned to read his report before WHBF-TV cameras in 1950, he did not feel the least bit daunted.

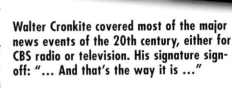

Walter Cronkite covered most of the major news events of the 20th century, either for CBS radio or television. His signature sign-off: "... And that's the way it is ..."

Not at first, anyway. But it wasn't long before Liggitt learned that the amount of air time a news item merited would depend largely on the visuals available to illustrate it. So he was outfitted with a Polaroid camera for capturing frames of flickering flames at fire scenes when no cameraman was on hand. Today, he recalls a courier holding newly developed film of an East Moline basketball game out of the window of his car so it could dry while it was being rushed to the Rock Island studio for broadcast.

Learning how to present "all-live" TV was fraught with misery. Anita Sundin, a WOC-TV performer and continuity writer, once spoke of a tongue-challenged weather person who transposed the "F" and the "P" in "fair and partly cloudy."

When WOC-TV did go live, some of its early performers and shows, besides anchors and newscasts, were "Mr. Weatherwise" (another puppet); Marjorie Meinert and George Sontag, musicians;

Johnny Carson was the "king of late-night television" for 30 years, but it was Jack Paar, left, who pioneered the format. Paar, who preceded Carson, ran afoul of NBC over a joke that censors deemed too risque for the airwaves.

Pat Sundine, variety show host; Warren Vasen and Ran Jansen; game shows; and shows that interacted with children like the Dixie Belle Showboat series with "Cap'ns" ranging from Vern Gielow to Ernie Mimms, and the "Circle 6 Ranch" with Wrangler Pete Vegenas.

Early live programming on WHBF is remembered as the Buddies of the Airlanes; Jim Olsen as Postman Petersen; Milt Boyd as Grandpa Happy; Chuck Harrison, newsman, and Don Wooten, weathercaster.

By 1950, the Tri-Cities had 40,000 TV sets. How many today? Stay tuned.

— **Ron Lorenzen**

Their last hurrah. Men and women of "M*A*S*H" pose for their last official portrait as the series calls it a wrap after 11 glorious seasons. The final episode in 1983 was watched by 50 million viewers.

A young Bill Cosby and Robert Culp in "I Spy," which ran from 1965 to 1968.

Ed Sullivan's Sunday night show originally was called "Toast of the Town" and eventually was renamed for him. It was Sunday night's highest-rated program. His guests ranged from puppets such as Topo Gigio to high-profile performers from Broadway. And, of course, The Beatles made their U.S. television debut on the Sullivan show.

In the early days, there was Pat ...

(For 18 years and six months, Pat Sundine was THE television personality in Quad-City Land. Now living in Naples, Florida, Pat says that she is 77 and could return to the air just as soon as she could get her hair done.)

Pat Sundine as hostess of "Especially for You." She was one of the first Quad-City TV personalities.

I suppose you could use the old cliché and say I've done it all: TV show hostess, talk show, phone show.

Talk show? Ha, I laugh and laugh when I think of this. Once, I had been interviewing the secretary to the governor of Iowa. I signed off for a commercial, and intended to say, "I'll be back to a busy switchboard." What I said was, "I'll be back to a swizzy bitchboard."

Life was like that in the long-ago early days of WOC radio and TV.

Commercials? Well, anything could happen. I had been working with Cap'n Ernie, and our sponsor was a dairy company. I did a lot of my own commercials and brought my 3-year-old son, John Patrick Sundine, to drink a glass of milk before the camera. Right there, on the air, he said:

"I won't drink it."

I gave him an anxious look and smilingly said, "Dear, drink your milk."

He just looked back at me and said, "I DON'T LIKE MILK."

That settled that. I drank it myself.

"When television belatedly found its way into the home, after stopping off too long at the tavern, the advertisers knew they had a more potent force available for their selling purposes. Radio was abandoned like the bones at a barbeque."

— Fred Allen, "Treadmill to Oblivion," 1954

Those were years with George Sontag, a dear person who saved the day for me so many times. Once, I cajoled Jack Sundine into bringing his grandfather on the air for his 100th birthday. I was going to do the whole show on him. We had a blazing salute of candles, and George played "Happy Birthday." Then grandfather said, "I've had enough of this" and walked off the set. That left me with 22 minutes of air time. Thank goodness for George. He filled the rest of the time on the piano and I showed slides.

So many of the funny things come to mind. I was to do a part in a commercial. The announcer was to say, "The best of bread." Instead, he said, "The breast in bed." I quickly came on, intending to say, "The best in bread." But it came out, "The best in bed."

During a live show we did everything — and I mean everything.

On the "Cartoon Showboat" set with Cap'n Ernie Mimms, 1970, WOC-TV.

Pat Sundine Edwards, today.

Dining with the stars

Television has changed it all ... including the way we eat. We were so hypnotized by the first TV that we had to dine in front of the set; hence, the birth of the collapsible TV tray, with its spindly legs. From that was born the TV dinner.

In 1954, Swanson introduced the world's first TV dinner: turkey, stuffing, mashed potatoes, gravy and peas. Ten million were sold the first year. Chicken TV dinners and other entrees soon followed.

In the 1960s, a fourth section was added to the tray, for brownies, cherry or apple cobbler or other desserts. That wasn't enough for a hungry guy. In 1973, Hungry Man dinners came to the market, offering bigger portions.

By 1987, we were so thrilled with microwaving that a new type of non-metal packaging was introduced.

The original Swanson aluminum dinner tray took its place in the Smithsonian Institution, a symbol of the way we have come to live in the television age.

We'd always go the Mississippi Valley Fair in Davenport, and one afternoon I went out there with Lorne Greene of the old show "Bonanza." He was driving, and he drove like a bat out of hell, right through Davenport to the fairgrounds. I never have had such a fast ride. But on the show, live, he was as calm as if plodding along on a horse.

Mine was a real homey show, the first of its kind in this part of the country, I suppose. WOC was the first TV station in Iowa. I'd give a daily household hint. Once, we had an apron contest. I got more than a thousand aprons in the mail, and I showed most of them on the air.

So many names come back to me as I think of those days, like Donna Scott of "Romper Room" and Ed Jones, who was my producer. I did a lot with live guests. In the 1960s and 1970s, Mantovanti and his orchestra were very, very big. He was to be on my show, all gussied up in his tails. He wasn't too happy to begin with about getting up so early, because I went on right after the "Today" show. To make matters worse, our floor crew forgot to pick him up, so he was late arriving. To placate him, Jones had arranged to put on Mantovanti's latest record. Things went from bad to worse. They used the wrong speed for the record to introduce the maestro's new, best-selling album.

Those were the days of very strong TV personalities, like Warren Vasen and Ran Jansen. And, for sure, B.J. Palmer, who owned the whole works. B.J. loved pretty ladies. Our first TV studio was a big garage building behind the place where everything is situated now atop Brady Hill. Early, very early in the morning, when we were rehearsing, B.J. would slip his trousers over his pajama bottoms and sit on the sidelines, smiling and watching.

Oh, gosh! Those were the good old days. And really, for longer than 18 years, they really were good. I feel like a pioneer!

— **Pat Sundine Edwards**

In living color —at a cost

Color television was a thousand-dollar gleam in the eye of every Quad-City watcher, but most waited until the mid-1950s when it became widely available and practical for the pocketbook.

Advertisements like this, for RCA models, were appearing in magazines by the late 1950s.

A group of 50 invited guests in the home of L.A. Baumgartner, Davenport, saw what was believed to be the first TV colorcast into the Quad-Cities. It was Easter Sunday 1954, delivered by NBC-TV via Channel 6, WOC-TV.

The program was devoted to the Easter Parade in New York City and a colorful parade it was, viewers said — though the set required to receive it cost about $1,000. By late fall, big-screen (17-inch) was coming on the market, dooming black and white within a few years.

Now that you're going to buy Color TV...

TV TONITE TILL 9

Relax, drink a Coke, watch the fights on the incomparable

SUMMER PATIO

Capehart TELEVISION with CX33 Chassis

Television Mart

BOYS! GIRLS!
Get your free chance on a Hopalong Cassidy Radio. Free cokes, free favors.

Brady at Kimberly
Davenport 3-9116

1616 15th Street
Moline, Ill.

Low Down Payment
15 Months to Pay

SUMMER PATIO

Saturday night with the spooks

TV fanatics of several generations recall when, in 1963, the new "vid" on the block, WQAD-TV, Moline, turned Saturday nights over to horror shows — "Chiller Theater."

An edited version of one newspaper's report of the premiere:

"The second feature Saturday, entitled 'Night Monster,' was rapidly approaching its climax with the monster about to be revealed when the video began to fail. All at once, an announcer's voice confided something weird was going on at the transmitter site. Then the monster and the movie vanished altogether. At length, the announcer could be heard saying that the station was ending its broadcast day."

Some were fascinated just to watch the test pattern

Everything must have a first.

In the days when "snow" was an accepted irritation of television-watching, the glaze-eyed thrill of owning the first set in Davenport — possibly the entire Quad-Cities — was a determined resident of 2326 Jersey Ridge Road.

Louis Thomas put down $895 for a 10-inch Capehart in 1949, plus $250 for a high reception tower, plus $130 for a long-distance antenna.

This was months before WOC would go on the air and Thomas pinned his hopes on receiving Chicago stations. He did, with fair to good reception.

Another 1949 TV pioneer was Russell Swartz of Jersey Ridge and Kimberly roads, Davenport. His reception was quite good because he had hired a wrecking crew to rip the top off an old windmill, where he installed an antenna.

Television was a novelty in its early days. Crowds would gather outside TV stores to watch the Friday night fights through big display windows. George's Radio & Appliance in Davenport mounted an antenna atop the grandstand at the Mississippi Valley Fairgrounds and had several sets in place for viewers to watch a baseball game from Chicago.

Reception was quite clear, but some were skeptical, claiming that it was a stunt — George's had put a movie machine in that box so people would think it was TV and thus enhance sales.

Harold and Irene Lincoln of Davenport were among the first to purchase TV sets, braving the annoyance of watching Chicago roller derbies through a blizzard of snow.

Mrs. Lincoln remembered: "We were so fascinated by TV that we would just sit and watch the test pattern."

When WOC went on the air, hundreds of Quad-City set owners were waiting. Clyde Clark, a one-time Davenport appliance dealer, said that on the first night of local programming, his store received 50 frantic calls from TV set owners who were too nervous to adjust the vertical or change the contrast for fear of turning the picture into flip-flops.

An early Zenith black and white model.

A Daily Times promotion calendar of 1931 was speaking of "television and airyplanes and such new-fangled things."

European crafts-
men were brought
to Bettendorf to
fashion the fine
woodwork in the
Joseph Bettendorf
mansion, which was
completed in 1915.
A set of silver gilt
dishes, made in
1808 for the Duke
of Cambridge, were
used as ashtrays
and a showpiece in
the mansion was a
coronation table of
King Louis XVI
of France.

The Way We Lived

"Let me tell you about the very rich. They are different from you and me ... they possess and enjoy early."

— F. Scott Fitzgerald

chapter seven

Mansions of the Mighty

In a pre-tax time, when a dollar earned was a dollar saved, mansion-building flourished in the Quad-Cities. Among the grandest ...

The Bettendorf brothers, William and Joseph, were kings in an industrial dynasty of building railroad car trucks and boxcar frames, which held the wheels to the railroad car. William was the first to build a mansion, a Spanish mission-type in the bluffs lording over the vast Bettendorf Co. plant. The cost was an astronomical $125,000 in 1908, but he died before moving in, and it now is the Iowa Masonic Home. His brother, Joseph, built an even grander, 28-room mansion, which is shown here during its prime years of family occupancy. It had a bowling alley, dancing hall, formal gardens, a swimming pool and a greenhouse for flowers and trees to grow bananas, his favorite fruit. It now is St. Katharine St. Mark Independent College Preparatory School.

Above, A lower level card room. Left, one of the two bowling alleys.

The staircase showcased the work of imported craftsmen. At left, The 17-acre mansion grounds had formal gardens and a lily pond.

The most glamored mansion around was Villa Velie, built by Moline auto manufacturer Willard Velie. Modeled after an Italian villa, it was built on a 500-acre tract, much of which now is Wildwood. Artisans were brought from Europe to build the 46-room mansion, which had 14 bedrooms and 12 bathrooms. The hills, sloping toward the Rock River, were vineyards, with plants imported from Europe. Velie had his personal wine label. In the

Nic Chirekos

depth of the Depression, the Velies moved to less grand quarters, and the place became a series of night clubs, the best-known being the Plantation. Suave Nic Chirekos managed the place in its heyday, visiting with guests and requesting "House of Blue Lights" from pianist Sinclair Mills. The mansion fell on hard times after Chirekos was murdered in his upstairs office by a burglar, but is majestic again, remodeled for use as a bank and office suites.

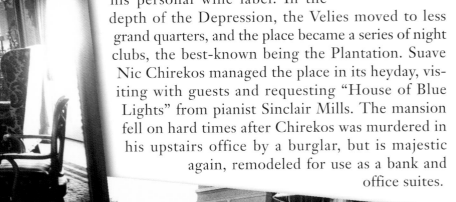

Villa Velie was a grand place to party in the 1920s and early 1930s. Top left, the living room. Lower left, a dance floor placed over the mansion's pool. At right, the ballroom. Despite one twice-told tale, the mansion — completed in 1914 — never had an indoor swimming pool.

The Plantation Tahitian Room

The original Velie sunroom, left, became the Tahitian Room, above, as it appeared in an old postcard. Below, the mansion's billiard room.

Garlic breath, anyone?

One of the tastiest ways to get garlic breath was to eat a Plantation salad. Mary Laing Haynes of Bettendorf comes up with the recipe for the dressing ...

1 quart Miracle Whip
1 pint Kraft French dressing
1 bud of garlic, chopped fine
3 teaspoons anchovy paste
1 small package Roquefort cheese
Add melba toast to salad just before serving

Movie theaters once were palaces, and one of the grandest in the Tri-Cities was the Capitol. The Davenport theater has gone through hard times, but retains most of the gilded glory that it had when these photos were taken.

Fake clouds floated across the ceiling of the Capitol, and stars twinkled in the gilt dome.

chapter eight

Gone to the Movies

"Movies are a dream world. Eat popcorn and dream."
— Sam Shepard, actor and playwright

● ●

Movies altered the way the Tri-Cities looked at the world ... Cruise, Gable, Harlow, Fairbanks, Streep, the Three Stooges ... cowboy shoot 'em ups of the West that never was ... the steady six-shooter aim of beady-eyed William S. Hart and the rolling gait of "The Duke" ... the silver screen land of Bogart and Bacall and Eastwood and Marilyn and Woody ... all spun into web of celluloid dreams.

Tri-Citians went wild for that amazing new amusement, the movies.

First, Julius Geertz stretched a sheet between two trees at old Pariser Garden, a beer garden in Davenport's West End. His movie projector was speedily hand-cranked, lit by a crackling arc lamp. On weekend nights, he reeled off flickering scenes like a speeding locomotive that appeared to be roaring right out of the sheet/screen.

"People screamed, thinking the train was coming right at them. No kidding, some women just about passed out," recalled Geertz, who went on to operate several "real" theaters.

Sultry Swedish movie star Ingrid Bergman's birthday was on an August 29, and the RKO Orpheum invited fans to sign this giant birthday card in the 1940s.

Fast forward, now, to a time we remember. Remember the romantic days of the drive-in movies and the ornate Capitol in Davenport, where stars twinkled on the domed ceilings while fake clouds floated by and ushers had golden epaulets on their crimson uniforms.

The Fort in Rock Island, with its flower shop on the corner, was a jewel. And every one of our cities had its hometown, neighborhood favorites.

But the most dazzling movie palace was the Orpheum, in Davenport.

"Show's over ... the crowd surges out over the brilliant red carpets ... a second show crowd fights outside the box office ... the first crowd melts into the night ... night restaurants are filled ... the streets are filled with crazy-driven cars like on New Year's Eve ... The Orpheum opening night is over," wrote columnist Bob Feeney in the *Davenport Democrat* on November 25, 1931.

Theater managers were masters of hyperbole. The Esquire promoted its cuddly love seats, a tight squeeze for two, and introduced "usherettes," the first women ushers in the Tri-Cities. Three hundred applied.

"I was one of the six chosen," says Shirley Glynn Rucker of Bettendorf. "We wore cute outfits. For one movie, we were dressed as cheerleaders."

The Capitol gave free tickets to big families when it showed "Cheaper by the Dozen." Milton "Uncle Miltie" Troehler was never without gimmicks at the Orpheum. An employee paraded out front in a drum major's outfit for "The Music Man." The Orpheum sent a desktop-size birthday card to Ingrid Bergman. When the first Beatles film, "A Hard Day's Night," played the Orpheum, the marquee billed it as "Floppsy, Moppsy, Cottontop and Ringo." Several girls stayed all night in sleeping bags on the sidewalk to be first in line.

Quad-City movie biz has always been good. "The Graduate" played 10 weeks; "Pillow Talk" packed the 2,000-plus seat Orpheum for six weeks. At the smaller Coronet, "The Sound of Music" played 72 weeks.

"I don't know where the people kept coming from," remembers Jim Stopu-

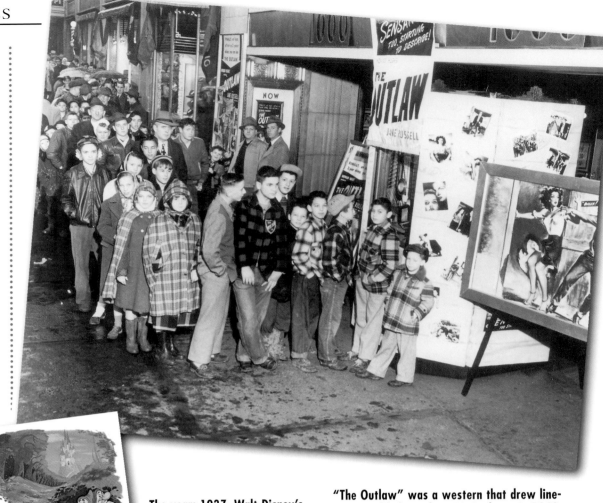

"The Outlaw" was a western that drew line-ups of kids to the RKO Orpheum in 1943. Walter Huston and Jane Russell starred.

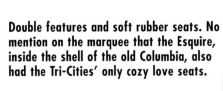

The year: 1937. Walt Disney's first feature cartoon, "Snow White and the Seven Dwarfs," appeared on local screens. Those in the movie industry said Disney's innovation wouldn't work.

Bargain admission in 1940 at the State, in the 200 block of West Third Street, Davenport.

Double features and soft rubber seats. No mention on the marquee that the Esquire, inside the shell of the old Columbia, also had the Tri-Cities' only cozy love seats.

First in line! This man slept on a cot in the foyer of the RKO Orpheum to get the first seat for a 1945 thriller about a man, supposed to be dead in the war, who returns with an altered face to find his wife has remarried. It starred Orson Welles.

los, who ran the Coronet.

When places like the Orpheum were not showing movies, they opened their stages to performers such as Liberace and French mime Marcel Marceau, the Beach Boys and Sonny and Cher. Before all this, our Rock Island princess, June Haver, sang on the Orpheum stage with the Ted Fiorito orchestra. That was before Hollywood lights lured June.

Rapid rewind, now, to the 1920s, when the movie craze was really catching. Davenport had 24 movie houses, all operating and doing business at one time. In downtown Davenport, the Mirror and the Royal stood side by side. The Zenith was only a block away from another shoebox-size theater, and reels were carried back and forth by bicycle. Admission to most theaters was a dime to dreamland, pre-popcorn. Some of these places were jitney houses, admission for kids was only a nickel, and for some, it was only a penny.

"I remember, so well, the old penny shows at the Davenport Friendly House. Movies were only one cent on Saturday afternoons," says Lillian Kunz.

Every town had at least one movie house. Theaters had catchy names, like the Roxy and Paradise and Mirror in Moline; the Ritz and Rialto and Rocket in Rock Island; the Majestic and Strand in East Moline. The Brotman brothers were the movie kings in the Illinois Tri-Cities, once owning seven theaters. Polly Brotman, with her pince-nez glasses, reigned as a queen-royal in the lobby.

With this came the come-alongs, Bank Night every Wednesday, where admission to the show was a chance on an astounding $250 or $500 or maybe — glory of glories — a new car. The dime-store patina on free dishes lured patrons to the State in Davenport; and Wahoo, a punch-card bingo game, brightened glum Depression-day hearts with a $1 nightly prize at the Majestic in East Moline.

Sound arrived, and the Columbia in Davenport was showing the first talkie, "The Jazz Singer." It wasn't long before audiences

Shaped like a shoebox, the Zenith Theater in Davenport first showed silent films. Neighborhoods were dotted with movie houses. The Washington was less than two blocks from the Zenith.

Movie houses never missed an opportunity for hoopla. Henry Plude, at far left, manager of the Capitol in Davenport, offered free admission in 1950 to the biggest Tri-City families for one attraction if they showed up all at once. After the film, he would treat them to dinner at the Blackhawk Hotel. At left, the family of Mr. and Mrs. Roy Stewart, 15 children (a few didn't make it to the movie). At right, the family of Mr. and Mrs. Herb Peters, 14 kids, all present. Both families were from Davenport. The film? "Cheaper by the Dozen," a movie adapted from the book about an efficiency expert who said it was effectual to have big families.

In small print, this midnight Spook Party poster said, "If you come alone, you'll be afraid to walk home."

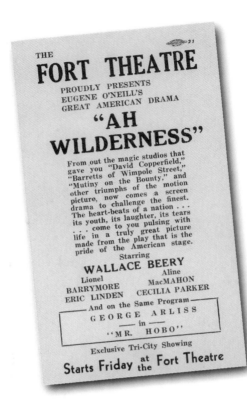

were transferred into a world of fantasy, with Rogers and Astaire and tons of feathers and gallons of glitter.

All tastes were considered. Said Ray Long, the Davenport movie historian: "Between 1930 and 1932, 58 gangster movies were shown in the Quad-Cities." The wounded Edward G. Robinson was growling, "Mother of mercy, is this the end of Rico?"

Fast forward again, through the years of "You Ought to be in Pictures" and "Hooray for Hollywood" and all of that good stuff. How can Quad-City Land top the years past?

It has, with the new Showcase Cinemas 53, all 18 screens of it and the biggest theater in Iowa. With stadium seating, Davenport's newest movie palace has made obsolete the old usher's call, "The best seating is now in the balcony."

When Shirley Temple's new film was on its way to the Fort Theatre, Rock Island, flyers were mailed to regular customers.

Cameras west — Our love affair with horse operas

When he managed the Garden Theater in downtown Davenport, the late Paul Ives used to groan, "I never knew where to put all the people when a Western was shown."

The fascination began with the trail-blazing "The Great Train Robbery" (the first Western filmed) and galloped through our-years-remembered to "True Grit" and "Cat Ballou" and "High Noon" and "Butch Cassidy and the Sundance Kid." Horse operas (as the early ones often were called) always appealed to Tri-City cinematic audiences.

"Come to think of it, I've never really seen a bad cowboy movie," says Donn Iogha, who was in the film business 55 years. "It's always the good guy against the bad guy, and the good guy always wins."

First into the saddle were William S. Hart and Tom Mix and his horse Tony. And then along trotted the superstars of the shoot-em-up westerns — Buck Jones, Ken Maynard, Tim McCoy and Hoot Gibson. To really estimate the star power of movie cowboys, Buck had a fan club membership of 3 million in 1934.

Every shoebox theater (rarely, the big local movie palaces) had weekly western serials, 15-minute cliff-hangers that made all the kids bug-eyed to return the next week. Serial night was always one of the biggest show nights at Tri-City movie houses like the Zenith or the Family or the Star.

Really, the Westerns never stopped coming; more sophisticated, yes, but always horse operas, with ever-smiling Hopalong Cassidy or the ever-brave Lone Ranger, "Hi-yo-o-o-o Silver, away-y-y-y," and then Gary "Yup" Cooper.

One can wonder about the universal appeal of the Westerns. Perhaps it is because things were simpler out on the prairie.

James Stewart, a stalwart gunslinger in notable Westerns such as "Broken Arrow," once observed, "The Western is an original. An American feels, this is ours."

Even though we don't have itchy trigger fingers, there is more than a grain of truth in that statement. Westerns always held a promise of good vs. evil, and they never broke the promise. That's why few of us ever missed one of those weekly serials, and why that movie about Butch and Sundance is the most-rented cowboy film in Quad-City video stores.

When Paul Newman and Robert Redford teamed up in "Butch Cassidy and the Sundance Kid," their antics filled Quad-City theaters on both sides of the Mississippi — and not because audiences were attracted to Katherine Ross, who rounded out the trio.

Life was simpler on the range. The good guys, those wearing the white hats, always won and the bad guys, in the black hats, lost.

Tim McCoy, a Western favorite, starred in this oater from the '30s. John Wayne had second billing.

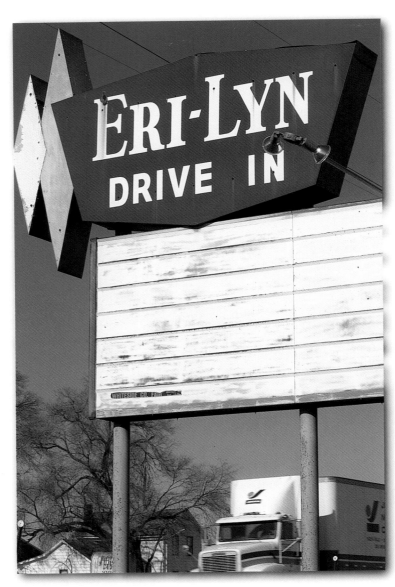

Farewell, Hollywood. The Eri-Lyn (so-named for Erie and Lyndon, Illinois) is closed, but the sign still stands forlornly on Illinois 78, south of Morrison, Illinois.

The biggest screen ever made

Sure, I remember the hot dog doing flips and the dancing ice cream. Five minutes to showtime. I remember eating popcorn from Eagle grocery bags and drinking green Kool-Aid in the back seat of the station wagon.

I remember electric in-car heaters that worked most of the time, kids sitting on the hoods of cars, triple features, making out in the back seat and smuggling in buddies in the trunks of cars.

But mostly, I remember movies.

Great movies, bad movies and some that weren't great or bad, just boring. Violent movies, cult movies, erotic movies, movies I would be embarrassed to mention because of their quality or content. Stinko sci-fi and the best of that genre. Kids' movies, adult movies, movies for the whole family — and all shown on the biggest screens ever made, those of the drive-ins.

Some films were meant for that big screen — the special effects of "The Ten Commandments" and "Star Wars" come to mind.

You get a whole new perspective on others like "The Godfather" and "The Dirty Dozen" when they are viewed with a group of young males who can speak their minds under a dome of silence like the roof of a '66 Ford Galaxie 500.

That was part of the drive-in experience too. It was a part of growing up.

I must have been about 9 when I woke up from a nap to see huge walls of water 30-feet high closing in from both sides. It swept away chariots, horses, men and the whole of the Egyptian army.

That's the earliest drive-in experience I can remember. The movie, of course, was "The Ten Commandments."

Dad took us to the drive-in quite a bit when we were kids and mom was working nights. We mostly went to the Bel-Air in Davenport because it was close to home.

We got a little older, and it wasn't cool to go to the drive-in with your parents. Then, one magic day, I got my freedom, more commonly known as a driver's license. It was back to the drive-in.

The first trip: the Semri in Silvis. The passengers: my brother, Kevin, and his girlfriend, Linda Hartman, and my sister, Lucinda, and one of our best buddies, Kevin Zuber. The car: a '65 Chevy Impala. Why we decided to drive all the way to Silvis, I don't know — especially when you consider the movies: "Grand Prix," starring James Garner and "If It's Tuesday, This Must Be Belgium," starring Ian McShane and Suzanne Pleshette.

Skip ahead a few years, and the party is more intimate — me, my wife, Nancy, and her Sugar Daddy. We popped the cork on some champagne in the parking lot of Illini Hospital and headed in. (Sugar Daddy is what Nancy called her '70 Chevelle.)

A couple of years later the car changed to a '76 Oldsmobile Omega, and we added a passenger, our daughter, Claire.

The drive-in was the Memri. The movies were "Alice in Wonderland" and "Pinnochio." We had just as much fun.

A few years later, I had my last, and satisfying, drive-in experience.

When he was 2, my son, Adam, sat completely still in a recliner for two hours, mesmerized by what he was watching on HBO. Every 10 minutes or so he would turn to Nancy and say two words, "Star Wars."

So when the "Star Wars" trilogy came to the Oasis in Davenport, it was a must-see.

Sometimes, Claire and Adam were in the front seat with us. Sometimes, they climbed into the back. I don't know whether they stayed awake through "The Empire Strikes Back," but I do know they were asleep early into "Return of the Jedi."

We decided to leave, a little disappointed that they couldn't make it through all three.

But then that's the way drive-ins were.

Exciting, adventurous, a little disappointing at times.

But all in all, a unique experience.

— **Mark Feeney**

The first (and last) picture shows

Memri, Milan, Illinois
Opened July 2, 1948: "Abilene Town"
Closed August 31, 1986: "Aliens" and "Big Trouble in Little China"

Bel-Air, Davenport
Opened July 14, 1948: "It Happened on Fifth Avenue"
Closed August 31, 1986: "Texas Chainsaw Massacre, Part 2" and "Re-Animator"

Corral, Moline
Opened July 25, 1950: "Oh, You Beautiful Doll"
Closed September 12, 1982: "Sorority Girls," "Voluptuous Graduates" and "Campus Teasers"

Semri, Silvis, Illinois
Opened June 29, 1951: "Give My Regards to Broadway."
Closed September 5, 1982: "Poltergeist" and "The Thing"

Oasis: Davenport
Opened September 1, 1961: "Konga" and "The Angry Red Planet"
Closed August 30, 1987: "Summer School" and "Back to the Beach"

The Corral Drive-In, near the Quad-City Airport in Moline, was called the Ski-Hi Drive-In during its first year. It was renamed the Corral at the start of its second season.

The Corral opened in 1950 with the family film "Oh, You Beautiful Doll" and closed in 1982 with the softcore porn triple-feature "Sorority Girls," "Voluptuous Graduates," and "Campus Teasers." Interesting sign of the times?

The last film to play a Quad-City drive-in was "Back to the Beach," a satire on the old drive-in beach films, with Frankie Avalon and Annette Funicello.

For the most part, the old drive-ins now are empty grass fields. The Oasis is the site of the Brady Street Showcase Cinemas. The floodlights tower for the Memri is still standing.

Today, the only remaining drive-in in the Quad-City region is the thriving 61 Drive-In in Maquoketa, Iowa. A sign of our times: Information about what's playing is available on its website, www.maquoketa.com/61drivein.

— **Contributed by Thomas George, Rock Island**

Grass, folding chairs, kids peeking out and blankets on a chill night at the Quad-City region's last surviving outdoor movie — 61 Drive-In on the edge of Maquoketa, Iowa.

A 1955 Ford and two root beers on the tray. Few drive-in variations, few menu offerings — root beer, burgers and fries — and always a car hop in saddle shoes.

From the Roundup to Mel's

"This day is ours ... won't you be mine; This day is ours ... oh, please won't you be mine; Hello, sunshine; goodbye, rain; She's wearing my school ring on a chain. She's my steady, I'm her man; I'm gonna love her all I can."

— Theme from "Happy Days"
(Norman Gomble and Charles Fox, Bruin Music Co.)

Many sweet summery nights began or ended at the drive-in. Mom and dad gave baths to the kids, who would be snuggled into their pajamas and driven to the A&W for a root beer.

Kids got a baby beer in a tiny mug, no charge. No one thought a whit about seeing kids in their PJs — in wood-sided station wagons or DeSoto sedans — waiting for a car hop to clamp a tray on dad's side and deliver four frosted mugs (two large, two minis) foamy with caramel-colored root beer, all for the princely sum of about 20 cents.

For the older kids — those sporty enough to have cars — the evening ended at the drive-in. That interlude followed a whodunnit movie like "Laura" with Gene Tierney and Vincent Price at the Fort or Capitol, or after a spring-fling sock hop at the Y.

You could tell the seasons had passed from winter to spring when the drive-in lights flickered on, and the car hops bought new saddle shoes. Guys who drove converts, envied by all, put their tops down and swooned with their girlfriends to languorous, romantic music like Glenn Miller's "Moonlight Serenade."

Car hops in cowboy outfits — a classic fast food drive-in, the Roundup. In the shape of a teepee, it was on Bettendorf's State Street, near the present City Hall. The picture was taken at the opening in the summer of 1941.

The first Tri-City drive-in was light years before McDonald's ever became a gleam in Ray Kroc's eyes. Was it an A&W or Maid-Rite or a White Castle?

McDonald's, with 45-cent meals, didn't come along until February 1958, brightening Moline's Twenty-third Avenue. The McDonald fast-foodery arrived the following June in Davenport, with golden arches and a winking waiter named Speedy as a logo; and in 1959, McDonald's came forth with a rush of business on Rock Island's Eleventh Street.

Good children who went to the A&W with mom and dad were given a free "Baby Beer."

In many ways, Dairy Queen had its birthing days in the Quad-Cities with the Medd family of Bettendorf. The Medds operated the first stores and originated "The Cone With the Curl on Top" slogan. Davenport artist Paul Norton did the Dairy Queen logo, still in use. Ron Medd says the family originated the Blizzard, one of the chain's big money-makers. This is one of the early stores, on Davenport's Rockingham Road near South Concord Street.

Whatever may be the measurement in medical journals of dyspepsia, the earliest drive-in eateries were the god-children of *all* fast food, and with it our hurry-hurry mentality. The car rolled us over the vast plain of life, stopping at the drive-in for a quick burger, fries with ketchup and a chocolate malt. Drive-ins were forerunners for all things that are drive-in or drive-up ... banks to phones and pizza delivered to your door, pepperoni or sausage?

Many lay claim to the fame of being the Tri-Cities' first drive-in. Who cares whose yellow neon lights went on first? All are scrumptious memories.

It could well have been the A&Ws, which pumped root beer from giant wooden barrels at black and orange stands. A&W foamed everywhere in this region, big towns and hamlets alike. The gimmick of the drive-in, delighting grandpa, was a charmer of a teen-age girl serving the meal while he waited in his car.

It was the land of the opportune. Early entrepreneurs reasoned that mundane curbside drive-up service was not enough to lure the car crowd. In Bettendorf, the Roundup was built, in the shape of a teepee, near the site of the present City Hall. Car hops dolled up in cowgirl outfits.

Earlier, Dave Palmer, the enterprising young man who grew to be chieftain of the vast Davenport-based Palmer empire, may have envisioned a franchise. In the early 1930s he opened the thatched-roofed Coconut Grove drive-in at the edge of the Brady Street chiropractic campus. On a bare campus wall, he projected movies for customers to watch while they downed root beer floats (called Black Cows) or knocked off burgers.

"I was one of the first car hops hired, and Dr. Palmer told me to go to Parker's and buy some beach-type pajamas to wear," remembers a one-time teen named Genevieve Conwell. "It was a gravel lot and I wore out two pairs of shoes one summer. It was so much fun, I would have worked for nothing. A nickel tip was a big thing."

Wheels brought the eternally hungry to drive-ins ... names steeped in the

East Moline's Maid-Rite offered a sign of welcome to the city.

Maid-Rite was born in 1926 in Muscatine, Iowa. This first Maid-Rite stand had a dirt floor. Muscatine's Maid-Rite quickly expanded to a concrete-floored fast food restaurant. To celebrate the new building, Sherman Phillips remembers, the owner hired him and other young musicians to climb on the roof and play, over and over again, "A Shanty, in Old Shanty Town."

Riefe's, in its early days on West Locust Street, Davenport.

Typical, smiling car hops and nickel and dime root beer: The Hi Hut, 1957.

Dancing the Chicken Delight

Chicken Delight — served with a little cellophane-wrapped mint in each plastic platter — became such a national phenomenon in the 1960s that a recording was made, "Dance the Chicken Delight Ring-a-Ding." A seven-inch cardboard, played at 33⅓, is a collector's item for those with a '60s fetish. Being cardboard, it had to be taped to the turntable to keep the disk from wobbling out of tune.

"Delivered free and hot right to your door, or picked up at the store," says one side of the record, which shows a teen dancing the Ring-a-Ding. Flip side of the record shows her demonstrating the dance ... "Push knees back and forth rapidly, swing arms from left to right ... wiggle hips ... right arm in the air for eight beats ... jump and turn around ... jump with feet spread ... pony with feet, and make like a chicken with your arms as wings, pecking in and out with your head."

Fun, eh?

sweet smell of french fries and tenderloins and pickle relish. Riefe's had such a promising hit in its first Bettendorf "hut" that it became big-league as a drive-in and a sit-down restaurant in northwest Davenport; the Hitching Post, near the place where Moline and East Moline meet; Hoagy's, on Moline's Nineteenth Avenue and Seventh Street; Ted's, a hustle-bustle drive-in and restaurant at Brady and Kimberly, Davenport; Moke's, on Rock Island's Eighteenth Avenue; and the big cheese of all Quad-City drive-ins, Deb's in Milan.

The longest-serving drive-in employee in our land may be Ethel Snyder of Muscatine, who began at the Cheri-Top there as a car hop at the tender age of 14. When it reopened in 1998, Ethel was back, figuring that she had been car-hopping or burger-flipping since 1966.

"We wore red skirts and white blouses with 'Cheri-Top' on the back. It was a lot of fun, and the boys tried their best to flirt."

At Muscatine's A&W, the owners had a strict policy, remembers Mary Tyler Askam Koehler.

"When we closed at 11 o'clock, Spin and Billie Dittman took you home, unless you had a note from your mother giving you permission to go home with someone else."

Fast food sizzled both indoors and outdoors

Symbol of thirst at A&Ws and root beer stands everywhere, giant wooden root beer barrels like this. The "R-J" stood for "Root Juice."

This advertisement appeared on June 25, 1958, thanking customers for dining at the new McDonald's on Brady Street, Davenport. A meal — burger, malt and fries — cost 45 cents.

and — hold on — even in the air. Enterprising Al Tunick of Rock Island founded and brainstormed Chicken Delight, shifting fast food from burgers to something unheard of — drumsticks and white meat. "Don't Cook Tonight, Call Chicken Delight." Gimmicky, he floated chicken dinners from planes, by tiny parachutes, to rural customers. By the time Colonel Sanders went nationwide, Tunick had 750 franchised Chicken Delights in North America. Always ready with a quick turn of the buck, he eventually sold out and switched from chicken to another form of fast food, Karmelkorn.

Maybe all this fast-food business began with loose meat on a warm bun. In 1926, Fred Angell, a Muscatine butcher, invented a sandwich. He steamed hamburger instead of frying it and slurried in some spices. He offered one of his sandwiches to a delivery man who was so enthused that he said, "Fred, you know this sandwich is made right." Voila! The name Maid-Rite was born. The first drive-up Maid-Rite fast foodery actually was a downtown "stand" with a dirt floor, the forerunner of the vast Maid-Rite chain.

Fast food places were like home to many, and Judy A. Colgan Fuller of East Moline maintains that the Maid-Rites made by her dad, Bernard Petrus Colgan, surpassed any other. "He had a special touch at his place in East Moline, where Maid-Rites were only 20 cents."

To catch a first in fast foods is an elusive claim. Dairy Queen had its origins in the now non-existent Green River, Illinois, and Cecil Medd of

Speedee was an early McDonald's symbol, beneath the golden arches.

Bettendorf was on the ground floor as one of its founders.

Medd remembered when McDonald's Ray Kroc would visit him in Bettendorf. "Kroc was studying our operation, and at the same time selling us multi-head malt mixers. He had a whole bunch of mixers in the trunk of his Cadillac."

Kroc's empire is a legend. There are 19 McDonald's in the Quad-City region, extending to Muscatine and Walcott. In the beginning, though, the Quad-City McDonald's were among the first. Moline was No. 90; Davenport, 114. That rather makes us pioneers, inasmuch as there are now 14,500 McDonald's.

"Your order, please? Burger with everything. Fine. Right up in a second."

That's fast food.

Few things change in drive-in land — car hops still wear poodle skirts at the Cheri-Top, Muscatine.

1956-57 CHERI-TOP DRIVE IN
Muscatine, Iowa

LICENSE NO.		GLASSES	WAITER NO.
Hamburger 35			
Cheeseburger 45			
Tenderloin 45			
Grilled Cheese 30			
Hot Dog 25			
Steak 50			
Bar-B-Q 40			
Hot Dog on Stick 30			
Chicken Sandwich 45			
Ham Sandwich 40			
Bacon, Lettuce & Tom. Sand. 55			
Fishburgers 45			
Pizzaburger 45			
Chicken 1.50			
Shrimp 1.50			
Fish and Chips — Sticks .95			
Chicken Giblets L G 95			
French Fries 25			
Onion Rings 45			
Dishes .10 .15			
Cones .10 .15			
Malts	CH. ST PIN VAN CHY		
Shake			
Phosphate			
Sodas			
Sundaes			
Banana Split			
Orange	8 UP		
Rt. Beer	Coke		
Coffee C B S	Root Beer Float		
Milk	Iced Tea		
	Pepsi		

Order from used by car hops at the Cheri-Top in 1956-57.

The barbecue and rib kings

Fast food is barbecue food, luscious ribs, oozing to your elbows with dripping ruby sauce of superb succulence. Or, for the more fashionable fingered set, buffalo wings.

James R. "Jim" Overton barbecues about 6,000 pounds of ribs a week, creating a mouth-watering essence that drifts all the way to the Government Bridge. Jim's Rib Haven got its start in Rock Island and is known the world over. Overton has shipped rib dinners and barbecue sauce to every state and many foreign countries.

"A guy took some to France once," Overton says. "I got a letter back saying, 'Just close up everything and come over.'"

Ribs are a food so fast that you can flip the bones over your shoulder after but a minute of gnashing. Impressarios of ribcraft give much credit for bringing it to the Quad-Cities to a husky chef, Wes Cooper.

Wes "Big Daddy" Cooper was an Army chef who had barbecued ribs for Gen. Dwight Eisenhower and, in his wartime travels, baked Ernie Pyle's last birthday cake. After World War II, he was chef at places such as the Davenport Club, Johnny Hartman's and the Ship's Wheel. Then, he took fast food on the road with a giant, wheeled, stove-hot charcoal barbecue rig at outdoor parties for Deere & Co. and at places such as Davenport Country Club and Short Hills, East Moline.

"Big Daddy Wes taught us all a lot of things," says Dempsey Miller, who fast-foods his barbecue ribs to parties within half-a-hundred miles of the Quad-Cities by way of a wheeled wagon, stoked with hickory logs.

Miller says, "Don't get me wrong, but I think I'm right. I believe I'm the one who introduced buffalo wings to the Quad-Cities. None are better than mine. I have sauces for my ribs and wings that are sweet as sugar, or will bite you so hard your eyes will water."

Davenport businessman Dempsey Miller is the driving force behind a day-long festival of music, entertainment and food each summer along Marquette Street.

With tears, many Quad-Citians remember the Rock Island Rockets that roared through these lands to points east and west and south and north. The first Rocket whizzed through in 1937; the last run from Rock Island to Chicago was in 1979.

When Rockets and Zephyrs crossed the prairie

" ... Oh, the Rock Island Line is the road to ride, the Rock Island Line is a mighty good road ... Get your ticket at the station of the Rock Island Line ... Well, I may be right, I may be wrong. You're gonna miss me when I'm gone."

— Hollis Music, 1956, adapted from a traditional American folk song

chapter ten

All Aboard!

Out across the prairie sped the Golden State Limited to Los Angeles and the "G-Whizz" to Kansas City. It was the great Age of the Railroad, which one day would see dozens of passenger trains arriving and departing from Rock Island, Davenport and Moline depots.

The throaty notes of the train whistle, the chuff-chuffing of an engine at work, and the hiss of escaping steam had replaced the echo of the steamboat calliope along the river bluffs, and soon there would be the streamliners, the Rocky Mountain Rocket, with fresh carnations on the linen-covered diner tables and lake trout on the menu, and the slant-nosed Burlington Zephyrs.

The great Age of the Railroad had arrived in the early 1900s, and prospered in the 1920s and 1930s and 1940s and into the 1950s, and a romantic age it was — every bit as romantic as the Age of the Steamboat which it had replaced.

Sleepers awakened in the middle of the night by a distant train whistle felt the same mix of loneliness and excitement the steamboat had elicited in another age. Boys and girls ran down to the tracks whenever a train passed much as Mark Twain had done on the river. They

A crane hoists a steam locomotive for repairs at the mighty Silvis yards of the Rock Island Lines. Before closing in 1980, it was the world's biggest locomotive repair shop.

Conductor's cap, his watch, and a teapot from the diner of the Rock Island Lines.

waved at the engineer and the man in the caboose, who always waved back.

Children soon learned they could press their ear to the track and hear the clickety-click of an approaching train miles away. Now and then a bad boy put a penny on the track so the wheels would flatten it.

For the very fortunate, there was a ride on the train itself — a ride that often began at night, a family standing on the station platform surrounded by suitcases and bags as the scheduled time neared.

No one wanted to miss the arrival. Every bit as much as a Shakespearean actor, a train knew how to enter and exit the stage dramatically, clanging its cars together, each crisp blue conductor hanging out from his own car, passengers looking out through every window watching for aunts and uncles, grandparents, children waiting to meet them, slowing so smoothly that one never knew exactly when the train stopped with a final puff of black smoke and the hiss of escaping steam.

When all the luggage was safely on, and the ladies helped up the steps into their cars, the conductor cried, "All aboard," and the process began all over again in reverse. The people waving goodbye on the platform grew smaller and smaller until they disappeared, and it was time for children to explore this new world of upholstered seats full of strange families, heavy curtains and dark mahogany trim — or chrome in the newer cars. In the rocking aisles, one almost had to learn to walk all over again.

Symbol of the bicentennial

Old 652, the Rock Island Lines locomotive chosen to carry the red, white and blue during the Bicentennial in 1976, was a proud standard bearer.

The locomotive, once a mainstay on the Golden State run, was hauling passenger cars between Rock Island and Chicago that year. The 20th Century Railroad Club of Chicago had a contest to select a design and repaint the locomotive. The winning design: a blue cab with a large white star on its nose and large white "Independence" painted on a red background on the sides.

Old 652, built in 1952, was one of the largest and last diesel-electric locomotives designed for high-speed passenger service. Its top speed was 117 mph.

By 1985, with the Rock Island in bankruptcy, Old 652 was headed for the scrap heap. It was rescued at the last minute, purchased for $6,500 by a group of railroad buffs from the Kansas City area. They restored the locomotive and put it to work pulling excursion trains in Baldwin City, Kansas.

Highlight of the trip: The dining car. One had to walk from one car to another to get there, a scary moment in the open air, but it was worth it to spend an hour in a world that could just as well have come out of a fairy tale. The crisp white tablecloth was set with china and silver, and the menu was plain, but it contained a selection of foods one sometimes couldn't even pronounce.

And the waiters. It was hard to remember ever being treated so politely. They stood at attention even while swaying with the train. And how could they pour coffee straight into the cup from a foot up — just the right amount, without spilling?

And then, to bed. Sometimes the train had a Pullman car at the end, but that was hardly necessary, with the soft clickety-click of the wheels and the rocking seats.

On through the night, out across the prairie, on toward Kansas City and

John Mey, rail crossing guard, surrounded by a garden at his shack, Third Street crossing, Moline.

In 1926, postal trucks await mail by train at the Rock Island Lines depot in Davenport.

Los Angeles, on through but hesitantly into the 1960s when the auto and the long, stretching interstates plucked the passengers and trucks pulled business from the freight trains.

Just as the steamboat had changed the landscape in the 19th century, railroads did the same, creating new towns like Matherville and Coal Valley in Illinois to meet their needs for coal or crossing points, and determining which small farm communities survived by selecting one route over another. Into the great rail hub of Chicago came lumber, coal, grain, and livestock from Davenport, Rock Island and Moline, and carloads of hides from Viola, Illinois, watermelons and ice from New Boston, broomcorn, bricks, and potatoes from Cambridge, Illinois.

The railroad was becoming the heart of the three cities. Rock Island Lines was building the world's largest locomotive repair shop on a 900-acre farm east of Moline. First called Vulcan, then New Shops, the name was changed to Silvis in honor of the farm owner.

The 1920s and '30s became the Golden Age of Trains in our region. By 1934, there was something new. That June, 20,000 peo-

A DRI Line steam engine defies high water along Davenport's River Drive during the 1951 flood.

A crew makes ready to pull out of Silvis Yards. Note the long oil can in the engineer's hand.

A lone hobo rides a flatcar in west Davenport during the Depression. Trains were a great free ride.

ple came to Rock Island to see the new Burlington Zephyr, the nation's first streamlined diesel train. The Rock Island Lines was not far behind. In the summer of 1937, the new streamlined Rock Island Rocket began its run between Rock Island and Chicago, with a remarkable time of 2 hours and 15 minutes. Other steam engines soon were replaced by the Rocky Mountain Rocket, the Texas Rocket, and the Minneapolis Rocket.

When World War II ended, the railroads prepared for an expected surge in travel. But it was not to be. As the steamboat earlier had lost out to the railroads, so the railroads now confronted their nemesis: the automobile. Cars were spilling out from factories in record numbers and everyone had a love affair with the car. By 1958, the first interstate highway had reached the Quad-Cities. Trucks and passenger cars quickly ate away at the railroads.

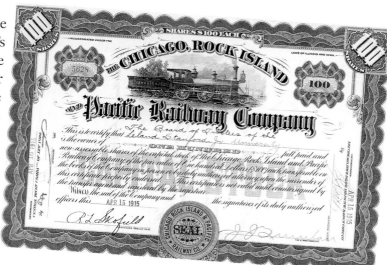

A 1915 Chicago, Rock Island and Pacific stock certificate for 100 shares at $100 per share, worth $10,000.

By 1960, the remaining railroads in our region could sense the end. Railroad tracks fell into such disrepair that trains often had to crawl across dangerous sections. The Rock Island Rocket's scheduled time of 2 hours and 15 minutes grew to 3 hours, then 4, until it was no longer possible to take the morning Rocket to LaSalle Street Station, shop, see a matinee, and return on the 5:30 train.

On January 2, 1979, the Rock Island Rocket — the last passenger train out of the Quad-Cities — made its final run. The mighty Silvis Yards closed in 1980, and on June 1, 1984, the Rock Island Lines, which had been so much a part of the Quad-Cities for 130 years, ceased to exist — the first major railroad in the United States to go bankrupt.

Even for those of us who were here when the great trains still ran, who considered a round trip on the Rocket to Chicago a special event, even for us, the sounds and sight and smells are growing dimmer and further away. We should have taken more photographs, we tell ourselves, we should have made notes, we should have made a scrapbook for our children.

Indeed, we should have.

— **Roald Tweet**

Chugging down the Fejervary Park grade in Davenport is old 2516, a Mikado, in about 1930. The locomotive is a 2-8-2, meaning two wheels on the front truck, four drivers, followed by two at the rear. The engineer is waving.

Old No. 1001, on the way to Silvis

By number, it was 1001, a rumbling string of old Chicago commuter cars that had outlived their class and usefulness. All were the same dismal color — tired red, about the hue of a retired boxcar. But No. 1001 carried more passengers than any other train — ever!

It huffed by steam, then growled by diesel, nearly uninterrupted for 60 years or so. First, it carried workers to and from the vast new Silvis Yards. Ultimately — almost as an act of convenience — it carried workers needing transportation to and from other Tri-City factories.

By name, it was the unglamorous Work Train, free for railroad employees, dirt-cheap for others. Ten-ticket books sold for a dollar.

In the summer months, about 450 workers rode the spartan cars, the old plush seats worn from too many years of Chicago commuter-train use; some seats were recovered with imitation leather or plastic. In winter, the daily passenger count reached 900. At one time, during World War II, 1,000 workers a day were riding the train. It was necessary in the years of three-gallons-a-week "A" stamp gasoline rationing.

The Work Train lunch bucket brigade had a camaraderie unlike any bunch who rode the rails. There were regulars like Q.W. Mott of Davenport, who took the Work Train for 21 years and, after retiring from his job, stayed on as its conductor for another spell.

Passengers read newspapers, jawed, dozed as the train lumbered through the cities, making scattered stops to pick up passengers on their way to work in early morning, or heading home in the twilight.

The Work Train left Taylor Street in the west end of Davenport at 6 a.m. each working day, picking up passengers at the crossing there. Next stop was the downtown Davenport depot, arrival time, 6:10. Then, International Harvester plants in Rock Island and East Moline. Stops, too, for Deere factories, and the last passengers alighted from the cars in the Silvis Yards at 6:40 a.m., capping their Thermos bottles of coffee from which they sipped on their short rail junket. The Work Train ran on time, nearly to the minute, because its riders could not be late for work.

For the return run, the conductor timed the locomotive's start from Silvis at 4:12 p.m. And when local industry swung into production overtime during World War II, a midnight run was added to accommodate late-shift workers.

But no longer does the Work Train run. Quad-City railroad buffs believe it ceased in the 1970s, its only period in the roundhouse during the dull days of Great Depression unemployment.

Old No. 1001 was not the Golden State Limited or the Orient Express, and no passenger had to worry about what to wear. Overalls were the accepted apparel.

The first trick (shift) roundhouse crew at Silvis Yards of the Rock Island, 1928.

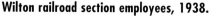

Wilton railroad section employees, 1938.

95

Riding the rails

"I began hopping freights when I was 13 and by the time I was 18, I had been to 40 American states and three countries — Canada, Alaska and Mexico. Maybe I was the youngest hobo on the road in the 1930s. We called it 'on the bum,' and in all those years, never spent a single dime.

Larry Frantz

"I'd be on the road for months at a time, then return home to Rock Island for a while. I met some of the greatest guys in the world when I was on the bum — doctors, bankers, just plain hoboes.

"My first trip, I ended up in Milwaukee at a hobo jungle. They were cooking stew in a five-gallon olive oil can. I asked for food, but they wouldn't give me any until I could throw something in the pot. I went to a grocery store and they felt sorry for me because I was just a punk and they gave me some bacon butts and cheese ends. I threw it all into the pot. It tasted pretty good.

"A smart guy on the bum could just about pick the direction to go. Trains with 2500 by the headlight would be heading northwest; 5000 series, to the southwest. My favorite was the Rock Island. I loved that railroad. If you saw two white flags on the locomotive, you knew it was a fast freight. Those could be dangerous.

"On one trip, I told a hobo to keep his foot off a coupling. He didn't. Two minutes later his foot was smashed flat as mashed potatoes.

"I came back to Rock Island, settled down at 18, got married and became a toolmaker at American Air Filter, Moline. But oh, I loved that hobo life. Those were the days of steam locomotives. Once you get cinders in your hair, you can't get them out."

— Larry Frantz, Davenport

Call it royalty on the rails

Regularly — he admits, likely a dozen times a day — Glen Pepmeyer of Galesburg, Illinois, closes his eyes and wistfully hears the clickity-click siren-song of the rails. He was an engineer on the gleaming Burlington Zephyr, one of the first of America's streamlined trains.

He describes making a hollow of his right palm, the precise size of the wooden spindle at the end of the whistle cord, before tugging a wailing hoot.

"She had a distinctive whistle, high-pitched I'd say. Two longs, a short and a long for a crossing."

As mariners call their ships "she," railroad engineers likewise refer to their locomotives.

Pepmeyer was a railroader from 1941 to 1984, "some of the finest years of my life," he says ... the most shining of those years as an engineer in the cab of the California or Denver Zephyr, gleaming 12- and 14-passenger car trains with diners that were rolling restaurants with white-jacketed waiters. Stern conductors in the cars held thin gold watches to keep the train on pace with their timetable.

"Up high, I was a true king of the road, a monarch in my cab," he says of the years on the Zephyrs. "They were such wonderful trains. I began with the shovel-nose Zephyrs, and when the more sleeker nose models arrived, I was engineer on those, too."

Railroaders are a certain breed, with a love for their craft that is unmatched in most any other profession.

"I dream of trains all the time. I was a Zephyr engineer. My train was my love and my responsibility. Why, I wouldn't have traded places with the president of

Above, Burlington Zephyr was a silvery streak across the plains. Right, a menu from the Zephyr.

ZEPHYR EVENING SELECTIONS—a la CARTE

Colorado Pascal Celery, 25
Green or Ripe Olives, 20
Tomato Juice, 20   Pickles, 15
Shrimp Cocktail, 20
Broiled Jumbo Whitefish, Maître d'Hotel, 75
Fried Lake Trout, Tartar Sauce, 70
Roast Leg of Lamb, Mint Jelly, 75
Baked Chicken a la Zephyr, 75
Burlington Dinner Steak, 90
Potatoes: Baked or Hashed Brown, 20
Baby Lima Beans or Sugar Peas, 20
Fruit or Crab Meat Salad, 40
Lettuce or Tomato Salad, 25
Sandwiches: Ham, Ox Tongue or Cheese, 20
Bread and Butter or Hot Dinner Rolls, 10
Ice Cream with Cookies, 25
Pie, 15; with Cheese, 20; a la Mode, 25
Half Grape Fruit, 20
Strawberry Preserves, 20
English Plum or Fig Pudding, Hard Sauce, 20
Cheese with Crackers or Ry-Krisp, 20
Coffee, Tea or Cocoa (Pot) 20
Coffee, Cup, 10
Individual Bottle Milk, 10

ZEPHYR PLATE DINNER

PRICE OPPOSITE ENTRÉE IS
COST OF COMPLETE MEAL

Shrimp Cocktail or Tomato Juice

Colorado Pascal Celery

Green and Ripe Olives

Baked Chicken a la Zephyr . . . . . $ .75
Roast Leg of Lamb, Mint Jelly 75
Broiled Jumbo Whitefish 85
Burlington Dinner Steak 90
Potatoes: Baked or Hashed Brown . . . 1.00

Baby Lima Beans or Sugar Peas

English Plum or Fig Pudding, Hard Sauce
Pie, Ice Cream with Assorted Cookies,
or Cheese with Crackers

Coffee, Tea, Cocoa, or Bottled Milk

Hot Dinner Rolls or Bread and Butter

the United States. You're like that, when you're a railroad man."

He recalls his regular Zephyr run, clicking off the 117 miles from Galesburg to Ottumwa, Iowa. At that division point, another crew took over on the routes of the California or Denver Zephyrs.

"Oh, those Zephyrs traveled. Technically, we were to keep her at 79 miles an hour, but we'd get it up to 90. It all depended on the section of tracks. I tell you, 90 is mighty fast on a train."

Zephyrs are gone now, their routes absorbed by Amtrak. Still, Pepmeyer squints his eyes, imagining once again that he can hear the nostalgic ding-ding-ding-ding as a train swifts through a gated crossing, with the red lights blinking like ruby owl-eyes in the dark of night. Gawking towners gazed with awe and jealousy on the passengers in the lounge cars, sipping their martinis and manhattans, or the diners lazing over apple cobbler (a Zephyr specialty).

Pepmeyer, like many railroad men, began as a fireman with the Chicago, Burlington and Quincy in the age of steam. He graduated to the billed cap and neckerchief of an engineer.

"When I was young, working on a switch engine, and going through downtown Burlington, I'd want to hang out the window by my waist and yell to people, 'Look at me, I'm an engineer.' I was so proud."

The pride will never fail, like the lost wail of an engine's whistle.

"Once a railroad man, always a railroad man. The day doesn't go by that I don't wish I was back in the cab of a Zephyr — a king, call it royalty on the rails."

How far aviation has come in the past decades. Members of the Northern Lights Aerobatic Team make Quad-City skies their personal playground as they practice for the 1998 Quad-City Air Show.

The novelty that became a roaring reality

"The Wright Brothers created the single greatest cultural force since the invention of writing. The airplane became the first World Wide Web, bringing people, languages, ideas, and values together."

— Bill Gates, CEO, Microsoft Corporation

"Switch off." "Switch off."
"Switch on." "Contact."

The pilot in the cockpit and ground crewman at the prop shouted the commands at early Tri-City airports.

"Airport" was a generous description. Flying fields of the 1920s were little more than cow pastures for pioneer aviators as they cranked up the engine of a Stinson or Curtiss JN4C "Jenny."

From Davenport's Cram Field to Moline's Franing Field to Bettendorf's Wallace Field, the likes of Rusty Campbell, Eugene Ely and Gus De-Schepper climbed clouds in their open-cockpit planes and charted a new industry. The greatest of the era — Charles Lindbergh and Amelia Earhart — put down flaps in our airports.

Today, as you board a sleek jetliner at Quad-City International Airport in Moline or look skyward as the Blue Angels or Thunderbirds

In September 1937, United Airlines began commercial flight service into the Moline Airport. The Boeing 247s carried 10 passengers

Iowa's pioneer aviator

Ada Phelps: It was bad luck to clean the helmet.

When, during the depths of the Great Depression, Glen Phelps came home one day and asked what color airplane his wife, Ada, wanted, she figured a ridiculous question deserved an equally ridiculous answer. So she gave one: "Orange."

A few weeks later, they stopped at Cram Field, Davenport, and Glen pointed out their new, bright orange Velie Monoprop.

As she recalled years later, Ada was stunned. Her husband didn't know how to fly a plane. And his reason for making such an extravagant purchase — to drum up business for his insurance agency — seemed outrageous in 1930.

Glen Phelps learned to fly his airplane. So did Ada. Together they were lauded as Iowa's "first flying couple."

Ada Phelps eventually joined the Civil Air Patrol, which required her to qualify as a sharpshooter. "Not too comfortable to learn to fire guns on my stomach when I was pregnant with twins," she recalled years later. And until her death in 1996 at the age of 96, she was a member of the Quad-City Airmen's Association.

As for the helmet and goggles she wore for this 1987 photograph, she explained that it was considered bad luck for a pilot to clean the helmet. So hers never was washed.

streak over Davenport Municipal Airport at the annual Quad-City Air Show, you forget that aviation was a novelty not so many years ago.

The drone of a radial engine was a siren's song for the crowds who craned their necks to see early mail planes land at Cram Field, now Northwest Park. Bettendorf was an aviation hotbed. Wallace Field, on the riverfront east of the downtown, was a busy flying school in the 1920s. The first Velie Monocoupe, in which pilot and passenger rode side-by-side in enclosed comfort, was produced in 1927 at a converted tabernacle at State and Fifteenth streets in downtown Bettendorf.

Quad-City International Airport has its beginnings in November 1922 when Gus DeSchepper, Floyd Ketner and Dr. C.C. Sloan formed a partnership and

One of the bizarre moments in the history of Tri-City flight. January 12, 1940, the pilot of a United DC3, flying from the West Coast, had engine trouble and tried to land at the Moline Airport. He lost altitude and put down on the frozen Rock River in front of what now is Harold's on the Rock. The five passengers and crew members crawled out, unhurt.

leased 30 acres of William Franing's pasture to create an airport.

A decade before, the site was serving as a control point for the first coast-to-coast flight by U.S. Army planes, an event that attracted throngs of rubberneckers. That same year, Lt. Eugene Ely, of Davenport, made the world's first flight from the deck of a ship.

On May 12, 1926, the Moline Airport, as it was known, became a stop on the nation's air mail route system when National Air Transport inaugurated regular mail flights between Chicago, Kansas City and Dallas, with a stop in Moline. Air mail pilots included Rusty Campbell, a familiar sight in his Curtiss bi-plane.

As the aviation industry continued to spread its wings, the Quad-Cities became an important link in the system.

"The Quad-Cities was the main refueling stop for transcontinental flights as well as a weather stop," said Joseph S. Kimmel Jr., one of the community's biggest aviation boosters.

It was inevitable that the Quad-Cities needed a first-class airport. Finally, in 1947, Rock Island County voters approved the county's purchase of the Moline Airport through a state act that created local airport authorities with taxing and bonding powers. The action laid the groundwork for today's Quad-City International Airport.

— **John Willard**

When flight was new and fascinating: An air show at the Moline Airport, October 28, 1929.

With its gigantic picture window, the observation deck in the old terminal at the Quad-City Airport gave generations of children and adults an up-close view of arrivals and departures.

Soaring stars

Charles A. Lindbergh took the Tri-Cities by storm when he landed his "Spirit of St. Louis" in Moline on August 19, 1927. Just three months earlier, the 25-year-old aviator had flown the aircraft from New York to

Charles Lindbergh

Paris, becoming the first person to fly solo across the Atlantic.

Shrieking whistles and clanging bells greeted the Lone Eagle as he approached. He circled downtown Davenport three times, dipping the wings of his Ryan monoplane in salute. In return, his excited welcomers tossed their hats and waved flags and handkerchiefs.

After his third pass, he headed up the Mississippi River to the Moline Airport, where he performed a touch-and-go landing, circled the field a couple of times and finally set his plane down shortly after 2 p.m.

His visit was part of a national tour to promote aviation. In keeping with the spirit, Davenport's Crescent Macaroni & Cracker Company cooked up Lindy Cookies in the shape of the "Spirit of St. Louis."

Another aviation star, Amelia Earhart, touched down at the Moline Airport, but little else is known about her visit. In 1937, she vanished in the South Pacific while trying to fly around the world.

Amelia Earhart

Charles Lindbergh is barely visible — he's the one without hat — beside his "Spirit of St. Louis," which he had just landed at Moline Airport.

A crush of admirers around Lindbergh's plane, pushed inside a hangar at Moline Airport. Crescent Macaroni & Cracker Co., Davenport, was so impressed by his Atlantic flight they turned out a line of Lindy Cookies.

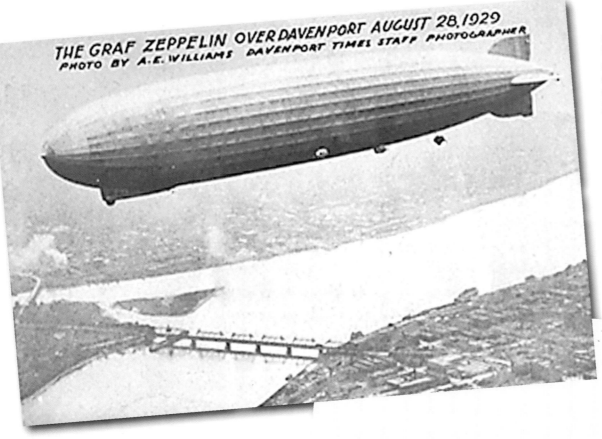

THE GRAF ZEPPELIN OVER DAVENPORT AUGUST 28,1929
PHOTO BY A.E. WILLIAMS DAVENPORT TIMES STAFF PHOTOGRAPHER

An epic event: The "Graf Zeppelin," from Germany, hovering over the Tri-Cities. The ship detoured to fly here to salute the large German population. Some detractors claimed the crew was spying, photographing the Rock Island Arsenal.

Cram Field in Davenport, 1935. It was named for Ralph Cram, publisher of the *Democrat & Leader,* who soloed in flight at the age of 62 and became a nationally known advocate of flight.

Big Ben Gregory's Ford Tri-Motor offered 50 cent plane rides over Davenport from Cram Field in the 1930s. At 9 each night, he shot fireworks from the plane as it roared over the city. He billed it as "The Ship From Mars."

Victory Celebration

Byron Burford
Special collections, Augustana College Library, Rock Island, Illinois

It was a very good night...

"The most memorable of my final days of performing was what I heard in Moline, Illinois. I forgot some lines and someone in the balcony yelled out, 'That's all right, Frank. We love you.' "

— Frank Sinatra, reminiscing on his
1994 performance at The Mark of the Quad-Cities

chapter twelve

Fun Fun Fun

I deal in fun; it's not reality."
Puffing smoke rings from a fat cigar, Milton Berle had that to say when he came to town to ring down the curtain on Davenport's old movie palace, the RKO Orpheum, in anticipation of its rebirth as the Adler Theatre.

Fun is never off-duty in the Quad-Cities, and one excuse is as good as another for having a good time.

Blustery John Ringling, who built a mighty amusement empire, is quoted in a biography:

"Those Tri-Cities can be depended upon as good show dates, even if the corn crop is bad."

It's fun, fun, fun: We've always known how to have fun. Kids rolled hoops, and now they whoop it up at the *Quad-City Times Hoopfest*. We used to run only if someone chased us; now, 20,000 run the *Bix* 7. We're so much fun that 40,000 women came here from all over the country in 1998 — just to go bowling.

"London Bridge is falling down" at the Korthaus farm between Probstei and Walcott, Iowa.

It's fun, fun, fun: parades and stock car races and bicycle races and—nearly lost in memory—Golden Gloves boxing matches and Soap Box derbies, baseball in the breezy bleachers along the Mississippi River, stilt-walking clowns and men fired from cannons at the circus, Monkey Island antics and at Fejervary's Mother Goose Land, and at Niabi Zoo. Liberace at Palmer, Andy Williams at the Adler, Elton John and Frank Sinatra packing The Mark of the Quad-Cities, that magnificent monster in Moline, with basketball in the afternoon and hockey at night. The John Deere Golf Classic is here, and Big 10 games are only an hour away in Iowa City.

It's fun, fun, fun: We've danced all night; Lawrence Welk called Fairyland in DeWitt, Iowa, the smoothest floor in America. On that same night, Augustana's Handel Oratorio Society may have been singing "The Messiah" and on that weekend, Tri-City Symphony could well have been accompanying a promising new singer, Mario Lanza.

Listen: The movies talked, Al Jolson in the first talkie ("The Jazz Singer") at the Columbia, with little kids so scared they cried, but the talkies never stopped talking, and Jolson ad-libbed in the film: "You ain't seen nothin' yet, folks."

It's fun, fun, fun: Pigeon racing and rolle bolle and Rock Island's revived lantern parade, with its watery counterpart, Venetian Nights Lighted Boat parade, riding the waves of the Mississippi.

It's fun, fun, fun: Hayrack rides and scope the top of the world and touch the stars from the Ferris wheel at the fair, with pickled beets and 4-H projects in the exhibition hall down below; and tractor pulls and astounding 24-horse hitches. The three-headed cow at Royal American Shows on the Davenport levee, where Gypsy Rose Lee defined the art of strip tease.

It's fun, fun, fun: Going mad for Midler; cheering McEntire; rocking at RIBCO; polka-dancing at Durant; Festival of Tree-ing to trumpet in the holiday season — and any day, simply hanging out at the mall.

The old Gus Kahn song is as good as the century turns as when written in 1920:

" ... *In the meantime, in between time,*
Ain't we got fun?"

Play time in the 1940s on the Watkins farm in rural Pleasant Valley, Iowa, found Beverly Cale Witmer in the backyard with a rebuilt pedal tractor and a coaster wagon.

Fun, fun, fun. Better than a swimming pool when a fire hydrant is opened for kids on a 95-degree day.

Everyone was pumping an accordion in the 1930s. Members of the Honolulu Conservatory of Music accordion band of the Tri-Cities gathered in June 1939.

Hide and seek

In a forgotten age, before beep-beep-buzz-buzz video "shooter" games blinked in the family room, ... before CDs and cable TV, things were different. Kids got out of the house and made their own fun. They were never underfoot, glaze-eyed with boredom, matching video wits with Crash Vandicoot.

"We were outside, yelling and playing games with the other kids," remembers Mary Sears of Davenport. "For some wonderful reason, we were enjoying life."

The games they played needed no batteries, no hookup with a television set. The packs of children who roamed neighborhoods were in search of fun-fun-fun. Their kingdom was someone's back yard or boulevard, a place to scream, "Red Rover, Red Rover, come over, come over" or "Pom Pom Pullaway."

For Spud or Kick the Can, an alley was heaven in concrete, with weeds growing through the cracks. Alleys were only infrequently traveled by neighbors — usually friendly and tolerant — putting their cars into single, unattached garages.

Playmates were pals forever. The girls (at times, the boys could be coaxed to take a turn) jumped rope on the sidewalk. "One, two, buckle your shoe. Three, four, open the door," and screams of "pepper" to signal double-time fast cranks of the rope. For the especially nimble, there was Double dutch, two ropes turning at once.

Generations not yet turning gray still hum "London Bridge is falling down" or "Ring around the rose-y, pocket full of pose-y, ashes, ashes, we all fall down."

A sandbox provided hours of innocence, enough to attract an entire neighborhood to build castles in the sand and, later, obstacle courses for Hot Wheels cars.

All of this, most certainly, must sound alien to today's turn-of-the-century generation. But the games we played were fun, cost-free and endless on shimmery summer nights — at least until the fireflies made their appearance.

Beyond the borders of one's own neighborhood, there were city parks and playgrounds. Every city had to have at least one swimming pool — with low and high diving boards. But it was nearly as quenching, on blistering days, when the water company or the fire department came to flush the fire hydrant on the corner, arcing torrents of water into the air.

Slowly, organized summer fun began to take over. Early on, there were swimming lessons — mandatory for those growing up in communities where rivers run. Little League and tennis lessons and gymnastics crowded onto the calendar.

Before the structured fun of soccer tournaments, a kid's life was "red light, green light," and "hide-and-go-seek." Games would be played until dark, when it came time for flashlight tag. That squealed on until mom yelled out the door, "Come on in, time to get your baths."

Leone Bredbecke, who once led the recreation department for the Davenport park system, sighs:

"Kids of today really don't know what they're missing."

No fancy playground equipment needed for the 1930s. Happiness was a tire swing on a long rope for Frances Rohwer in a farmyard near Donahue, Iowa.

Snow on the ground, Flexible Flyer sleds and three boys. Winter fun! They had been belly-flopping in a pasture north of Welton, Iowa. From left, Gilbert Ryan, Dale and Ralph Brooks.

Round and round it goes

In the prime time of innocence, when arrival of a merry-go-round was the thrill of the summer, Gem Steam Riding Gallery was not merely child's play, but a delight for all ages.

Galloping wooden horses in a tented circle turned by steam played on vacant lots in small Western Illinois and Eastern Iowa towns.

"For both old and young. Come and bring the children. Open every evening and on Saturday from 3 to 10 p.m.," enticed the flyer announcing a four-day September visit to Bishop Hill, Illinois. "Tickets, 5 cents each."

The reverse of the broadsheet offered testimonials, touting, "It is everywhere highly recommended by the press and the people."

Iowa Journal, Wapello, Iowa:

"No other amusement has been more agreeable than this late invention."

Orion (Illinois) Times:

"The Riding Gallery is first class in every respect. The young, middle-age and old alike vied with each other in participating in this innocent sport. The proprietors are pleasant, agreeable and genial gentlemen. They go from here to Alpha, Illinois, and carry with them the esteem of the friends made here."

Geneseo (Illinois) Republic:

"Everybody seems to be patronizing the merry-go-round, as they call it, and are loud in their praise of it."

Our favorite toys

"Go get Kissy if you want a little kiss ... press her arms like this ... you get a little kiss."

Kissy is but one member of the doll family that includes illustrious cousins such as Betsy Wetsie and Raggedy Ann and Cabbage Patch Kids and Mrs. Beasley and, it seems eternally, Barbie.

Dolls and Lincoln Logs, Daisy air rifles and Davy Crockett coonskin caps, Bill-Ding blocks and Creepy Crawler makers, Pong and Donkey Kong, Stretch Armstrong and Twister, Tonka trucks and Big Wheels — everyone has a favorite toy, a must-have from a holiday or birthday long past that remains shelved in the memory corner of the mind, if not in the dusty corner of a closet.

Once, toys were simple, marbles and jacks. Like life, they have become complicated, Nintendo and Hot Wheels volcanoes or collectors items, Beanie Babies.

Does anyone remember their Kibbies, Cat's Eyes, Mibs or Moonies? As the century turned into the 1900s, kids in every city and hamlet could be found kneeling, squatting and knuckling down to play marbles. Marbles were mostly glass, but some smart aleck might try to bring in a steelie, a metal shooter that was never too accurate, slow, and tough on the shooting thumb. Unpaved alleys were best for play. Dirt was a must to scratch out a ring. Marbles were played for fun, but if you shot someone's marble from the ring, it was a keeper, your marble for keeps.

Boys don't play jacks any more than girls shoot marbles. Usually, that is. Jacks is a game of great skill and dexterity. In its simplest explanation, the ball is bounced, and jacks are picked up, or scooped up, in pattern set by rhyme or number. Only one hand may be used to catch and pick up jacks. All jacks must remain where they fall when scattered. Games vary. You pick up one, then two, and so on. There are many versions, but the main idea is to have fun.

Davy Crockett ("King of the Wild Frontier") may have been the first action toy, but he wasn't the last. The four-star general of the regiment always will be GI Joe. A non-com in fatigues, his birth — combat-ready, of course — coincided with escalation of the war in Vietnam. Like Beetle Bailey, GI Joe seems destined to be a military man forever. But what a guy! He's been a Green Beret, a Navy SEAL, a jungle fighter, a demolitions expert. His descendants are Transformers. But in most toy boxes, he always will be, simply, the ultimate fighting man, from head to toe.

There's only one name for a doll that presents a figure of such unnatural proportions to girl-children: Barbie! Today's youngest grandmothers were yesterday's first generation of Barbie owners. Barbie made her debut in 1959; more than 1 billion dolls have been sold since. She spent her earliest years as little more than a clothes horse, but recently Barbie has become a career chick: Among her end-of-the-century professions is School Photographer Barbie. She also is venturing out of her Dream House as Working Woman Barbie, complete with a day planner, play laptop computer and a cell phone.

Rubik's Cube was one of countless brain-teasing toys that have tested the mettle of youngsters and adults. There always have been individually challenging toys, linking rings and Tri-opoly. But games requiring "2-4 players" endure: checkers and pick-up sticks and dominoes and chess and board games such as Battleship and Monopoly and Scrabble. In the '90s, most favorite games of the past are being adapted for computer play. Best thing about that development: You can't lose the game pieces.

THE
LITTLE
KING
BY
OTTO SOGLOW

© 1998 KING FEATURES
SYNDICATE, INC.

IF I DON'T GET
$10,000 TODAY
UNDER THE
OAK TREE, THE
KING WILL BE
HURT.
SLIPPERY GUS

HIS MAJESTY WISHES
TO KNOW IF YOU'LL
SETTLE FOR $5000

©King Features Syndicate, Inc.

"The Little King" was a character who never spoke. He was always a playful king in a nameless land usually was shadowed by a puffed-up attendant. The strip began in 1934 and lasted until 1975, when its creator, Otto Soglow, died.

"Thimble Theater" began in 1919 with the Oyl family and its stick-slender daughter, Olive. Ten years later, it received its leading man, an oddly built, pipe-smoking sailor who loved spinach. E.C. Segar was the cartoonist.

When the comics were known as funnies

Once, comic strips were called "the funnies." When he was mayor of New York City, Fiorello LaGuardia read them every Sunday morning, over the radio. He took special delight in the Katzenjammer Kids and Popeye, whose muscles bulged after eating a can of spinach.

Comics are an American art form that spread throughout the world. They go into almost every home in Quad-City Land, a quick read that reflects not only the world we live in, but the way we think.

Comics began with a single panel, "Down Hogan's Alley," in 1895. The main character was a buck-toothed kid wearing a long nightshirt. Printers wanted to experiment with yellow ink, and put that color onto the kid's nightshirt. It wasn't long until the comic became known as "The Yellow Kid." Other comics came to be and they burst into newsprint with the first flashes of color in the black and white newspapers.

Without the comics, would Mickey Mouse ever have been born? Walt Disney originally was a cartoonist. Comics gave us Nancy and Charlie Brown and Pogo and super-sleuths Dick Tracy and Kerry Drake. The early humor of "Toonerville Trolley" was to bring on Dagwood and Blondie and Camp Swampy, where Beetle Bailey perpetually serves in the Army. Without comics, kids and grownups never would have known the beauty of the artwork in Prince Valiant — or the wonder of the Arthurian legend.

Many comics stay with us forever, from childhood to today-hood. Others stay frozen in a past that confounds in the present.

Times change. The world changes. And now the comics turn contemporary with life as we know it ... Doonesbury and Sally Forth and Dilbert.

By reading the comics we better understand ourselves and — all the better — we can laugh at ourselves.

©Universal Press Syndicate

In 1968, Garry Trudeau, an undergraduate at Yale University, began drawing a comic strip for the *Yale Daily News*. A representative of Universal Press Syndicate saw it and saw opportunity. He offered to put the strip, retitled "Doonesbury," on the market. Doonesbury brought a different perspective to the comics page or, in some cases, to the editorial page where editors, concerned about the strong political bent of the strip, chose to print it. Trudeau made history in 1975 when Doonesbury became the first comic strip to win a Pulitzer Prize, journalism's highest honor. Art Buchwald said: "It is not only the best comic strip, but the best satire ... "

"The Katzenjammer Kids" is the oldest strip still in existence. It began in 1887, and continues to the present, centering on pranks pulled by the blond Fritz and dark-haired Hans, who torment Mama, Papa and their guest, The Captain. It was created by Rudolph Dirks.

©King Features Syndicate, Inc.

"Bringing Up Father" began in 1913 and is one of those rare strips that survives to the present. The formula remains the same, top-hatted Jiggs, in a battle of wits with his social-climber wife, Maggie. The strip usually ends with Jiggs leaving the house in a hail of dishes or rolling pins. George McManus, the originator, died in 1954, but others have continued the panel.

©King Features Syndicate, Inc.

Why the circus will always come to our towns

"Everything but the circus is supposed to be bad for you. It is the only spectacle I know that, while you watch it, gives the quality of a truly happy dream."

— Ernest Hemingway

No one ever said that Hemingway was a true lover of the circus, but how else would he have written those so-perfect words for a Ringling Bros. and Barnum & Bailey Circus program?

The sawdust and pink lemonade has fascinated a variety of writers: Galesburg's Carl Sandburg, Thomas Wolfe, William Saroyan and even George Will, to mention a few circus buffs.

It would appear all of the Quad-Cities is a circus buff, too.

When tented, the Ringling show customarily set up its big top on the Rockingham Road showgrounds in the west end of Davenport. Cole Bros. often chose to play near the Dasso truck gardens in Rock Island.

Whatever may be said, the circus in the Quad-Cities has survived chautaquas, minstrel shows, Howdy Doody, Cinerama and drive-in movies. Why?

The late Bob Parkinson of Cambridge, Illinois, one of the founding godfathers of the Circus World Museum in Baraboo, Wisconsin, put it this way:

"The circus is the full gamut of life, the drama of balance and losing your balance.

Cat man

Terrell Jacobs, who was nearly as famous as Clyde Beatty, once worked a record 48 lions and tigers in one steel arena. In his waning years as a wild animal trainer, he was working only a handful of cats on the Davenport levee with Royal American Shows carnival. On June 6, 1949, his whip snapped back into his face and caught his eye. It was so severely lacerated that it was nearly out of its socket and was removed at Mercy Hospital. He joined the show several weeks later with a patch over his eye, but his career as an animal trainer was washed up.

The immense spread of the Ringling Bros. and Barnum & Bailey Circus, playing on Davenport's Rockingham Road showgrounds in 1940. This layout would be raised in a new town in the morning, then torn down at night to be hauled by train to the next showground.

To laugh at clowns and life itself, and bite your fingernails over some-one falling from high places, not unlike your own survival of winning or losing at whatever you do and the sheer dream of everyone to say, oh hell, let's run away from life and join the circus."

After a too-long absence, big-time circus is back again in the Quad-Cities, full-blast and spangled, and for the moment, playing every Labor Day weekend at The Mark of the Quad-Cities.

Long ago, when the circus played under canvas, it was unfettered by color and blare. The Ringling show would put at least 5,000 posters into a city like Davenport. Ralph Heninger, who lived across the street from the Rockingham showgrounds, remembers carrying water to the elephants and listening to the rhythm of the rousters pounding stakes ... "Hammer, five, six-bit; beat 'em, split 'em, don't get hit."

By noon, the big top was pulled into the sky by the brute strength of man, elephant and Mack truck, to be followed by the matinee. After the last night performance, it would be the haul back to the circus trains. Naptha flares lined the street and there was the mysterious sound of a bullman (elephant keeper) herding his shuffling string of mammoths, trunks to tails, their leg chains clinking upon the bricks as they passed dark-ened porches of awed kids. He called, "Ho, Babe. Here, Ruth."

Next day, the circus was gone, the old banquet of peanuts and popcorn had disappeared. Patterns in the sawdust were all that remained, as if trying to make the children of all ages cry.

"For every soul is a circus,
And every mind is a tent.
And every heart a sawdust ring,
Where the circling race is spent."
— Vachel Lindsay

This, the most widely used poster in the history of the American circus, features the image of Clinton's Felix Adler. Poster © Ringling Bros. and Barnum & Bailey

"I lack the adjectives,
verbs
And nouns,
To do full justice
To the clowns."
— Ogden Nash

Davenport's B.J. Palmer fell in love with this old Barnum & Bailey Two Hemispheres bandwagon when it was abandoned and falling to pieces at the Iowa State Fairgrounds in Des Moines. He restored it, and had a small museum built to house it on the Palmer College of Chiropractic campus. The building was long ago razed; the bandwagon is at the Circus World Museum, Baraboo, Wisconsin.

The Clown of Presidents

This circus poster face made more people laugh than any known man, woman or child.

Felix Adler was the King of Clowns, a Clinton, Iowa, kid who became "The Clown of Presidents," He entertained Hoover, Roosevelt and Truman.

As a lad, he ran away from his Clinton home with a troupe of circus acrobats. He was so clumsy that they laughed him out of the ring, so he became a clown with Ringling Bros. and Barnum & Bailey Circus. When he died, the *New York Times* gave him two solid columns of type, far more than an ex-U.S. secretary of state who died the day before.

Like Yoric, the timeless Shakespearean jester, Felix (real name, Frank) Adler was a man of infinite jest, but really a shy person when out of makeup. During our many visits, he down-talked himself, and often just stared at his giant clown shoes.

Variety magazine said he had made at least 2 million people a year belly laugh for 50 uninterrupted years. The big top came to a halt during his fabled walk-arounds with trained piglets. Their reward was a slurp or two from a baby bottle of milk.

Since the piglets outgrew their usefulness after a month or so, Felix had to train hundreds of them during his long career of clowning. He would leave them with friendly farm folks, and maybe a year or two later, they would write to say that his young trainees now had piglets of their own. He was proud of his former pupils.

Once, when the Ringling show was playing Davenport, Jimmy Oakes invited Felix to appear at the Davenport Exchange Club. He did more than expected. He showed up in full costume, accompanied by a midget clown. They did a barbershop gig in the Gold Room of the Blackhawk Hotel, throwing buckets of shaving lather onto Exchange members. It turned into bedlam.

Felix disavowed the false sentimentality often associated with his profession. "None of this 'laugh though your heart is breaking' stuff," he would say. He never saw a clown with a broken heart, and once said, "Clowns are a carefree, jolly bunch of good fellows, full of the devil."

Felix is buried at Springdale Cemetery, Clinton. During funeral visitation, his widow told friends that he last wore his clown makeup during off-season at a Christmas celebration at Wanamaker's store in Philadelphia. He told children he was Santa's son. When one child asked about his mother, he replied, "Why, her name is Mary. It's Mary Christmas."

All the stars in our eyes ...

Stars are like shining clusters on Quad-City stages. There have been no dry spells and fame has created its own standards. We've had sellouts and turkeys. Once, at intermission of a local show, Dorothy Lamour (Bob Hope's sidekick in the "Road" movies) looked out on an almost empty house and groaned: "There's no business like show business except in Davenport when there's no business."

Yet Eric Clapton came around years later to gross $600,000 at The Mark of the Quad-Cities. And Frank Sinatra remains the biggest-grosser for ticket-tab. The Chairman of the Board had no trouble selling out with a $75 "top" at The Mark.

They've ALL been here, some in the early quest for fame, on that "tour of one-night stands."

Frank Sinatra

A sampling of entertainers who have played here:

Aerosmith; Alabama; America; Paul Anka; Eddy Arnold.

Burt Bacharach; Ethel Barrymore (insisted on having her own dressing room built at the edge of the stage); The Beach Boys (They've played everywhere, from John O'Donnell Stadium to The Mark. In 1989, promoters got into trouble for cutting down a tree on Davenport city property because it blocked the stage); Bix Beiderbecke; Harry Belafonte; Louie Bellson; Tony Bennett; Jack Benny; Edgar Bergen; Sarah Bernhardt (Offended by "the poisonous air" of downtown Davenport, she had her private railroad car parked on a siding far out on Eastern Avenue); Harry Blackstone, Jr.; Blue Oyster Cult; Michael Bolton (with Wynonna); Victor Borge; Boston Pops; Boyz II Men; Brandy; Brooks & Dunn; Buffalo Springfield.

Eddie Cantor; George Carlin; Mary Chapin Carpenter; The Carpenters; Carrot Top; Johnny Cash (He was "born again" after a visit with Tommy Barnett, charismatic preacher at Westside Assembly of God, Davenport); Harry Chapin (Delighted fans waiting for the doors to open at Davenport's Orpheum by walking along the line, guitar in hand, and chatting); Cheap Trick; Cher (with and without Sonny); Chicago; Eric Clapton; Dick Clark; The Clash; Phil Collins; Aaron Copland; David Copperfield; Bill Cosby; Counting Crows; The Cranberries; Crosby, Stills & Nash; Sheryl Crow; Billy Ray Cyrus.

Charlie Daniels Band; John Denver; Neil Diamond (At least three times, once as opener for the '60s one-hit-wonders Strawberry Alarm Clock, once to open The Mark); Phyllis Diller; Doobie Brothers; Bob Dylan.

Emerson, Lake and Palmer; En Vogue; Simon Estes; Melissa Etheridge.

Arthur Fiedler; Fleetwood Mac; Dan Fogelberg.

Kenny G; George Gershwin (The audience applauded "Rhapsody in Blue" but not "An American in Paris"); Vince Gill; Benny Goodman; Robert Goulet; Amy Grant; Cary Grant; Great White.

Merle Haggard; Jascha Heifitz; Jimi Hendrix; Katharine Hepburn; Herman's Hermits; Bob Hope (Four appearances, one to receive an honorary doctorate from St. Ambrose University); Buddy Holly (Winter Dance Party 1959, with Richie Valens and Big Bopper, played the Col days before the "day the music died"); Marilyn Horne.

Jose Iturbi; Burl Ives.

Janet Jackson; Mahalia Jackson; Jane's Addiction; Byron Janis; Waylon Jennings; Joan Jett and the Blackhearts; Billy Joel; Elton John; George Jones and Tammy Wynette; Spike Jones and his City Slickers.

R. Kelly; Sam Kinison; KISS.

Patti LaBelle; Ann Landers; Mario Lanza; The Lettermen; Jerry Lewis; Huey Lewis and the News; Liberace; Gordon Lightfoot; Little River Band; Lovin' Spoonful.

Reba McEntire; McGuire Sisters; Don McLean; Ed McMahon; The Mamas and the Papas; Barry Manilow; Mannheim Steamroller; Marcel Marceau; Steve Martin; Johnny Mathis; Dave Matthews Band; John Mellencamp; Robert Merrill; Metallica; Bette Midler; Steve Miller Band; Liza Minnelli; Eddie Money; Moody Blues; Grace Moore; Lorrie Morgan; Motley Crue; Anne Murray.

Willie Nelson; Nirvana; Ted Nugent and the Amboy Dukes. Ozzy Osborne.

Paderwski; Dolly Parton; Pavlova; Peaches & Herb; Itzhak Perlman; Peter, Paul and Mary; Bernadette Peters; Tom Petty and the Heartbreakers; Prince.

REO Speedwagon; Paul Revere and the Raiders; Jason Robards; Dame Margerita Roberti; Paul Robeson (After a performance, he ordered a Scotch in the Blackhawk Hotel bar, a place where blacks never were seen at that time. The bartender told him it would be $20; Robeson responded by putting two twenties on the bar and asked the bartender to have one with him. The bartender did); Kenny Rogers; Rush.

Bob Hope, commencement speaker at St. Ambrose.

Lalo Schifrin; Willard Scott; Pauly Shore; Sylvia Sidney; Simon & Garfunkel; Red Skelton (He shopped for underwear at Target and Kmart); Smashing Pumpkins; Smothers Brothers; Starship; Rod Stewart; George Strait; Tom Sullivan.

James Taylor; The Temptations; Tesla; Third Eye Blind; Mel Torme; Jethro Tull; Tina Turner; The Turtles.

Van Halen; Luther Vandross; Stevie Ray Vaughn; Bobby Vee; Bobby Vinton.

The Wallflowers; William Warfield; Fred Waring; Andy Williams.

Yanni.

Rob Zombie; White Zombie.

Heaven couldn't wait

B.J. Palmer — the father of Palmer College of Chiropractic — was ceaselessly intrigued by the hereafter, but he couldn't wait to get there. Thirty-seven years before his death, B.J. built his own version of heaven alongside his mansion atop Brady Hill in Davenport. It was an outlandish garden of pebbles and ponds, petrified wood, stone snakes and weird objects with monkey heads, temple bells and Buddhas and a greenhouse of exotic plants.

He called it Little Bit O' Heaven, built in 1924 with two-ton mosaic gates, supposedly in the style of those of the Taj Mahal. B.J. called this entrance Purgatory, and the keeper of the gate to his Heaven was a cigar-smoking attendant nicknamed St. Peter.

When anti-smokers complained about St. Peter puffing cigar smoke in their faces, B.J. — an inveterate cigar smoker himself — would counter that the original St. Peter just might have used tobacco, and dared anyone to disprove it.

Whatever detractors may have said of B.J.'s Little Bit O' Heaven, it was a prime Tri-City tourist attraction for decades, heavily promoted on Palmer's pioneer radio station, WOC. It was a time before TV and other distractions, and every out-of-town visitor found it mandatory to visit Palmer's Heaven. Records show that during Heaven's lifetime, it attracted 3 million visitors.

B.J., who loved to loll words around in his mouth, and in his dozen books, explained his Heaven in personal prose: " ... A bit of a spiritual dream, a place where man can muse with the gods."

Inside, Palmer built the smallest chapel in the world (so he claimed, it being 8-feet

An Oriental vase is nearly the size of B.J. Palmer in an annex to his Little Bit O'Heaven, once a major Davenport tourist attraction.

When visitors asked Palmer where the water originated for this waterfall, he would answer, "It comes from a spring." He would then take them behind the waterfall and show a rusty bedspring.

square) and thousands were married there, allowing them to claim they had been wed in heaven.

After B.J.'s death in 1961, his Heaven went downhill. It was closed to the public in 1981, and two years later was dismantled. Some of the pieces went to the Palmer wing of the Putnam Museum in Davenport.

Heaven itself became a patio for students. On quiet warm nights, some contend they still smell B.J.'s cigar smoke.

Davenport's Col ballroom, in the 1960s. It has changed little at this turn of the century.

"Sometimes dancing and music can describe a true image of the customs of a country better than the words in a newspaper."

— Gene Kelly, the most talented dancer of our time,
in a 1964 *New York Times* interview, "On a Culture Safari"

When they danced all night

O n a back wall of the Col, queen mother of all remaining ballrooms in America, are scribbled the autographs of generations of music-makers who performed at the old palace in west Davenport.

There are the scrawls of stars such as Jimi Hendrix and Louis Armstrong (who signed, simply, "Satchmo") and Johnny Cash, who was such an unknown that he was backed up by a local band, Hal Wiese.

There are the signatures of leaders whose thin batons waved before big dance bands ... Wayne King and Guy Lombardo and Lawrence Welk; the toothy Stan Kenton, who brought a band of 23 to the stage; musicians from the Glenn Miller band; Duke Ellington; Harry James. Also, one remarkable diminutive signature, left by a new singer with Les Brown and his Band of Renown. Her name: Doris Day.

All the names are faded, almost indistinguishable, but it was a tradition for band leaders and musicians to sign the wall by the dressing room, says Don Wachal, long-time owner of the Col.

We've always loved to dance. In the days when the trolleys ran through the Tri-Cities, bringing the young to the Col, they followed the rhythms of the Turkey Trot, the Charleston, waltzes with dips and the old banjo step, the Big Apple.

I n the jitterbug days, a thin-as-a-rake young singer joined the big-time Dorsey band at the Col. It is documented by Kerker family members, who once owned the Col, that Frank Sinatra joined Tommy's band in Davenport ... "I'll never smile again, until I smile with you."

As with all in life, we've gone the complete circle. We're dancing again here in the Quad-Cities, but then, did we ever quit? Swing dancing is the pop pleasure; at the Sweetwater along Moline's River Drive, the marquee offers beginning and advanced lessons in line dancing.

"It's wonderful that we're dancing yet today — not just the seniors (*Quad-City Times Plus 60 Club* dances easily will attract 600) — but the young, too. But nothing like the way it was in the 1920s and 1930s and 1940s," Wachal says of his long memories running the Col.

"There were years when the trolleys ran 1 a.m. specials from the Col to Rock Island so people would have a way home. Interurbans had cars nicknamed, 'Show Me the Way to Go Home,' which were after-midnight

The five-foot posters, on heavy cardboard, are all originals, painted for the Col by Davenport police officer Mell Warren and commercial artist Jerry Berry. They are among dozens on the walls of the Col.

Megaphones, banjos and a scenic painting on the bass drum. Wayne Rohlfe and his serenaders at Danceland, where there was dancing every weekend — and often at midweek, too. Rohlfe is the only one with glasses and a mustache.

specials from Davenport to Muscatine."

Mention dancing, and the talk always rhapsodizes to the Col, called the Coliseum in its palmy days, which began in 1914. Always, it was a wonderful, romantic romp. It remains the center of the universe of dancing in MidAmerica, maybe all of America. Outside, the big neon sign still glares: "The Col — Dance and Romance." Most American ballrooms are gone, but the Col lingers — a sweetheart that keeps coming back like a song.

"Who knows how many people met at the Col, and ended up husband and wife?" Wachal asks. "Once, we tried to find out. We asked for affidavits of proof, wanting to have a party for couples who first danced together and ended up going down the marriage aisle together. We had more than 1,000 people that night, one of our biggest turnouts ever. No question that is a low figure, because thousands of others are scattered all over America."

How would a shy fellow and a bashful girl meet at the Col? Sometimes, there would be a scamper line, with a rope stretched across the shiny ballroom floor. Gents on one side; women on the other. The

Tom Owen and His Cowboys were a regional dance band favorite, and Don Wachal, now of Blue Grass, Iowa, played with them. That's Don with his foot on the rear wheel of the stagecoach.

Out on the range with Tom Owen and His Cowboys

Of all this region's bands, none was more popular than Tom Owen and His Cowboys. National trade publications hailed the boys in chaps as the band without fatigue; from 1937 to 1951, they toured MidAmerica ceaselessly. They may have been forerunners of Riders in the Sky.

They did the impossible, performing or playing dances nightly within 150 miles of Cedar Rapids. But they had to be back, every noon, to perform live — six days a week — on WMT radio, Cedar Rapids, Iowa. The radio station was their sponsor while they trailed the range of MidAmerica.

"There were six of us in the band bus, plus Tom, who owned the band and was the booker," says Don Wachal, who played with the band all of its years. They were in and out of Cedar Rapids, three or four months in a row, without a break.

"There were times when we wished winter weather would strand us, just so we could have a day off," Wachal says. The pace was grueling, but the pay was good. Tom took 70 percent, the hall got 30 percent.

"I know every small town within 150 miles of this area," Wachal says. "I know, I've played there."

Band members dressed in Wild West outfits, but Wachal says it was just for an image. "We played all kinds of music, besides western style."

Tom Owen and His Cowboys was a good band, so good they backed up Gene Autry at some dates. At one show, an unknown comedian dressed up as a cowboy and Tom Owen and band played for him. It was for George — Lonesome George — Gobel.

When Major Bowes and his top-rated radio amateur hour played Cedar Rapids, the choice for the house band on national radio was ... Tom Owen and His Cowboys.

YOURS FOR DANCING
Sheriff TOM OWEN AND HIS COWBOYS OF RADIO STATION WMT CEDAR RAPIDS, IOWA

Broadcasting Every Day 12:30 Noon Except Sunday

music would begin, and whoever they faced, they danced with. Never the mind that the guy had two left feet.

The waxy floor, the shiny mirrored ball sparkling circles on the floor, will never retire. The romantic never tire of dancing ...

"Waltz me around again, Willie, around and around.
"The music is dreamy, it's peaches and creamy.
"Don't let my feet touch the ground."
— Will D. Cobb, *"Waltz Me Around Again, Willie,"* 1926

Tossing pennies into the tuba

Dance jobs ... gigs ... is what they were called, and musicians like Bill Perry and Bob Lofgren found themselves living two lives. They worked regular jobs during the day, and they played gigs at night.

"How can I forget a job at Danceland in Davenport," says Perry, of Rock Island. "We played the infamous jumping 'Bunny Hop' for a Palmer dance of graduating chiropractors. The ballroom was just above the Eagle Lodge clubrooms and when club members saw the ceiling vibrating, they went into panic and ran to the firehouse across the street. They called police and the dance was called off. The students and grads went into a near-riot."

Mention of the Jack Manthey band puts Lofgren, an East Moline pianist, into a swoon. "Manthey had a smooth, all-reed band, beautiful, 12 pieces. We played at Beulah's Beautiful Club Belvidere, out Eleventh Street in Rock Island."

Dance halls were jumping everywhere, in little towns and at the end of distant roads and at places like Starlight Ballroom at Mississippi Valley Fairgrounds, Davenport. Along the happy-go-lucky Rock River, where cheap gin flowed in the speaks, dancers crossed bee's-knees to the Charleston in the river's biggest dance hall, Poplar Grove. Another romantic name, Moonlight Gardens, was attached to a dimly lit ballroom at the edge of Davenport.

"At the Green Lantern, out Harrison Street in Davenport, dancers would get wild and toss pennies into the tuba." Perry says. "Fairyland in DeWitt, was — and still is — one of the great ballrooms in the Midwest. Welk (Lawrence, of course) played there lots of times. The Top Hat ballroom at the LeClaire Hotel in Moline had the best view of any ballroom in America. The tea dances were the ultimate in class, with Hal Wiese and his big band playing that great old medley with 'April in Paris.'

"Bobby Hansen, who went on to big things as CEO of Deere & Co., played with Wiese. A fine trumpet player, he was. Bands couldn't play slow enough at the Top Hat. It was THE place for slow dancing."

Swingy stepping — a couple at the Voss Bros. company picnic, 1947, Mississippi Valley Fairgrounds, Davenport. The ballroom came to be known as the Starlight.

Kenneth L. Prestley

"Oh Sinner! Consider the future danger you are in. It is a great furnace of wrath; a wide and bottomless pit, full of the fire of wrath."
— Jonathan Edwards, an itinerant minister who traveled along the Mississippi River in the 1920s

The wickedest city in America

"Early to bed and early to rise, and your girl goes out with other guys."
— Stephen Longstreet, *"Sportin' House:*
A History of Sinners and the Birth of Jazz"

chapter thirteen

Sin, Shame, Rackets & Raids

Davenport was hard as a diamond in the early 1900s. Rock Island was little better, as the righteous fought — and ultimately won — the battle against the hoodlum lawyer John Looney and his cohorts.

Bishop Henry Cosgrove, of the Catholic Diocese of Davenport, called the city "the wickedest in the nation," aiming at Bucktown, an early 1900s carnival of sin transgressing from Perry Street and the river to the Government Bridge and up to Third Street.

After years of perdition, Bucktown finally was cleansed. But soon to be uncorked were the hooch havens of Prohibition, when bootlegger Nic Coin was gunned to death by shotgun sprays from a speeding car while he waited for a city bus on Davenport's peaceful West Locust Street.

Sin reared its head repeatedly in the Tri-Cities through years of on-again, off-again sleazery, gaming and girls and corner pickups and police stings. It has a habit of coming back like a long overdue bill.

Plush bar-eateries like Marando's in Milan and the Plantation in Moline are recalled for defying the law. Those of a generation ago still talk of walking down the maroon-carpeted stairs to the Plantation's lower level where, in the corner, a short-skirted young woman was dealing blackjack and, on the opposite wall, the slot machines jangled in spins for three cherries in a row.

In the late 1940s, Rock Island cracked down hard on gambling. Slot machines were seized at private clubs. With confiscated one-armed bandits, Rock Island detectives Max Jennings, left, and Tom Donnelly.

Jul's Danish Farm, now the Moline Elks clubrooms, was knocked off for possession of a giant gambling table. The defense claimed it could have been used for ping-pong. Jul's lost the case.

Two battling sisters from Moline, Marie and Mathilda VanMeulebrock, were hell-bent on halting gambling because Rock Island County was not doing enough to help homeless pets. In 1948, *Life* magazine called Marie "Joan of Arc" when she tossed bricks through bar windows, sat in jail, and was the fuse for blasting authorities into action.

Bernard J. Moran, Rock Island County state's attorney, came to realize the seri-

Bishop Henry Cosgrove

ousness of the problem when, during one raid in the county, 1,293 violations were found.

All-out gaming was being brought to its knees.

When it was at its worst ...

Sin in Davenport was at its most evil nadir in the early 1900s. The Catholic bishop scored points for berating Davenport as the wickedest of cities. Soon Mayor Waldo Becker and city aldermen went slumming in Bucktown; they claimed surprise at the evil they found.

By count, this downtown "Barbary Coast" had 51 bars, plus prostitution dens, dime-a-dance parlors, boxing rings and gaming spots for poker and faro games.

Davenport newspapers of the early 1900s took up the cry against the sins of Bucktown. A *Democrat* editorial said:

"It will take more than a religious campaign or a church crusade to clean up Davenport. The city must have a wholesale movement of decent people."

One critic of the city administration claimed:

"The late-night Owl Car trolley from Davenport to Rock Island is a scene of debauchery. This last car is invaded by loud, lewd, tough and disreputable men and women."

Crackdowns were inevitable. State police repeatedly raided the brothels and wine rooms, small, curtained, booth-like nooks. Patrolmen began riding the Owl Car.

Mayor Becker yielded to public pressures and ordered the closing of dance halls and brothels in the Tenderloin. But when the mayor learned that the Hackmans Ball (for livery drivers) had been scheduled at one of the locked-up dance halls, he ordered a period of grace for the hall to reopen.

A reporter for the *Democrat* joked in print: "The farewell function was the swellest event of the season for the Tenderloin District's social set."

The closings were short-lived; it soon was business as usual, but ...

The final call for debauchery came in 1918 when the U.S. Secretary of the Army issued an order:

"All saloons and bawdy houses within a half-mile of Rock Island Arsenal must close within 36 hours."

The order shut down the 51 bars in Bucktown and 27 wholesalers. The age of shameful sinning was never to revel again.

The Quad-Cities of today is relatively sin-free. Gambling has returned — legally, this time — in the riverboats along the region's shores.

What goes around, comes around.

Thirsty patrons line up for a last drink at Phil Schwab's bar, Rock Island. All bars within a distance of the Rock Island Arsenal were closed on May 2, 1918, ostensibly by federal decree. In headlines, the *Democrat & Leader* said: "Sound taps for thirst parlors in Rock Island. 'Wettest' town in Illinois ready to pass into the dry column. 40 bars go out tonight."

Cheese it, the cops!
Super Bowl Sunday — the biggest raid of all

A film writer could not have scripted a scenario quite like Super Bowl Sunday 1980, a super-size gambling raid at Mr. Kelly's, a downtown Davenport bar.

More than 150 people were arrested. In that group were a Davenport police officer, a Scott County magistrate, the director of a law enforcement training center, a college football coach and several people previously linked to gambling.

Attendance was by invitation only. A uniformed police officer stood at the door to ensure there would be no intruders. Tickets — sold weeks in advance — cost $200, and each buyer could bring one guest. Ticket sales were limited to 100. Something for all: Blackjack tables, roulette, poker — everything needed to create a raunchy Las Vegas for one Super Bowl Sunday.

The winner of a pool on the outcome of the football game between Pittsburgh and Los Angeles was to have netted $15,000 in cash.

Fun and games came to a stunning halt when 40 uninvited guests pushed into the party, members of the vice squad from the Davenport Police Department, the Iowa Division of Criminal Investigation and the Iowa Highway Patrol.

The raid was such a surprise that not even the mayor, the chief of police or county attorney were told in advance. Afterward, the chief of the Division of Criminal Investigation was to say: "The fewer people who know, the better."

The raid brought months of headlines. Davenport Mayor Charles Wright bitterly denied that he was in Mr. Kelly's shortly before it was raided. A police captain was transferred in connection with the raid. Alderman-at-large Larry d'Autremont said, "It was not one of the police department's finer moments."

The tip-off about the party came from angry wives of men who planned to attend. When it all shook out, Scott County Attorney Bill Davis said that charges against 111 of the 158 people arrested would have to be dropped. A month before the raid, the city council had repealed the ordinance under which they had been charged with patronizing a disorderly house.

The Super Bowl Sunday raid of 1980 made headlines for months afterward. In the end, charges against 111 of the 158 arrested had to be dropped because the ordinance under which they were arrested had been repealed.

Jolson, Blind Billy, Brick and Bucktown

Al Jolson

What tales the old brick streets of downtown Davenport could tell if the asphalt paving were stripped away.

One of the celebrated clubs of the early 1900s was Brick Munro's Pavilion at the southwest corner of Pershing Avenue and Second Street in Bucktown.

Munro, so the memories tell, ran a straight place — no girls, no gambling, just a saloon and good music.

The legend has been handed down so many times that there must be some truth in it.

Once Munro hired a young man by the name of Al Jolson as a singing waiter. In later, more prosperous years, Jolson returned to Davenport to star on the stage of the Burtis Opera House. At intermission, he called out to the audience:

"You paid three bucks to hear me tonight. A couple years ago, you could have heard me for the price of a beer at Brick Munro's."

High-salaried performers from theaters around the Tri-Cities regularly would wind up the night singing or playing at Munro's. One of them was a piano player named Blind Billy, who appeared on many vaudeville stages across the nation and made much to-do about his claim that — though blind — that he could play any song called to him from the audience. Without music, of course.

Billy enjoyed the atmosphere of Munro's and stayed for nearly a year.

The story goes that one day a bartender called to Munro:

"Hey, Brick, Billy wants to see you."

Munro yelled back: "He'll have a heckuva time seeing me, he's blind."

Customers in the place laughed, and that became a part of Blind Billy and Brick Munro's nightly routine.

The 'Great Bingo Raid'

In the annals of Quad-City raids, none likely will compare with the bingo bash of 1965 at the Capitol Club in downtown Davenport. Into paddy wagons and squad cars were herded 144 bingo players — 139 of them women.

The Capitol Club was such a popular bingo parlor that city bus driver Charley Clark would shout, "Bingo Junction," when he stopped to unload riders at West Third and Harrison streets.

The raid made headlines all over the nation after a zealous county attorney decided that bingo, however innocent, was illicit. Money was changing hands; it was a game of chance.

By 1965, most gambling was gone in Scott County, but bingo sinfully malingered in Davenport. So, on the sunny afternoon of June 4, 1965, police moved in on the Capitol Club, 222 Harrison Street, arresting the 144 bingo players and charging them with being inmates of a disorderly house.

An 87-year-old woman who walked with a cane was arrested. So was a 12-year-old girl. The "criminals" were frightened, many of them weeping. One elderly bingo player was helped to her husband's car by a detective and booked at the scene. The remainder were taken to the police station where most were released on bonds of $25 to $50.

Scott County Attorney Dave Miller staged the raid on the premise that bingo was gambling, and gambling was not legal in Iowa.

Court appearances were staggered, apparently because judges had no intentions of facing so many angry bingo players at the same time. Fines generally were small.

The bingo raid made the front pages of the *Chicago Tribune* and *San Francisco Examiner*.

When bingo fell (only to be legalized seven years after the 1965 raid), it was a portent of the end to all gambling in Scott County. For a time, even pinball machines were banned. Frightened druggists and grocers hauled pinballs out of their stores in coaster wagons, hiding them in sheds and garages.

From the wrong side of the law ...

The last of the major Davenport brothels of old still standing has been restored and now is the law offices of Michael Liebbe. Located at 116 East Sixth Street, it operated from the early 1900s into the 1940s and was best known as Geraldine's Place. Liebbe has restored the old place to its jasmine-scented splendor, with florid wallpaper and a mirrored stairway where customers could eye "the girls" as they descended. It is the only known brothel on the National Register of Historic Places, Liebbe says.

Capitol Club, site of the infamous bingo raid of 1965. A paddy wagon and squad car are out front; in the background, a helmeted officer carries armloads of bingo cards as evidence.

John Looney: The wickedest man

Alternately, he looked the type of a lawyer (which he was) or a hobo — more frequently, the latter. Sometimes, he was disguised by a black beard. Weasel-faced, he had the lips of a frog.

Whatever the portrait, John Looney was the most evil man in the long history of our cities. He was a killer and a con man; an extortionist, bootlegger, pimp and — of all unlikely vocations — a newspaper publisher whose bogus, libelous headlines and stories would blare:

"Hospital Hiring Prostitutes As Nurses"

Looney was a festering boil on life in Rock Island, beginning with a boast of his hoodlum power in 1910 or so and sleazing into the booze-running 1920s. In 1912, the Illinois Militia (a version of what now is the National Guard) had to be called in to quell the Market Square Riot, a Looney-inspired bloody melee in which dozens were injured and one bystander killed.

Looney was king-boss of the Rock Island rackets, and the fear of him stretched through the Tri-Cities. He was a friend, but not a confidant, of Chicago mobster Al Capone.

Looney's eating habits were as eccentric as the man. He snacked on raw liver and crackers in his office, a sparse room in his Mirror Saloon at Second Avenue and Seventeenth Street. In the back was a brothel; in between, he ran his *Rock Island News*. "Truth, Good Government and Protection of the People," the masthead ridiculously claimed.

Extortion kept his pockets full. Prostitutes would fling themselves into the arms of innocent men on the street, a photographer would snap a picture, and Looney would demand a payoff to keep it out of print.

The racketeer was at constant war with the *Rock Island Argus*, making vile claims in print about the morality and

CINCINNATI CLEVELAND   HOUSTON INDIANAPOLIS   NEW ORLEANS NEW YORK   RICHMOND SALT LAKE CITY   ST. PAUL TORONTO   SCRANTON

$2000 REWARD

DESCRIPTION:

Age - 60 years
Height - 5 ft. 8 in.
Weight - 125-135 lbs.
Build - Slender
Complexion - Sallow
Hair - Jet Black
Eyes - Dark (Beady)
Nose - Prominent
Slightly twisted toward right side, indicating break.

Remarks:

Walks like an Indian, toes straight forward.
At times uses a disguise.
May wear a natural black beard.
He is a lawyer by profession.
Is well versed in horses and horse racing
Has conducted a newspaper
He is a telegrapher
Owns a large ranch near Chama, New Mexico

JOHN P. LOONEY

Indicted for Murder in Rock Island County, Rock Island, Ill.

The above reward is offered by the Citizens Committee of Rock Island, Illinois, for the apprehension and return to Rock Island, Illinois of John P. Looney. Any information regarding Looney can be telegraphed at our expense to the nearest of the above listed offices.

Postmasters, Police Officers, Sheriffs, Hotel Proprietors, and all persons receiving this circular will confer a favor by posting it in a conspicuous place.

Under its rules PINKERTON'S NATIONAL DETECTIVE AGENCY does not operate for rewards, therefore will not accept, nor permit any of its employees to accept this reward or any part thereof.

Pinkerton's National Detective Agency

Reward Expires February 1, 1924   137 South Wells St., CHICAGO, ILL.   Telephone Main 2828

A replica of a Pinkerton Agency "wanted" poster for John Looney.

honesty of its editors.

Looney railed not only against the *Argus*, but battled with gunfire others muscling in on the booze-girls-extortion underworld. The gangster's pride was his young son, Conner, who boasted that the goal of his life was to kill a man before reaching the age of 18. Looney's enemies — eager to take over the rackets — made sure that Conner didn't achieve his wish. On October 6, 1922, Conner was shot to death by rival gang gunmen.

Looney vowed revenge. But before he could mete it out, he was charged with the murder of a saloon keeper who had balked at paying protection money. He served nine years in the state penitentiary in Joliet, Illinois. When he was released, Looney retreated to his New Mexico ranch where he died of tuberculosis.

Directly, or indirectly, the hoodlum was linked to at least eight Tri-City murders.

Typical front page of John Looney's scandal sheet. His *Rock Island News,* boasted to be a morality newspaper, made scurrilous attacks on citizens. The weekly was sold for a nickel. Once, 18 young paper boys were herded into court for offering an indecent newspaper for sale.

The short life of the 'longest bar in the world'

Of all the bars in America, the New Billburg in Rock Island was alleged to be the longest. "Longest," though, is a record claimed by any saloon with a bar longer than 50 feet.

In all truth, the New Billburg may have held the record — 117 feet of shiny mahogany.

The New Billburg's life was short, and its owner — Anthony Billburg — ultimately ended up in prison for murder. Billburg, once a henchman of hoodlum John Looney, came to be his enemy and was one of the gunmen charged in the slaying of Looney's son, Conner. Despite the efforts of his attorney, the noted Clarence Darrow, Billburg went to prison.

Billburg was within the law when he built his legendary bar in 1915. He commissioned architect Arthur Ebeling — who designed edifices such as the Kahl Building in Davenport and the mansion of J.W. Bettendorf — to draw plans for the "Longest Bar in the World" at the northeast corner of Twentieth Street and Third Avenue. A marble trough with constantly running water ran the length of the bar, eliminating the need for cuspidors. One of the New Billburg's admiring customers was said to be Chicago gangster Al Capone.

In 1918, to focus workers' attention on the needs of World War I, the federal government closed all bars within a half-

Scrolls on the ceiling of the New Billburg were fashioned after the design on dollar bills.

mile of the Rock Island Arsenal. The New Billburg was padlocked. Prohibition soon followed, and it never reopened. The "Longest Bar in the World" was dismantled, and is said to have been taken to Chicago. The corner building had an array of uses, as including a soft drink parlor, an auto agency and a service station. It was razed in the 1960s.

"We're still trying to locate that bar," says Anthony Billburg's great-granddaughter, Lynne Cutler Gronke, Torrance, California.

Rock Island's Mecca of Music

It was the jazz-me-blues Mecca of Music, no greater slot for big-time jazz than Second Avenue, Rock Island, in the 1940s and into the 1950s. "It was an unexpected oasis that drew the best talent in the land to a relatively obscure city in America," says Bob Cramer, Quad-City jazz buff.

It was a block of music, cornered by the hottest of all spots, the Horse Shoe Lounge. There, through the fog-haze of cigarettes, the smoky tones of Sarah "The Divine" Vaughn, silenced the crowd with "My funny valentine, sweet comic valentine." Ella Fitzgerald murmured her memorable "Poor Butterfly ... " three times nightly.

The Horse Shoe, at 1601 Second Avenue, was the hangout for jazz lovers who came here from as far away as Cedar Rapids and Peoria.

There was music all along the block. Next to the Horse Shoe, dancers weaved as if they had downed one too many bourbons. Eddy's New Yorker had a bobbing dance floor; actually, springs under the floor to give the illusion of dancing on a ship at sea. Up a few doors, but with lesser talent, was the dim Buvette, where jazz fiddler Speck Redd shouted "Abba-dabba-dabba-dabba" as he played.

A few doors away was another hot spot, Hollywood Supper Club, good food and good music, with Woody Cather glad-handing at the door. Two regulars were top performers of the 1950s, Les Paul and Mary Ford, whose "World Is Waiting for the Sunrise" topped the charts.

But it was the Horse Shoe, which came to be called the Paddock, that was the triple-valve favorite. Why and how did all the nation's No. 1 attractions come to Rock Island?

Al Barnes, who ran the showplace from 1941 to 1952, knew how and where to book the best. Customers paid $1.25 to get in, and the waiting line would stretch a half-block. The oval bar was long, a place where at least a hundred could elbow, while the stars performed in the middle. Tables filled the rest of the place.

Barnes paid anywhere from $500 to $1,000 a week. Louis Armstrong and his all stars got $4,000, with $1,000 of that going to Satchmo himself. They'd stay at the Horse Shoe for a couple of weeks.

But for all their stardom, the black entertainers who played to sellout crowds had to stay at boarding houses because area hotels were closed to them. Even the great Nat "King" Cole was refused a room at the Fort Armstrong Hotel. Most entertainers stayed at boarding houses in Davenport.

Once, when Louis Armstrong was playing the Horse Shoe, Jack Benny had a one-nighter at Moline's Wharton Field House. Benny's sidekick, Eddie "Rochester" Anderson and band leader Phil Harris hired a cab to catch Satchmo's last show. When they got there, they were told he was at a funeral home down the street. Rochester and Phil feared the worst until learning that Satchmo had taken up lodging at Nicholson Funeral Parlor, a place where blacks were put to rest.

That same night, after Benny's show, Rochester and Phil went back to the Horse Shoe, climbed to the stage and gave the fans an added bonus. The show went on until about 4 a.m. Benny was furious when he heard what he had missed.

Among other entertainers who awed Horse Shoe audiences were Moline's Louie Bellson, the Mills Brothers, Velma Middleton, Nellie Letcher, Doc Evans and his Dixieland band and Earl "Fatha" Hines.

The club saw its best years between 1949 and 1951. Barnes sold the Horse Shoe in 1952 after realizing that the days when the big jazz entertainers could draw large crowds were just about over.

Rock 'n' roll was on its way in.

— **Thomas Geyer**

Louis "Satchmo" Armstrong was a regular at the Horse Shoe, later called the Paddock, in downtown Rock Island. His quintet was paid $4,000 a week; Armstrong kept $1,000 of it.

Emotions were high when America entered World War I. Posters urging men to enlist went up at post offices and recruiting stations throughout the Tri-City region.

You're in the Army now

"This is the Army, Mister Jones. No private rooms or telephones.
You had your breakfast in bed before but you won't have it anymore.
This is the Army, Mister Jones."

— Words and music by Irving Berlin

chapter fourteen

Living Through Our Wars

Always, we are at war. From the doughboys in the barbed-wire-rimmed muddy trenches of World War I to the sodden jungles of Guadalcanal and the blood bath at Iwo Jima ... from the bullet-riddled beaches of Normandy to the sad skies of B-24s and B-17s, streaking down in flames ... from the bitterness of Saigon and Hue to Desert Storm and the "smart bombs" hammering Iraq. Always, we are at war. Peace, it would seem, is an elusive stranger ...

World War I

"Over there, over there, send the word to beware over there ... the Yanks are coming, the Yanks are coming ... We'll be over, we're coming over, and we won't be back 'til it's over, over there."
— *Words and music by George M. Cohan*

With fervor for the doughboys to "Kick the Kaiser" and "Fight the Huns," the Tri-Cities marched to World War I. Never in the history of our communities had there been such zeal and enthusiasm to fight ... but not without tight-lipped bitterness in many homes and businesses.

"KP" — service jargon for "Kitchen Police" — was their temporary duty in World War I. Among those peeling potatoes at a U.S. Army post was Edward Haut, Davenport, left. In 1918, he volunteered to carry ammunition to a machine gun emplacement at Chateau-Thierry, France, and was killed by an artillery blast.

A zealous editorial in the Davenport *Democrat & Leader* described our doughboys as ... "Akin to the Crusaders, fighting off to war, as if rushing forth to redeem Jerusalem."

Brightly colored flags waved from the streets. Citizens were dazzled by the bunting and slogans of "Give 'til It Hurts" — and they did at repeated war bond drives. Our cities were afire with the spirit of a war that brought fat paychecks along with lightless, heatless nights and a new astonishment — classes at Davenport's Lend-a-Hand Club for women to become auto mechanics to fortify the starved work force.

The Rock Island Arsenal showed its muscles for the first time, employing nearly 15,000 people. Some of the workers, stupified by higher-than-ever-seen salaries for 10-hour days, displayed their largess by wearing silk shirts in the machine shops.

On the April day of 1917 that America entered the war, the all-male Augustana College band marched — hup, two-three-four — to a recruiting office that had been set up

And then it was over ...

Armistice Day, November 11, 1918, caught the Tri-Cities fast asleep. It didn't take people long to wake up.

Ed Buckner, the Associated Press telegrapher for these cities, had been at his key for 48 hours without sleep, awaiting the Armistice "flash." At 2 a.m., the news clicked on his receiver:

"ARMISTICE, PEACE."

Telephone operators were called. Within minutes, every factory whistle in the Tri-Cities was hooting. By 3 a.m., wedges of delirious citizens were jamming downtown streets. At the head of one group was the usually conservative Ludwig Becker, director of Tri-City Symphony. He led a tin can and wash tub band from Davenport across the Government Bridge to Rock Island.

At noon, 10,000 Rock Island Arsenal employees were furloughed from work to march in one giant, raucous parade first through Davenport, and then winding into Rock Island. An old black hearse, pulled by several young men, bore a sign: "We Got Him." Delegations from Palmer College carried skeletons with signs proclaiming the bones "Kaiser Wilhelm."

For months, Petersen's had been waiting for the moment. On the Second Street side of the department store, a 60- by 100-foot flag was unfurled from the rooftop to nearly street level.

A few months later, Davenport roared a welcome to Iowa's heroic Rainbow Division. It appeared that half the city greeted the battle heroes of the Rainbow, ending their long journey from the River Rhine and setting foot, after two long years, on the soil of their native Iowa.

"Famous 42nd Division marches with fixed bayonets while the whole city shouts welcome," said a *Democrat* headline. It was an imposing spit-and-polish parade, from the Davenport depot and through the city, 481 men and officers. There was no command. The men filed into formation by instinct.

In the next year their commander, Gen. John Pershing, visited Davenport to a tumultuous welcome. The city was so awed that it changed the name of Rock Island Street to Pershing Avenue.

As the general toured the Rock Island Arsenal, he paused to visit a rest room. There, a bronze plaque later was fastened to a wall:

"General of the Army John Pershing (expletive deleted) here."

With bayonets fixed, members of Iowa's heroic Rainbow Division marched off the train and through downtown Davenport in a parade after the end of World War I. In step were 481 officers and men.

in Rock Island's Spencer Square. The band enlisted in a group, stayed together, and bolstered enthusiasm for our soldiers in France.

J.H.C. Petersen & Sons department store in Davenport mandated that all clerks — when they were not waiting on customers — knit sweaters, scarves and wristlets for the boys. The store supplied the yarn and needles.

For the little girls, a popular cartoon figure — with the rosy face of a Campbell kid — was Dolly Dingle. Dolly Dingle cuddly dolls and paper dolls were on the racks at F.W. Woolworth's, and toys for boys all were tanks and play rifles.

In the wave of hysterical patriotism, dissenters were swept aside. But bitterness smoldered. Davenport, and much of the rural Iowa farmland, had been developed by the immense rush of German immigrants.

Germans, many of them prominent citizens, went into the closet. German, a mandatory second language in Davenport schools, was banned. Davenport's German Savings Bank became American Commercial Bank. *Der Demokrat*, a respected German language newspaper since before the Civil War, ceased publication. Davenport Public Library trustees debated whether to lock up, at least for the duration, books by German authors.

While John "Black Jack" Pershing swept to

Frank Callant, Moline, hammered and carved a vase from this World War I artillery shell, which he brought home. "He was a Belgian immigrant who enlisted in the American army," says his daughter, Marie DeKezel, Moline.

In formation, World War I soldiers filed off a troup train in the Nahant, Iowa, railroad yards, and marched through the John Brocker farm to bathe in the Mississippi River. It's curious why they carried their rifles.

True War-Time Style: By Grace G. Drayton

The Christmas Spirit

By JOHN DAVIDSON

SPIRIT of Happiness, Spirit of Mirth,
Spirit of Love for the children of earth,
Yours are the gifts that bring pleasure and joy
Into the heart of each wee girl and boy—
Eagerly waiting to see you appear,
Yours is the happiest day of the year.
Come, gentle Spirit, and bring once again
Peace upon earth and good will to all men.

Dolly Dingle was a popular dimpled character on the home front during World War I. There were Dolly Dingle paper dolls (left) and she was the spirit of goodness on a 1918 magazine page.

'Will you supply eyes for the Navy?'

victories, the bitterness spread locally against German citizens. The neighborhood atop Harrison Street hill in Davenport was tagged "The Hindenburg Line" by anti-Germans who named Northwest Davenport, with its beer-drinking Germans and Turner Hall, "Sauerkraut Hill." Animosity swelled when the Scott County Protection Association encouraged patriotic citizens to paint yellow the doors of all citizens of German heritage.

Those days, so often laced with bitterness between the patriotic bunting, were tragic as the death lists grew. Battlegrounds like Saint Mihiel and the barbed-wire of no-man's-land took 194 young Tri-City lives, but the fatality rate was even more deadly on the home front. In three months between October and December of 1918, 7,500 cases of Spanish flu were reported.

Dr. W.C. Goenne, Davenport, speaking for all the Tri-Cities, told a news conference:

"We had 105 cases reported today. Only God knows how many will have pneumonia by tomorrow morning."

The *Democrat* said that time was the only cure, but boiled onion poultices to the chest and laxatives might help. At least 800 people died, among them the commandant of the Arsenal and William "Fatty" Orendorff, Long Grove, the fattest man in Iowa, who weighed 700 pounds. He was buried in two wooden piano boxes, spiked together.

And then, World War I was over. *The Daily Times* and the *Democrat* had war "Extras." "Kaiser Shivers" claimed one bold headline.

It was called the war to end all wars.

But it wasn't.

Big posters of a blindfolded Navy officer standing on the deck of a ship appeared all over Davenport and Clinton and Muscatine and Geneseo during World War I. It was a plea for citizens to supply binoculars to the U.S. Navy.

The posters proclaimed: "Navy ships need binoculars and spy glasses. Glasses will be returned at termination of the war, if possible. One dollar will be paid for each one accepted. Tag each article with your name and address and express or mail to:

Hon. Franklin D. Roosevelt, Assistant secretary of Navy, c/o Naval Observatory, Washington, D.C.

The posters bottom-lined: "Will you help us stand watch on a destroyer?"

Fall of '41

Michael Blaser

Downtown Davenport looking down from the top of Ripley Street hill in 1941.

When life tasted oh, so sweet

The fall of '41 — nothing was ever the same again.

Everyone was 18 in 1941 and a dozen passenger trains were in and out of the Tri-Cities every day. Hoot, hoot, all aboard-d-d. There's the Rock Island Lines Rocky Mountain Rocket right on time at the big, sandstone Davenport depot that looked like Elsinore from *Hamlet*. Downtowns were hustling.

There was Hoagy's "Stardust" playing on the juke at Davenport's Zoom Inn and slow-dancing on the minuscule dance floor of the old Antler's Inn on the Twenty-third Avenue outskirts of Moline. Convertibles and girls far prettier than Hollywood starlets and wearing tremendously high heels and smoking long cigarettes with red tips.

We took 1941 for granted in our idyllic time that the wise among us now pontificate was our Golden Age. As Robert Frost "carried on a romance with life," so did all of us. It was an easy and fun time to be young, and each day had no limits.

The fall of 1941 was clear and autumnal lovely. If there was an uneasy feeling about the shooting war across the Atlantic, our hearts were still young and gay.

But there was hope in Davenport in the fall of '41, with a kind of strained and modified joy in making the good times roll. Was America on the hit list? Maybe it all would pass over quickly. Hadn't FDR designated our Four Freedoms earlier in the year?

That October and November continued fine and dry. And later a purpling haze came and stayed and trees of the city turned so that it was like an imagined place out of a Utrillo painting. One wondered how anyone could ever be lonely or unhappy in such a place as the Tri-Cities, hard by the pewter-gray Mississippi.

The rise of the fall of '41 was here and gone and then December 7. Apocalypse here — and the days to come.

The young kids in Tri-City high schools were soon to become grown guys, marching off to war. Time was running out. After the fall of '41, nothing would ever be quite the same again. But none of us knew that in those days, the fall of '41.

— William Perry

> "Nothing would ever be quite the same again."

World War II

"War's very objective is victory. There is no prolonged indecision. In war, there is no substitute for victory."
— *Gen. Douglas MacArthur*

"Before going into combat, we were always issued new shoes. On Iwo Jima — where we had 6,800 young men killed — I looked down at a dead comrade, covered with his poncho. My size shoes were sticking out. I said thanks to God for not being in those shoes," remembered John Goodall of Davenport. As he talked, his present grimly segued to his past as a teen-age Marine.

"Once, in a bombardment, I was fully buried with a buddy. On Saipan, I wrote a V-Mail letter home to my mom. I said it was pretty nice over here. I didn't mention that I had dug my sixth foxhole that day."

World War II switched the psyche of the Tri-Cities as well as it did the world. The recall of the once-young Marine, John Goodall — now a successful Quad-City advertising man — is what that war was all about. It was a horrible, bloody carnage that brought at least 400 dead from Scott and Rock Island counties alone. It was Victory Gardens on courthouse lawns and ration coupons for gas, canned peas, sugar and coffee; and half-block lines when the Martha Washington candy shop in downtown Davenport got a rare shipment of chocolates; and endless flowing tears for the maimed and the dead; and Rosie the Riveters at Rock Island Arsenal and Grace Fields singing hopefully "There'll be bluebirds over the White Cliffs of Dover, just you wait and see."

Just you wait and see ...

From Scott and Rock Island counties, 24,000 men and women were called to duty during World War II. It was the central point of their lives. No experience ever had compared.

"These were the years of triumph, the days of sadness," wrote World War II chronicler Geoffrey Perrett.

Shaken, confused, the Tri-Cities was at war on December 7, 1941. A few days after Pearl Harbor, Weir Sears Sr., president of Sears Saddlery in Davenport, wrote the commandant of Rock Island Arsenal, offering to do whatever necessary to help defeat the enemy. Within a year, at least 90,000 Tri-City civilians were involved in the war effort.

We had all the war's fads and fancies:

Home on leave — precious times for servicemen. Gerard "Jerry" Heidgerken, Davenport, with his dad, Claude. In the background a U.S. Navy "Donald Duck" hat.

Just a few days after Pearl Harbor, Sears Saddlery Company (now Sears Manufacturing) offered its services to the Rock Island Arsenal.

THE SEARS SADDLERY COMPANY
218-222 Perry Street
Davenport, Iowa

December 11, 1941

Commanding General
Rock Island Arsenal
Rock Island, Illinois

Dear General Ramsey:

Since this war was embroiled or included the United States, we want you to know that if there is anything in our line or anything that we could possibly make that would help your production schedules over there, no matter how large or how small, please call on us. We have had considerable experience on Ordnance work and we have turned down jobs that looked too small or too difficult, but that is all over now, and we want to do our part any way, shape, or form.

Yours respectfully,
SEARS SADDLERY COMPANY

IWS:GJW

By: /s/
I.W. Sears, Vice Pres.

The wreckage of a German Messerschmitt 109 was displayed in downtown Davenport to boost sales of War Bonds during World War II.

'Hey, don't you know there's a war on?'

Everything went to war after December 7, 1941. The government set prices on everything from the rent on an apartment to rationing limits on practically all consumer products. An "A" stamp glued to the inside windshield allowed the owner of the car three gallons of gasoline a week. That allowed few, if any, Sunday rides, and the car pool was born for workers needing to get to the job. Food was rationed by points. A pound of hamburger was three points; a pound of ham was eight points. Points varied by the availability of the product, and a family was fortunate to have 25 or 30 meat points to "spend" a week.

Jim Dockery, a St. Ambrose College coach, says farewell to his wife, Barbara. He enlisted in the Marines, rose to the rank of major and was a hero at Iwo Jima.

women using leg makeup because there were no silk hose; a ban on weather reports in newspapers, lest the enemy be inclined to bomb the Tri-Cities during fair weather; and the belief that Japanese mini-subs might be lurking in the Mississippi River to torpedo Locks and Dam 15 and the Government Bridge, thus crippling Rock Island Arsenal, and then making their way to shell the U.S. Ordnance Depot in Savanna, Illinois.

Every guy under 38 was getting drafted. Entire families went to war.

"We were unique in that my dad, Robert Baugh, and five of my brothers were all in the service," recalls Marie Thomas of Davenport .

Always, time for news. In a battle-torn New Guinea slit trench, Sgt. Ray Pasvogel, Davenport, right, and a comrade type news for their unit newspaper.

Stores hailed anyone in uniform as a hero. Mr. and Mrs. Frank Kapsan had no children, so they treated every GI who ever had been in the Davenport Schlegel drug store that he managed as one of their own. She kept a foot-thick scrapbook of all their service pictures. The book still exists today.

So many guys gone ... so many jobs to be filled. Rosie the Riveters eagerly saved the day. By 1944, nearly 40 percent of the Tri-City work force was women.

When Hector "Tony" DeKezel of Moline went off to war, his new bride, Marie, tied back her hair, picked up his black lunch bucket and went to work at the Arsenal.

Sadie King, Davenport, was 59 and had 11 children. She worked seven days a week as a junior laborer at the Arsenal which counted an astounding 18,675 on the payroll, rolling out tanks and artillery pieces. The river valley rumbled like thunder as weaponry was tested at the tip of the island.

It was an era of rationing, shortages, "Turn in

'Oh, yes, I remember it well'

Dorothy Adams, a 21-year-old Davenport brunette, was selected by the crew of the USS Davenport, a frigate named after her hometown, as the pinup girl for their ship.

Her brother, Allyn Adams, who still lives in Davenport, was in the Navy during World War II and Dorothy felt it an honor to be selected as a Navy pinup girl.

The crew had conducted a contest, and scores of young Davenport women entered.

Dorothy Adams, pinup girl for the U.S.S. Davenport.

When Dorothy was selected Miss Pinup, the Davenport Retail Merchants Bureau gave her a $100 war bond. Dorothy provided the ship with a large color photograph, which was framed for the officers wardroom.

"I distinctly remember hearing from several men on the ship, and one of them even painted my portait, which he sent me. That was long years ago," says Dorothy, the mother of three who now resides in Eureka Springs, Arkansas."

"I wonder whatever happened to that painting. Really, it was a big thrill for a young woman."

Dorothy Adams married the late George William Orr, a career Air Force officer who retired as a colonel.

Each time one of her grandsons returned home from World War II, the words of Swedish immigrant Anna Palmberg, Monmouth, Illinois, were the same: "Let another one come home." This photo was taken in 1947 when all seven were safely home. With grandma, from left, Bill Palmburg, Gerald Linman, Herbert Johnson, Robert Linman, Glenn Nordstrom, James Nordstrom and Eldon Tinsman.

your old Ipana (or any other) toothpaste tube before you can get a new tube" and "Pour your kitchen grease into coffee cans and turn it in to help make munitions."

There was a hysteria of sorts, a united hysteria, because — for perhaps the first and last time — the Tri-Cities had its head screwed on. Entire communities joined together for scrap drives and bond rallies; the renaissance of spirit spread from ordinary Janes and Joes to the biggest of bosses. Everyone needed ration coupons for sugar or meat. The nabob from Rock Island's Watch Hill got no more gas for a Sunday drive than did the guy living on Ninth Street.

Tuesdays and Fridays were meatless day. At restaurants, butter was only on the table for breakfast.

Bill Hickey, the emperor-czar of MidAmerica lunch counters, liked to tell how he posted signs that said "One Pat To A Customer." A salesman got a slap when he said he thought that meant waitresses.

Farmers were buying war bonds to pay for bombers; movie stars stood on street corners peddling bonds. So unique was the local effort that *Life* magazine did a big spread on "How Davenport Sells War Bonds."

In the fervor and fanfare, there were farces, like those fears of Japanese subs off Rock Island.

Lookout posts, manned by helmeted Civil Defense volunteers, were mounted atop buildings like Moline

This German hat was given to Lloyd Speak of Davenport by a German soldier who had parachuted near an allied foxhole and was taken prisoner. The young German was grateful that the American soldiers did not kill him.

Stores filled their windows with pictures of servicemen and women from their city who were serving in World War II. This Eagle food store — one of the first in the Tri-Cities — was on the south side of State Street, Bettendorf, near the approach of what now is the Interstate 74 bridge.

All ages, and only a single smile in one of the first groups to be drafted from Scott County, July 1, 1942.

Caught in the draft

"Greetings."

What a disarming, frightening, anticipated word that was for the young guys in the 1940s. "Greetings" came in the mail, and it was the way Uncle Sam said you were about to be drafted.

ITEM: English lit class at Davenport High School was 10 minutes into Chaucer. Hortense Finch, who had a reputation for strictness, was upset when a student slipped into class.

"You're late," she scolded. "Where have you been? Don't you know classes start on time in Room 27?"

The student spoke up, hesitantly: "I had a study period and after that was lunch hour, and so I went down to register for the draft. I had to run back up the hill and couldn't make it here in time."

Miss Finch grew silent. She bowed her head and said to the young student, "I'm sorry."

The student remembers that she burst into tears and, upon regaining her composure, ordered everyone to stand up and sing "God Bless America."

ITEM: Bob Dafflitto, who now lives near Donahue, Iowa, was a young punk working as a gandy dancer (rail hand) for the Rock Island Railroad when he got his draft notice.

"We were working between Silvis and Lafayette, Illinois, when our draft notices caught up with us. We were to register by a certain date in Wyoming, Illinois.

"We hooked a ride on a freight, but when we got to Wyoming the draft board was closed. Nothing to do but wait until the next day, so we went into the depot and were going to sleep on the floor. We flopped down and discovered that the floor had just been oiled. They used to slosh oil on wooden floors to keep them looking nice.

"We spread out a bunch of wrapping paper on the oily floor. All of a sudden, the station master came storming in. He yelled at us, 'I'm not running a hotel for hoboes.' We told him we didn't have any money to stay anyplace, and had to be there the next day to register for the draft.

"You never saw such a sad station master. He said, 'Boys, please accept my apology. I have a son in the Air Force.' He called the draft board. A woman came down, opened the office, and registered us that very night. The station master said there would be a freight coming through in an hour, and we could hop it and get back to Lafayette so we could work the next day."

A letter from an icy foxhole

The letter reprinted here is yellow, brittle; it is in ink, interrupted in the middle of sentences by a switch from pencil to pen because the ink would freeze in the fog, snow and icy cold of World War II's Battle of the Bulge.

It is a letter from a foxhole, written by Jack Townsend, an infantryman, to his wife, Kay, in Davenport.

Scores of Tri-City GIs were in frozen foxholes along icy tracks in Hurtgen Forest, a nightmare that some had nicknamed the Witches Lair because it was such an eerie, haunting place. Not far from where Pfc. Townsend was hunkered down, two GIs unexpectedly found themselves in the same foxhole, chilled to the bone, but happy to discover they were both from the Tri-Cities — Karl Wagner of Davenport and Herb Doden of Rock Island.

This "foxhole letter" of Pfc. Townsend to his wife describes those bitter days, and a typical soldier's love, and yearning to be back home.

Dearest Darling: I'll try to drop a few lines and let you know that things are still OK.

First of all, don't mind the pencil or the writing because if I use the pen my fingers will freeze and also the ink. So, if I use a pencil I can write with my gloves on. It must have been 10 below zero last night. It makes no difference. We just stay out in the weather, like it or not.

I really think your new glasses make you look nicer, and so do the rest of the boys. You see, our pictures are passed around, because that is as close as we can get to home. Everyone enjoys everyone else's pictures.

(At this point in the letter, he switched from pencil to pen.)

"Well, it has warmed up enough to take my gloves off and use my pen, so maybe it will be a little easier to read. I still have a cold, but feel OK.

Well, honey, until I have another chance to write, just wait without too much worrying until my next letter arrives. All my spare moments are with you and home.

Yours, now and forever with all my love and care.

Your hubby, Jack

Some came home, some didn't ...

A joyous homecoming scene, repeated thousands of times in the Tri-Cities during and after World War II. Capt. Ted Corry, Davenport, is embraced by his wife. Corry, a decorated war hero, left the service and the National Guard as a one-star general.

So many servicemen were being returned for burial to National Cemetery on the Rock Island Arsenal that mass services regularly were held. This is the largest, for 29 men, in 1950. Ten were members of a single plane crew.

Public Hospital and Davenport Bank. Lookouts were to scan the skies for enemy bombers, which assuredly could not have hit this far inland. Blackout nights were strictly observed, with wardens patrolling block by block.

It was eerie to walk darkened streets with a warden. At one house on Davenport's West Fourth Street, the warden rapped on the door after seeing a flash of light. The occupant had opened and closed the fridge to get a bottle of beer.

By 1945, the jubilation of victory screamed into the streets. Joshua Roberts, a Davenport City Hall custodian, climbed to the belfry to manually clang the giant bell which had been silent through the war. Crowds stopped traffic; a sailor shinnied to the top of a traffic light in front of Rock Island's Dutch Inn; merry-makers snake-danced across Davenport's Orpheum stage, silhouetted against the screen with the movie still running.

"World War II ended with euphoria," says Quad-City historian Roald Tweet. "By war's end, the cities had become one place — to live, shop, work — one urban community. What had been the Tri-Cities became the Quad-Cities, with Bettendorf among them."

And from Perrett, the much-quoted World War II chronicler:

"It was the supreme collective social experience ... for in the unity of wartime, a disparate people was fused into a community, and that community was cemented in victory."

In 1944, with wartime demand stretching the workforce at the Rock Island Arsenal, 438 Italian prisoners of war were put to work there. Clemma Isenberg, Davenport, worked with this crew: Angelo, Aldo, Sgt. Angelo, Mario and Johnnie. At right, one of the POWs, sporting an Arsenal T-shirt.

Our WWII POWs

They had been shifted from one prisoner-of-war camp to another, and now 438 Italians came to their best "tour of duty" in the long years of World War II.

In 1944 they were assigned to the Rock Island Arsenal as laborers, living a relatively good life.

The commandant of the Arsenal ordnance depot said they did valued work, and that deadlines would have been missed without them. Still, some in the community protested their presence and the liberties they received.

The Italians were allowed to march off the island to church in Rock Island on Sunday mornings. But during these marches, they often were jeered by citizens. On some Sunday afternoons they were permitted to join Tri-Citians of Italian heritage for picnics on the island.

Captured in North Africa in 1943, the prisoners lived in comfortable Arsenal barracks, built a soccer field on the island, and each month were given a small amount of cash equivalent to exchange for their personal needs.

When the war ended, the prisoners went home. Several made their way back to the Quad-Cities, though. One, Victor Favati, earned his doctorate in chemistry during the four post-war years he spent in Italy. Then he returned to Davenport to marry a woman he had met here. He worked in the Rodman Laboratory at the Arsenal and later became chief engineer at the Army munitions plant in Burlington, Iowa. He died five years ago. His widow, "Alfie" Favati, lives in Davenport.

Flying 'The Hump'

"We were young and dumb and didn't know enough to be scared."

Gordon Fowler of Davenport is recounting his 103 traumatic missions in China, Burma and India over "The Hump," the most miserable of all places to fly during World War II.

Few airmen in the CBI Theater had flown as many missions as Lt. Fowler. At the ripe age of 20, he was in the left seat, command pilot of a C-46 transport, the biggest twin-engine plane flying in World War II. In that hurry-up war, Uncle Sam took soda jerks and gas jockeys and turned them into pilots of complicated aircraft.

"Flying The Hump was always a 10-hour mission," Fowler says somberly. The planes were in sightless mist and fog over a mystic earth where land maps were marked in pink as "uninhabited."

His is a familiar story to veterans of The Hump.

"In a break in the weather, when we could see the mountains below, there was a trail of aluminum, all crashed planes. We called it Aluminum Alley."

Time magazine once estimated that 3,000 C-47s crashed in the mountains. Practically all crews died. On a flight on Christmas Day 1944, Fowler remembers a break in the weather and the sickening sight below, the long trail of wreckage. The shattered aluminum glistened in the rare sunlight. To a homesick kid like Gordon Fowler, it reminded of Christmas tinsel and ornaments.

It was the weather, not the enemy, that brought down most American planes flying "The Hump."

"We were unarmed. The only weapon was my .45 sidearm pistol. Japanese Zero fighters came so close we waved at each other. They knew we were no particular combat threat," Fowler says.

"If you were in bad trouble, you could bail out, but that was a horror. Some guys walked out. It could take a year. One buddy, even though injured, made it along a trail marked with human heads on long poles. In one spot, villagers had warred and killed an entire settlement, men, women, cats and dogs. But they were friendly to Americans."

Fowler, a Davenport advertising executive, remembers the spooky voice of Tokyo Rose, who broadcast from Japan to alienate GIs. At 11,000 feet, Lt. Fowler would turn his radio band to Rose because she always broadcast Glenn Miller music. On every mission, she would break in, "Hello, Lieutenant Fowler. Don't you wish you were home in Davenport, where those 4F slackers are running around with all the girls?"

There was a spy in Fowler's headquarters — never found — who dispatched flight data to Rose. "How she knew me, and Davenport, still gives me the shakes," he says.

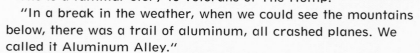

Lt. Gordon Fowler: Tokyo Rose knew his name.

HUMP PILOTS ASSOCIATION
CHINA·BURMA·INDIA

Fred and Opal Gruemmer: Love found a way.

Even in war, love triumphs

"My husband, Fred, and I were high school sweethearts in Wilton, Iowa. We dated for three years and then the war broke out. Being a good American, he enlisted in the Navy.

"Just before he was to leave, my sister, Alta Buennig, suggested we get married. In those days you couldn't be married and go to school, so we set out for Kahoka, Missouri, to be secretly married.

"Of course, there was tire and gas rationing at that time; so we started out in Fred's 1937 Chevrolet in a blizzard on a bald tire and no spare.

"We reached Kahoka about five minutes before midnight — November 21, 1942 — on Alta's birthday. We were pronounced man and wife by a justice of the peace about two minutes before 12. I was 17 and my new husband was 20.

"On the way home we were very low on gas. In those days people lived above their little stations. We pounded on one poor man's door about 3 a.m. and he got up and gave us some gas.

"We did make it home on a wing and a prayer (and a bad tire). Our wedding night was spent at the Blackhawk Hotel, Davenport. I kept my wedding ring in my mother's safe so I could finish high school.

"We have been married 56 years now, and have four children, nine grandchildren and four great-grandchildren."

— Opal E. Gruemmer, Durant, Iowa

'I didn't like the idea of surrendering'

R obert Lapham was a war hero with a story like no other. His was not a front-line battle, but an in-the-shadows, hit-and-run, always-in-danger struggle for nearly three years in the Philippines.

It began in May 1941 when the Davenporter was assigned to the Philippines to help train the Philippine Army.

The Japanese invaded the islands in December 1941 and because U.S. policy was to first defeat Hitler in Europe, the men in the Pacific were left to fight a months-long losing battle without reinforcements, food or medical supplies.

When Gen. Douglas MacArthur withdrew to the Bataan Peninsula, Lapham slipped behind enemy lines to take his chances with the Filipinos rather than surrender.

Davenport's Robert Lapham: He led an army of 13,000.

B efore the war ended, he emerged as a major guerrilla leader, commanding a force of nearly 13,000 Filipinos and wielding dictator-like authority over a large chunk of Luzon, military men and civilians alike. He was a hunted man with a price on his head.

Although it was hinted that he had been selected for guerrilla duty by MacArthur, there was no direct link.

"I didn't like the idea of surrendering," Lapham said in a 1996 interview. "I felt I had better chances on the outside than in a Japanese prison camp."

He had no idea it would take three years—not the three months he assumed—for the Americans to return to the Philippines. It was three years of malaria and dysentery, of scrounging for food and shelter, of sabotage, of holding together a 10,000-plus army dubbed "Lapham's Raiders," of dodging the bickering and jealousies of other guerrilla groups.

In Davenport, his family knew only that Bob was "missing in action." It wasn't until October 1944 that he had a chance to let them know he was all right.

W hen the Philippines was liberated in 1945, and a Signal Corps photographer snapped a picture of Lapham that ran big in newspapers all across the country, his friends and family went wild. Wearing a scarf and rosary around his neck, a campaign hat on his head and a .45 automatic strapped to his belt, the tall blonde fighter was the stuff of movies. When Lapham did return to Davenport, he was greeted with a hero's parade. He was the third American, behind President Roosevelt and MacArthur, to receive the Philippine Legion of Honor.

S till the war retained its hold, and he had demons to fight. "I had been the premier figure among a lot of people for a long time," Lapham wrote in his 1996 book. "A one-man court of law with virtual life-and-death power over my domain, and I was emotionally reluctant to step down. I actually ran a section of that country and that feeling of authority grows on you. You get to like it."

But Lapham survived, just as he had in the Philippines. He married, reared a family and retired in 1975 as vice president for industrial relations from Unisys in Detroit. Now in his early 80s, he and his wife, the former Sharlott Junge, live in Arizona. And in places like this book, his story — "that phase of life from so long ago" — is remembered. Remembered, and treasured.

— Alma Gaul

The women go to war

Old-fashioned ways no longer applied to women after we got into World War II. While the Andrews Sisters were singing, "Don't Sit Under the Apple Tree With Anyone Else But Me," Tri-City women were mustering into the service or filling in for the guys on the assembly line.

FRANCES EILEEN BRANDT, who had just graduated from Mercy Hospital School of Nursing in Davenport, enlisted in the U.S. Army as a second lieutenant and fell in love with an enlisted man. They had to keep it a secret and she couldn't wear a wedding ring on her finger.

Eileen met a fellow Davenporter, Charles "Chuck" Brandt, when both were stationed at Jefferson Barracks, Missouri. It was taboo at that time for officers and enlisted personnel to fraternize. "Our plans to meet had to be discreet because I was an officer and he was not." There were times when they had to walk by each other, and whisper plans to meet in the next block when no officers were around. They secretly wed on Valentine's Day 1942, but she had to wear her wedding ring on a necklace so no one would know she was married. While at Jeff Barracks, she recalls regularly working 18- to 20-hour days, caring for the thousands of draftees who were inducted there, and who had reactions to inoculations. She resigned her commission to officially become Mrs. Chuck Brandt and rear a family. Eileen shakes her head today and says, "My, how things have changed for women in the military since then."

Eileen

MARGARET DAVIES STUTSMAN, a Navy nurse from Muscatine, Iowa, had a long career in the service that took her to Guam and Japan and she ended up with the rank of full lieutenant.

Margaret was an experienced nurse when she enlisted in the Navy in 1943, an ensign assigned to San Diego (California) Naval Hospital. Vividly, she remembers the day the war ended. "The word flew through the hospital; there was jumping up and down, tears of joy." She wondered what would be next for her. Her Navy career would take her to several Pacific tours of duty. She opted to stay in the Navy reserves and in 1946 found herself called up to active duty in Korea. She wasn't discharged until 1954 — one nurse's long stint for Uncle Sam.

OPAL (CHARLENE) LENNON was handed a flashlight and promoted to inspector for aircraft parts at Deere & Co. in Moline.

Charlene was working as a riveter at Deere when six women were brought in for special training. She was asked if she would consider being an inspector. "I accepted," she says, "and they gave me a flashlight. Women were working on parts for the Douglas A-26 plane. The other women would be provoked when I told them to remove the rivets and do the job over."

Margaret

MARY KIRSCHBAUM was in the Navy WAVES and still recalls a frightening dream that was an all too-real experience for her husband, also in the Navy.

Mary and Roland Kirschbaum, like so many young lovers during the turbulent World War II, decided to be married in 1943 when he was home on leave from the Navy. Roland had no problem with her enlisting in the WAVES. "An experience my husband and I would never forget was a dream, so vivid I awoke, frightened for his life. I wrote him about it the next day. I dreamed I was hovering in the sky over Roland's ship, the Lindsey, when it suddenly disappeared. Little did I know that very night, his ship had been hit by two kamikaze attacks. It destroyed the hull of the ship, the damage stopping just before my husband's quarters. Roland returned to Oakland, California, shortly thereafter with my letter in his hand." By the end of 1945, both were discharged and began rearing a family of three sons.

(Charlene, Eileen, Mary and Margaret reside at Friendship Manor, Rock Island)

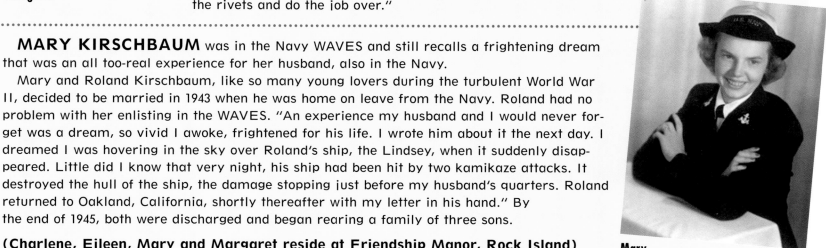
Mary

THE DAVENPORT DEMOCRAT
AND LEADER
Hereby
Enrolls Lt. CLIFFORD A. EGERT, Chaplain
of the UNITED STATES   Army
in the "Dear Joe" Club
[Exclusively for Service Men whose
letters or interviews have appeared
in this Newspaper War Feature]
P. S. No Dues, No Officers, No Meetings, No Collections. Membership Period: Forever.
John O'Donnell Sports Editor

Above, at the microphone, Barbara Dockery, whose husband, Jim, was in the Marines, during a salute to John O'Donnell in Davenport, Below, after the war was over, veterans hailed O'Donnell at an all day party. From left, Rena Bonnicker, Dick Froeschle, Roger "Gabby" Crow and Caryl Makeever, all of Davenport. Many ex-servicemen still carry their "Dear Joe" cards.

Dear Joe ...

He was a mythical person — one of the unifying phenomenons of World War II in the Tri-Cities — "Dear Joe." Dear Joe was a phantom, non-existent person, an image from the mind of John "The Coach" O'Donnell, sports editor of the *Democrat & Leader*, a relative of the *Quad-City Times*.

Knowing that the families of GIs frequently mailed newspaper clippings to their men and women serving overseas, O'Donnell occasionally began his Sports Chats column with a short, homey note to anyone in the service, addressing it simply to "Dear Joe."

Typical: "The town had a taste of big league baseball last week and the weatherman furnished the only sour note, which he did with vengeance. One week ago, it was so hot the golfers were playing in shorts. The other night, the Browns and the Pirates built fires in their dugouts outside the stadium ... "

In double-time, those in the service responded by writing letters to "Dear Joe ... " the first from Lt. Jack Roche on August 7, 1942.

Before the war was over, letters to Dear Joe turned into 2,250,000 words stretching over two full pages of solid type every Sunday in the Democrat.

Men and women in the service were lonesome for news of their pals. They wanted to know what they were doing and where they were doing it. First, it was weeks, then months, and then years that had separated them. Through Dear Joe, the GI shivering in the Aleutians heard about his hometown buddies who were sweating in the Marshalls; the Marine in the hellhole of Guadalcanal read about his ex-first baseman who was in the Merchant Marine off the coast of France. The Waves, the WACs, the Spars, the Army and Navy nurses had happier days when mail call brought them Dear Joe pages from the newspaper.

Once, O'Donnell remarked — from his letter-strewn office — "Dear Joe grew from an infant to quite a man."

It was a vast understatement. O'Donnell was the consummate hometown hero. He was picked as Davenport's "Man of the Year" and the women whose husbands and boyfriends and fathers were in the service once had a grand party for him as their favorite pin-up guy.

It soon came to be that O'Donnell formed a Dear Joe Club, sending membership cards to GIs in 30 countries. Many — among them, the Reverend Cliff Egert, a retired Diocese of Davenport priest who was a chaplain in the service — still carry dog-eared Dear Joe cards in their billfolds. It is a sentimental link to more than a half-century ago.

Those letters were the heart of Dear Joe. O'Donnell's novel idea had a weekly minimum of 7,000 words.

Servicemen and women cherished Dear Joe.

Wrote Cpl. Ed Burlingame from Belgium: "The Dear Joe pages are really morale builders. Morale is the greatest thing in the Army."

Wrote Cpl. Cliff Peterson from the Aleutians: "Your Dear Joe pages are like a breath of good Midwest fresh air."

Wrote Lt. Richard Corbin from Germany: "Our division has been fighting, dying and winning the Huertgen Forest, but will you please make me a member of the Dear Joe Club?"

That little membership card meant so much to so many. After being wounded in Europe, Pvt. Lee Roy Hennings wrote from a hospital in England: "I'm just getting caught up in my Dear Joe reading and my Dear Joe membership card arrived yesterday. Gee, Johnny, that's really swell and thanks a lot."

The war ended but that was not that. The GI Joes and Janes did not forget. Everyone pitched in, and there was an all-day Dear Joe party followed that night by a dance at the Mississippi Valley Fairgrounds. In thanks, they gave O'Donnell the keys to a new Hudson, the first new car he had ever owned.

He smiled, shook hands and hugged everyone, and spoke the tight words that said it all:

"Thanks for saving the world."

A Japanese-American who did not give up

As a kid growing up in Sterling, Illinois, in the 1930s, Kenje Ogata was so fascinated by the small planes flying over the airport near his home that he earned his pilot's license.

The day after the Japanese attacked Pearl Harbor and plunged the nation into World War II, he tried to enlist. He figured his country could use someone with his flying skills.

But the Army didn't see it that way. Blinded by his ethnic origin, recruiters did not welcome him into the Air Corps or any other branch.

Eventually, he was allowed to join other Japanese-

Kenje Ogata, Sterling, Illinois: One of two Japanese-Americans allowed to fly for the United States during World War II.

Americans in the Medical Service Corps. He was assigned to a base near Rockford, Illinois.

Still, Ogata never gave up his dream of flying. After he was rejected for flight status, he launched his own personal war against discrimination, writing letters and enlisting the support of prominent people in Sterling. He believes that Gen. Henry "Hap" Arnold, Air Forces commander, ultimately approved his transfer to the Air Corps.

After a two-year fight, he was accepted for aerial gunnery training and transferred to the 451st Bombardment Group in Italy. He survived 35 missions as a ball turret gunner aboard B-24 bombers, bailing out once and crash landing another time.

He was one of only two Japanese-Americans allowed to fly for the United States during the war. He says he experienced no discrimination or harassment in combat, with one exception. Once, on an outing at a Red Cross canteen near his base in Foggia, Italy, he encountered a major who busted him from staff sergeant to corporal for not having a button fastened.

Ogata, 79, still lives in Sterling. He retired two years ago after practicing dentistry for 42 years. The former Wilma Reiff, who used to go flying with him before the war, has been his wife for 56 years. Their daughter, Kenjalin, 52, has been on the administrative staff of Harvard University for 25 years.

The flak-filled skies over Europe seem remote today, but he still gets together with his former crew members. He thinks of what his parents taught him so long ago.

"They always told me that if you wanted to do something, you do it. You don't give up."

— John Willard

The death of a soldier

The last known letter that William Louis Slowie wrote to his wife, Jane, ended, "I love you lots ... " Then, he was killed in the jungles of Luzon, the Philippines, in World War II.

He left a widow and two small daughters, back home in Clinton, Iowa.

Pvt. Slowie was an infantryman. There are fewer tougher, more dangerous assignments than being with a line company.

He was 27 when he died, a handsome young man who had known the terrible rumble, grumble and roar of the Pacific battlegrounds.

The only reference to a date on the penciled last letter to his wife is "7 p.m. Thursday."

The postmark on the envelope was dated January 1, 1945, and was passed by a U.S. Army examiner who did not stamp approval on it until February 13, 1945.

Jane Slowie received the traditional "deep regret" telegram on April 3, 1945. It said that Pvt. William L. Slowie, 169th Infantry, 43rd Division, was killed in action on Luzon on March 4, 1945.

The letter that followed, from the U.S. War Department, was dated April 5.

"We've never known what happened to our dad, other than he is buried in a U.S. military cemetery in the Philippines," one of his daughters, Kathie Robertson of Davenport, says.

Jane Slowie is dead. Pvt. Slowie's daughters, Kathie and Linda Nolan, Chicago, have established a fund so that every Memorial Day, his grave is decorated with flowers.

His death reinforces the words of ex-president Herbert Hoover: "Older men declare war. But it is the young that must fight and die."

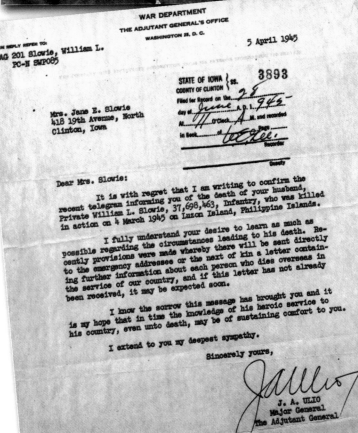

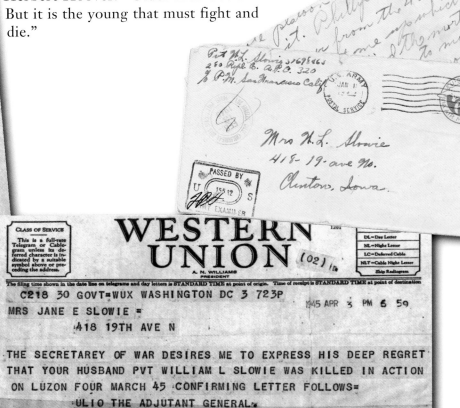

WILLIAM L. SLOWIE
PVT 169 INF 43 DIV
IOWA MAR 4 1945

Dear Jane:
   Just a short note as the mailman is ready to leave and I want him to take this with him. We didn't get here until 10 o'clock last night. Boy, is it a job pitching a tent in the dark. I am again the sergeant's messenger. I have to get him up and also the whole platoon if you can imagine it ... fired mortar all day today and the same tomorrow. If there's a flash-light around, would you send it to me right away ... The chow is awful, so I didn't eat today. I didn't have time to write yesterday. I got your swell letter yesterday. Tell Leon thanks for the buck; they always come in handy.
   Well, honey, I have to stop now so the mailman can take this. I love you lots.

                    Always, your Bud

We never quit fighting ...
The voices of 'Other Wars'

"In all wars, weather and mud are the common denominators."
— Lt. Richard S. Corbin

Global crusades of World Wars I and II gave way to a new kind of fighting for Americans in the second half of the century. Unlike earlier massive mobilizations that touched nearly everyone, the new wars were limited in scope ... but they were just as bloody deadly.

With the same sense of duty they showed at places like Belleau Wood, Chateau-Thierry, Guadalcanal and Anzio, Quad-City men and women marched off to Korea, Vietnam and finally the Persian Gulf.

The Korean War came too soon. When North Korea invaded South Korea on June 25, 1950, the veterans of World War II were settling into jobs, going to college, and buying homes at places like Glen Armil in Davenport and Riverdale and Molette in Moline and a burgeoning Bettendorf. They were raising families, too; the Baby Boom was here!

But five years after The Big War ended, many were back in combat again.

Korea

Richard S. Corbin, twice wounded in World War II while training French underground forces in radio communications, was called up in January 1951 to go to Korea. He was married, had a child, and was getting accustomed to the workaday world of his native Davenport.

The Army had other plans. Critically in need of Signal Corps wire communications officers, they pulled him out of the inactive reserve and sent him to the 51st Signal Battalion, I Corps, near Uijongbu. The area was infested with enemy infiltrators bent on destroying U.S. telephone wires, and Lt. Corbin frequently encountered them as he struggled to keep vital communications lines open.

In April he suffered a severe head injury, likely from being clubbed. The impact split his steel pot (helmet) and he was left for dead. A passing soldier noticed he was alive. After treatment at hospitals in Hawaii and the United States, he received a medical discharge.

Corbin proudly displays his Silver Star and three Purple Hearts in the living room of his Davenport home. He was disappointed about going to Korea, but not angry. "If your country says you are needed, you go," he says.

At the top, Robert Van Winkle winds up a furlough in Davenport and heads for Greenland, assigned to service with a fighter squadron during the Korean War. Saying goodbye is his mother, Helen Kemp. Telegrams such as this, notifying Alice Bates Kemp that her son was missing, were received by too many families. The Kemps were lucky: Robert Kemp was taken prisoner, but survived to come home.

War in Korea was half a world away, but Al Keppy, left, of Davenport, was assigned to an anti-aircraft installation in Virginia, for defense of Washington, D.C. The shoulder patch is Washington Military Defense.

Greg Gutgsell, Davenport, answered the call to Korea after serving as an infantry squad leader in the Pacific during World War II. Like Corbin, he was in the inactive reserve when he got his notice in June 1950, only a couple of weeks after his marriage. He was on orders for Korea, but ended up serving in the Second Armored Division at Fort Hood, Texas.

Korea often is referred to as "The Forgotten War," a label that Ken Criger, Davenport, knows too well. He enlisted in the Marines in 1948 and, in September 1950, was in Korea's Inchon Landing. Two months later, he and fellow Leathernecks of the First Marine Division were battling 120,000 Chinese Reds, whose orders were to annihilate the 15,000 allied ground troops.

Battling frostbite from the 30-below-zero temperatures as well as the Chinese, Sgt. Criger and his fellow warriors emerged from the ordeal with a Presidential Unit Citation. He came home to an indifferent nation, but his experience as one of the "Chosin Few" lives with him a half-century later.

Moments with Korean children provided a respite from war. Ken Criger, Davenport, at left, who was with the First Marine Division, shot this photo.

Pals forever: They went into the Army together, and served together in the Korean War. From left, Roger Nevins, Carbon Cliff, Illinois; Robert Cramer, Milan, Illinois; and M. Wayne Erickson, Taylor Ridge, Illinois. Wayne was wounded at Pork Chop Hill.

Vietnam

John Lavelle saw combat in Vietnam as a sergeant with the 523rd Signal Battalion, American Division. Thirty years later, as a language arts teacher at Bettendorf High School, he is using his experiences as a teaching tool. In a course examining wars of the second half of the century, his students interview veterans of the Korean, Vietnam and Persian Gulf wars and write short stories based on their interviews.

Lavelle created the course after sensing how interested his contemporary literature students were in Vietnam War writings. Not only is the course satisfying students' hunger to learn more about wars that have not been examined in depth by historians, Lavelle said, but it has helped him become more open about his own experiences in Vietnam.

"It was one of those things you didn't talk about," he said.

John Lavelle, left, a sergeant, and fellow soldiers entertain Vietnamese orphans on Christmas Day 1968. Thirty years later, he is using his Vietnam combat experience as a teaching tool at Bettendorf High School.

The Vietnam War's unpopularity placed an added burden on families whose sons and daughters fought it.

Robert and Helen Rae Knight, Davenport, sent their son, Robert C. Knight, into that war. And they carried the burden of divisive public opinion.

"What bothered me was that there were so many opinions on the war," Bob Knight says.

A Vietnam service medal.

Robert C. Knight received the
Distinguished Flying Cross in Vietnam.

William Cleaver during the
Persian Gulf War.

"When you have a son in the middle of it, you get a little tired of the objections that you read and hear about. We worried about him, where he was."

Robert C. Knight, an Air Force pilot, received the Distinguished Flying Cross for heroism while completing a reconnaissance mission. After completing his assignment in Vietnam, he served as a pilot with the Strategic Air Command and followed his father into the insurance business. He died of pulmonary hypertension at age 50 in 1993.

Persian Gulf

Whenever Iraqi dictator Saddam Hussein is in the news, William Cleaver, Rock Island, remembers leading the 150 members of his medical company into combat during the Persian Gulf War.

Cleaver, 49, is a Moline lawyer and a colonel in the U.S. Army Reserve. In 1990, he was a major and commander of the 209th Medical Clearing Company, a National Guard outfit based in Iowa City.

He left behind a family and a successful law practice when his unit was called to active duty on November 11, Veterans Day. During their four months in the war zone, his soldiers braved Scud attacks, knife-like desert winds and primitive living conditions. Fortunately, none of his soldiers was hurt as they handled 3,000 allied and enemy casualties.

— John Willard

'Without regard for personal safety... '

Steve Phillis of Rock Island was a hero in a war of heroes.

Phillis, an Air Force captain, was flying an A-10 "Warthog" when he was shot down during a 1991 attack on the Iraqi Republican Guard in the Persian Gulf War.

His wing man's plane had been hit by ground fire and crashed. The pilot bailed out and Capt. Phillis circled the zone to make certain he had landed in a safe area. There was thick flak and Phillis called in other A-10s for support, firing at enemy ground units to protect the pilot who was parachuting to the ground. Phillis' plane was hit. He died on impact when his A-10 crashed in the desert. The other pilot was taken prisoner and later released.

"Without regard for personal safety, Capt. Phillis protected his downed wing man and began a search and aid mission," said Lt. Gen. Thomas Baker at services for the captain at Rock Island Memorial Park.

As the services ended, four desert-camouflaged A-10 warplanes swooped over the gravesite. One of the planes disappeared in a sweeping arc to nowhere — the missing man formation.

Steve Phillis, an Air Force captain, was
a hero of the Persian Gulf War.

National Cemetery, Rock Island Arsenal, is a vast, silent plateau of heroes. Twenty-two thousand are buried there; more than two-thirds of the dead, possibly three-fourths, are service veterans. The remainder are spouses.

"Time is flowing by now and I am going back into battle. And I hear, far off, the buzz-saw roar of the planes and feel the quick shiver of the earth and the obiliterating crash of shells. I sense my power wasting from me while the battle rages and the deathless ... there is always still time to die."

— Jack Belden, a noted World War II wire service correspondent in his book, *Still Time to Die*

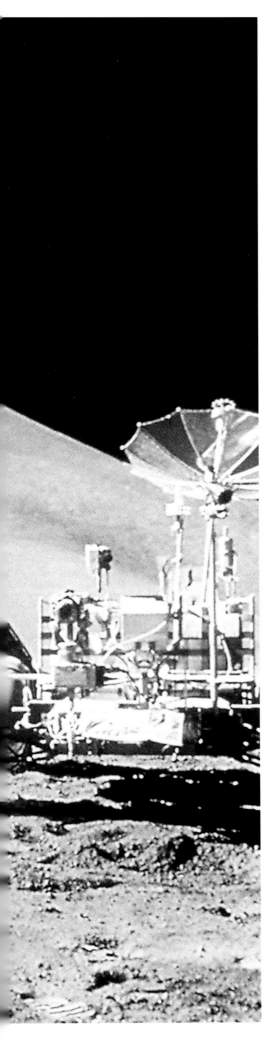

Innovators and inventors

"People think of innovators — people who develop new products — as strange or sometimes even odd. Remember, the Wright Brothers flew right through the smoke screen of impossibility. Where would we be without innovators and inventors, the people who tried and dreamed and made industries and businesses happen?"

— Charles Kettering,
vice president of research, General Motors

For generations now, much of who we are as people and community has been defined by the work done here.

Even before the area was known as the Quad-Cities, jobs in the Tri-Cities were planted firmly in manufacturing and industry. Along the way, our hands and our heads have produced inventions and technologies that have helped us to better work the land, travel the land and even protect the land.

For generations, the fruits of our labor flowed from the assembly lines and factory floors. The ingenuity that built John Deere's original plow evolved into today's awesome tractors and combines. International Harvester, J I Case and Caterpillar completed that industrial block.

The Bettendorf brothers built railroad car trucks and boxcar side frames that revolutionized railroading.

And on Arsenal Island, which remains the area's second-largest employer, workers made 167,000 155mm howitzer shells to aid the World War I effort. For several decades, beginning in the late 1960s, the Arsenal produced more than 2,300 M198 howitzers, some of which were used in Operation Desert Storm.

The arrival of Alcoa on the banks of the Mississippi in the 1940s did more than transform 453 acres of onion and

Long ago, a minor traffic jam of bicyclists leaving the Rock Island Arsenal at quitting time.

Aluminum from Alcoa Davenport Works was a major component in the Saturn V rocket and the Apollo spacecraft. In 1971, Alcoa Alloy 2219, made at the plant in Riverdale, Iowa, was used to build the Lunar Rover, the space buggy that explored the moon's surface.

corn fields into a mile-long factory. The world's largest aluminum sheet and plate rolling mill gave birth to its own town, Riverdale, Iowa.

Over the years, thousands at the Davenport Works have played roles in casting aluminum for use in the world's aerospace, automotive, railroad, trucking, lighting, defense, computer and printing industries. Today, the plant employs 2,700 people.

Long before we flew in space, Moline and East Moline companies were introducing us to the automobile with cars such as the Midland, the Deere-Clark, the Moline-Knight and the Drednought, which sold for $1,700 in the early 1900s. Hundreds of Velie cars, invented by Willard Lamb Velie, Deere's grandson, rolled off production lines. Velie even dallied with the manufacture of a Velie monocoupe airplane, one of which hangs at Quad-City International Airport.

On the ground, steam locomotives were built at Davenport Besler Corp.; Quad-City travelers still find them in use in the South Pacific.

We also have been responsible for supplying more common products for everyday use. At the turn of the century, the Davenport Broom Works made brooms in its factory at 1450 West Lombard Street. Tilley Ladder Co. in west Davenport was the world's largest manufacturer of wooden step ladders. Bricks for streets and buildings were churned out by Black Hawk Brick Co., Bettendorf Brick Co. and the Davenport Brick Co.

Boot and shoemakers such as William Bredfeld and Davis Zeffman could be found

In 1962, Alcoa trumpeted production of the largest aluminum coil ever made. Paul Griswold and Harlan Henzen measure the coil as it left the Davenport Works, bound for General Motors.

Hallmark of the industry — one of the "Big Green Machines" made at John Deere Harvester Works, East Moline.

on almost every corner. Directories place 34 of them in downtown Davenport alone in 1908.

Back then, George J. Gimbel and Mason's Carriage Works supplied the main source of transportation. And 35 different cigar manufacturers, among them Peter N. Jacobsen, were helping men to light up a smoke. It was the major industry to employ women at the turn of the century. But by 1930, there were only a few, thanks to the increasing popularity of the cigarette, the cigar industry's mechanization and cheaper labor pools in Florida and Cuba.

In Moline, A.E. Montgomery acquired riverfront property in 1912 to build the headquarters for his elevator company. It still dominates the downtown today. An escalator division was built in 1960 in Moline, then moved in the early 1980s to Coal Valley, Illinois. It is undergoing an $8.1 million expansion at this turn of the century.

Montgomery Elevator was a fourth-generation family business until it was sold in 1994 to Kone, a Finland-based company, and renamed Montgomery Kone Inc. Moline remains the company's North American headquarters.

In decades past, the best-dressed women were calling on dressmakers such as Davenporters Miss Fannie Gill and Mrs. Alice M. Nagle. Skilled seamstresses were supplying the racks of McCabe's Department Store in downtown Rock Island or were at work at Seaford Clothing Co., which remains in business today. Bradford Co., on Davenport's Harrison Street, made most of the blue uniforms worn by America's police officers.

Those who could afford it likely were washing their clothes in a wooden hand-operated contraption invented by the Voss Washing Machine Company of Davenport. In 1912, it was one of the five largest washing machine manufacturers in the country. But 33 years later, production shifted elsewhere with the company's closing.

In 1923, Servus Rubber launched its Rock Island manufacturing plant; by 1940, the payroll was 1,000 workers. Now owned by Norcross Safety Products of Oak Brook, Illinois, NSP remains a stable employer with 500 people who manufacture personal protective equipment.

Flour mills provided one of the key ingredients for much of the food we put on the table. The former Crescent Macaroni and Cracker Co. introduced us to a new product, pasta. However, since pasta still was relatively uncommon, the company started making soda crackers and cookies, "just like mother used to make."

Along Davenport's River Drive, once referred to by a neighboring radio station as "Twinkie Boulevard," Continental Baking Co. has been baking Wonder bread and Hostess snacks by the truckload since 1927. Over the years, it has changed hands a few times and was bought four years ago by Interstate Brands Corp., Kansas City. In the

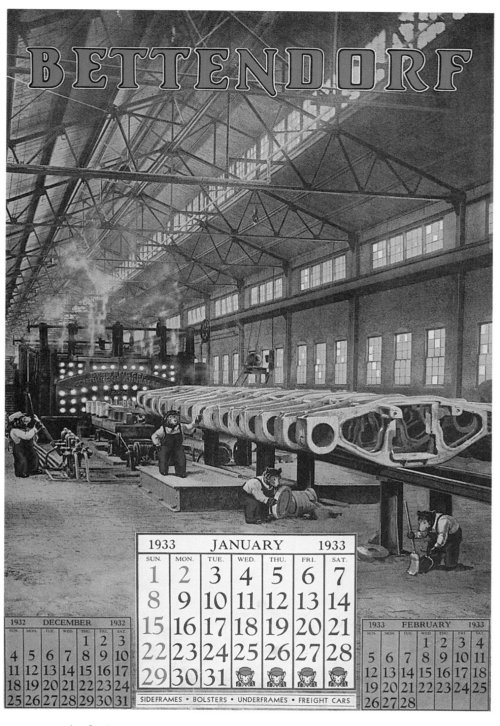

A page from a 1933 Bettendorf Co. calendar. Little bears work throughout the plant in this illustration. Bears were the official mascots of the company; the firm's baseball team was known as the Bettendorf Bears.

Tootle-oo-la. An Oscar Mayer wiener whistle from the 1960s.

Quad-Cities, Wonder Bread-Hostess Cake Division employs about 250 people.

The company once was owned by Ralston Purina, the world's largest pet food maker and another Quad-City manufacturer. Ralston, with operations in Davenport and Clinton, Iowa, announced plans late in 1998 for a $22.6 million expansion of the two plants.

Food workers also have found steady employment over the years preparing meat products and Lunchables at Oscar Mayer's plant in Davenport. Bulk gelatin for the confectionery, bakery, dairy and pharmaceutical industries has been made since 1979 at Leiner Davis Gelatin, the former Hormel Foods Corp. The gelatin plant in north Davenport, employing 140 people, was bought in the late 1990s by Goodman Fielder Ltd. of Sydney, Australia.

When prohibition ended, breweries such as Zoeller Brewery again were offering jobs. Zoeller's evolved into Blackhawk Brewery, Iowa's largest, and was a vital business when Albert Uchtorff acquired it in 1952. But just four years later, nationally promoted ales drove him out of business.

In the 1920s, Alexander F. Victor changed how we began to record history by creating more than 150 different models of picture-taking and projection equipment. He produced the country's first 16mm projector and camera; his inventions led to a standardization of film and equipment in the non-theatrical motion picture field. Walt Disney once applied for a job there as a calligrapher/cartoonist, but wasn't thought talented enough.

The face of our workforce changed dramatically in the past century. As the nation's men were sent to war, an untapped labor force — women, minorities and the handicapped — helped the Arsenal hit its peak in 1943 with 18,675 workers, many found by recruiters who went door-to-door searching for every able body. A year later, women held 32 percent of

Before Pepsi: At the turn of the century, A.D. Huesing lost the sheriff's race in Rock Island County and needed a job. So he began bottling root beer, ginger ale and other soda pops. In 1912, as a side business, his company began selling ice from wagons such as this, house to house, store to store, soda fountain to soda fountain. In 1935, when Pepsi-Cola Company was faltering, the manufacturer appealed to Huesing to begin bottling its line. The rest is history. Today, A.D. Huesing Company of Rock Island is one of the major independent Pepsi bottlers in the country.

Slices and spices

We take the little things for granted, like sliced bread. But were it not for a Bettendorf creation, we might still be hacking away at loaves (not to mention thumbs).

Otto Rohwedder, a jeweler, introduced a bread-slicing device to bakers in 1927 and 1928. It was called the Slicemaster and popularized the sale of bread in grocery stores. In later years, along came Art Kottman, an engineer/inventor who worked for Micro Company, an adjunct of Bettendorf Co. He refined a machine that sliced bread, wrapped it in wax paper, folded the ends and sealed the wrapper. Bread slicing remains fundamentally the same today, thanks to Otto and Art. The blades are manufactured by Hansaloy Corp., Davenport.

And then there is Boetje's mustard, one of the spices of Quad-City life. It has been around since before the turn of the century, a product sold around the world. Fred Boetje, a Dutch immigrant, invented Boetje's (pronounced boat-jees) mustard in 1889. Boetje's remains a sinus-clearing blast, modified from the recipe of its creator. Manufactured in Rock Island, a typical week's production is 9,000 jars. Boetje's is sold in every state; there are regular shipments to Korea, Hawaii, Japan and Germany.

Thanks to Bettendorf, we have sliced bread. And thanks to Rock Island, we have Boetje's mustard, which is shipped around the world.

the jobs at the Arsenal and 37 percent of the positions in other local shops. Post-World War II prosperity lured families from the economically struggling South. Not only did we offer good jobs for the sons and daughters of black sharecroppers, but there also was better housing and decent schools.

By the middle of the 20th century, we had become known as the farm implement capital of the world with thousands of workers building Deere, Caterpillar, IH and, eventually, Case Corp. equipment. Thousands more were employed in businesses necessary to help fuel the implement manufacturers.

The industry was struck hard by the labor strikes, a poor farm economy and inflation of the 1970s. In the 1980s, the farm crisis nearly devastated a community built around the American farmer. In 1981, IH sold its agricultural equipment to Tenneco, the parent company of J I Case. The last "Big Red" rolled off the Farmall production line in May 1985. The Rock Island plant closed a year later.

Caterpillar, too, fell victim. Its Bettendorf operation closed in 1986; the Mount Joy, Iowa, plant in 1987. Case announced plans that year to close in Rock Island and Bettendorf. Deere had its share of cutbacks and a six-month strike in 1986. But it was not profitable until the late 1980s.

Painful as it was, the crisis taught its victims and the entire community to value diversification and we have emerged stronger as a result. Even the Arsenal embraced diversification; today, that facility and its 40-some tenants employ 6,600 people. The largest number — 1,500 — work for the Rock Island Arsenal itself.

"The health of the industrial sector in the Quad-Cities is quite sound," said John Gardner, president of the Quad-City Development Group. "I'm very optimistic about the future. We have demonstrated there is a real agility and ability to adjust, a knowledge that was hard-earned in the 1980s."

— Jennifer DeWitt

A flatcar of "Big Red" tractors rolls from the International Harvester Co. Farmall Works in Rock Island, early 1980s.

Tough hard work for women in the 1900s — sand shovelers in the foundry of Union Malleable Iron Company, East Moline. Sand shoveling for castings usually was a job for men. Notice, there are few smiles.

Patriotic and opening their pocketbooks: During World War II, workers in the forge shop and steel shed at Deere & Co. subscribed 100 percent in a war bond drive.

Generations of shoppers who climbed the main staircase at Petersen Harned Von Maur's downtown Davenport store were greeted by this giant leaded-glass window on the mezzanine. Originally, it was in one of the marble buildings at the World's Columbian Exposition of 1893, in Chicago.

The reason for retailing

"The shopper, the buyer, is the reason for retailing. The lawyer calls him a client; the doctor calls him a patient; the banker, a depositor. No matter what the store or shop owner calls him, he is the most important person in their life."

— Advertising Age

chapter sixteen

The Way We Shopped

T he string for wrapping packages hung down like a spiderweb from a little cone-like gadget on the ceiling of the grocery store; the paper bags were opened with a quick snap of the aproned clerk's hand; orders were taken on the telephone, and delivered the same day — likely, within hours, if you lived in the city.

If you were in the country, it was a Saturday ritual to visit the general store. There, you could buy galoshes and Fels Naptha soap in thick bars, and half-a-round of cheese, and a hundred-pound sack of seed for the chickens, and cotton for a new dress, and thread, and thimbles, and a half-dozen bananas, and a sack of oranges, and a new bonnet for sister Sue.

Perhaps, just perhaps, we've gone the complete circle. We have strong signs of a shift in what we thought was an irretrievable era of shopping. We're shopping, in so many ways, the way we used to shop. The super-stores in our cities are the general stores of our yesterdays. The configuration is not quite there; yet, today you may go into one of these sleek-slick-sell-everything places, stroll with your shopping cart and, yes, buy a pair of galoshes, and thread and thimbles, and drop off your dry cleaning, and pick up a half-dozen bananas and a sack of oranges, and a new bonnet for sister Sue. A hundred-pound sack of seed for the chickens? Well, no.

Refrigeration? Not exactly. A calf, just dressed out, hangs in the butcher shop of George and William Efflandt, brothers who were in business at 165 Fourth Avenue, Moline, in the 1920s.

B ut for a moment, stroll into the shops of yesterday, where, as the old "Cheers" litany goes, "... everybody knows your name." A customer was sacred, to be addressed by a first name or with some dignity, if they wished to be called Mr. or Mrs. or Miss. Most shops

Sanitary Dairy cottage cheese came in a little carton with a wire handle; Kohrs Crown Lard was packed in tin pails. Both were Davenport companies in this mix of items to be found in a Tri-City grocery store of the 1930s.

were small with a faithful core clientele. Only the downtowns had the big stores.

In the long ago, we shopped from peddlers. The Watkins Man was a kind of traveling druggist who also sold extracts such as vanilla and lemon. The Fuller Brush Man got his foot in the door by offering a free gift, a small brush or a comb cleaner. His spiels were enchanting, and how cleverly he discovered hidden ground-in dirt in the carpet. He produced a brush that would magically remove it.

The magazine salesman was always working his way through college. Same for the encyclopedia salesman, who always painted a grim picture of how children in the family would grow up in shameful ignorance without a set of his encyclopedias, easily financed by monthly payments.

We did a lot of shopping that way, door-to-door. Who can overlook the milkman? Everyone had a milkman. The Omar man is remembered for his cream horns and jelly berliners. Before that, neighborhoods were visited thrice weekly by the Walcher truck and its driver who announced his presence by waving a ding-ding, ding-ding bell out the window while slowly cruising the streets.

In our neighborhoods, there would be a grocery store every few blocks; all, mysteriously, made a

Above, a plodding dobbin pulled this trim wagon to deliver groceries for Ernest Utech's grocery store at 1804 Division Street, Davenport. Practically all stores delivered.
At right, "If It Swims, We Have It," was the slogan of Feiner Fish Co. at the edge of downtown Davenport.

Up until the late 1960s, home milk delivery was the norm throughout our communities. This milkman carried for Levetzow's Model Dairy, Davenport.

living. In the grocery stores of old — where you didn't need a road map to find the Morton's Salt or Halligan's Coffee — there WAS string, hanging down from a cone-like gadget on the ceiling, for the clerk to carefully tie the top of your dozen eggs, which were counted into a paper sack. Not a carton, but in a sack!

You did not wait on yourself, *anyplace!* Grocery store, variety store, any venue of retailing. There was no self-service. Everywhere, there were clerks. That was the way we shopped. At the grocery, there was someone with pencil behind the ear to take down your order while you stood before the counter. It was neatly sacked, not in a plastic bag tumble, but in a 20-pound-weight brown Kraft bag. There was an art to packing a grocery bag. The heavy stuff, the blue label cans of Karo syrup went at the bottom, along with the Super Suds box — the one with a free dish inside — and the lighter corn flakes at the top, and always, the celery at the very peak of the bag. Grocers took pride in their sacks; leaves of the celery stalk were a flowery touch peeking from the top.

"I cannot forget the old Norton's grocery store in Orion, Illinois, with the narrow aisles and the butcher behind the meat counter wrapping your purchase in white paper," says Lori Sampson, the Orion village clerk.

"During the Depression, my parents, Walter and Ann Hoffmann ran a mom and pop grocery store on Washington Street in Davenport," says Anita Lowe. "Grocery stores sold a lot of penny candy; I remember filling the penny candy case and having a few samples, too."

Eleanor Koenig remembers the wooden dill pickle barrel, stored in the walk-in ice box, and the big keg of sauerkraut positioned near the front door, the better for the essence to drift out the open door, at the old Koenig's market in Davenport.

Stores had an aroma of their own, but then, so many stores were "their own." They sold but a single item. Richter's in Davenport and Mosenfelder's in Rock Island were the class stores for menswear and they had a whiff of moth balls to protect the woolens.

Knueppel & Ott, the leather goods store, was redolent with the sweet smell of harness and saddles and reins on Second Street in downtown Davenport.

In the top photo, a typical grocery store of the 1920s, this one at 801 Twelfth Street, Rock Island. H.C. DeBois stands by the front door. The deliveryman is Robert Laedeke.

Milk bottles from Waage Dairy, Davenport, displayed in a milk promotion at Kresge's, downtown Davenport.

An advertisement for Rub-No-More Soap, painted on the window of Bernard Schwener's Fancy & Staple Groceries, 817 West Second Street, Davenport. Suppliers would paint the store's name on the glass if the owner would allow a plug for the product.

Big band members always stopped at Elmergreen's Music Store on Harrison Street, Davenport. Oscar Elmergreen, right, took pride in that he once sold a trombone mouthpiece to Tommy Dorsey. At left, his son, Bob.

The formal 1927 opening of Doden's Drug Store, Rock Island

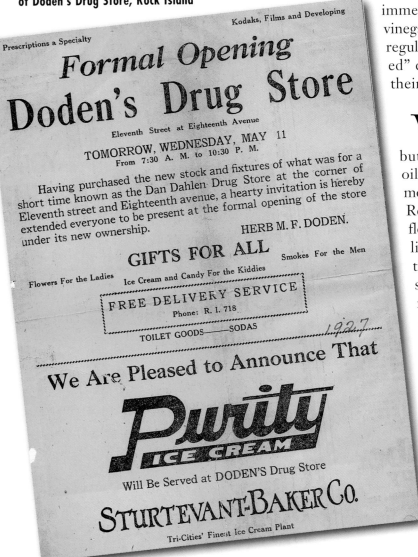

Neighborhoods had a plethora of stores. Hellman's Dry Goods was a corner store for house dresses and sheets and pillow cases and pearl buttons. The same for places like Halpern's in Rock Island.

Customers could close their eyes and instantly tell that they was in one of the 15 Schlegel drug stores in the Quad-Cities, or Herb Doden's pharmacy on Eleventh Street, Rock Island, from the healthy essence of phenol that made them feel they would be cured of anything bothering them just by sniffing lustily.

Butcher shops invariably smelled of sawdust. "Ma" Winterlin, who ran a landmark butcher shop on Davenport's Washington Street, would daily measure the sawdust on the work floor. She mandated that it be four inches deep. The pickled pigs feet — in immense open crocks — added a tangy vinegar essence to the air. Butcher shops regularly would hang racks of "denuded" chickens and ducks and geese on their walls.

Variety stores — most stores, for that matter, save the butcher shops — regularly had an oily odor. Before tile and carpeting, most retail places had wooden floors. Regularly, sometimes monthly, the floors were oiled, sloshed down with linseed, to doll them up and keep the dust down. Nabstedt's jewelry store was like that in downtown Davenport and the jewelers — most of them fine craftsmen — paid little heed if a minuscule flake of gold fell to the floor. When Nabstedt's, on the ground floor of old downtown Davenport Masonic Temple was razed, foxy Bill Vale, the wrecker, boasted of reclaiming thousands of dollars from bits of gold that had been embedded in the oiled-over wooden floor.

If a customer shopped for a 76 rpm record at Schmidt's in Davenport or a 45 rpm at Van Goor's in Rock Island, there was a clerk to remove the record from an album or rack and point him in the direction of a little listening booth — much like a phone booth — for the shopper to catch the sounds before buying. If he bought.

S&H Green Stamps were a come-along at many Quad-City stores, primarily supermarkets. Stamps were given for amounts of purchase, and could be redeemed for everything from silverware and dishes to new tires. King Korn stamps also were popular.

THE WAY WE SHOPPED

While we pat billfolds and purses that are thick with plastic, credit without cards was de rigeuer in the long-ago days of shopping. Charge accounts were the norm at most grocery stores. Petersen's and Parker's in Davenport; McCabe's in Rock Island; and Block and Kuhl in Moline had personal shoppers who would do your shopping for you — a courtesy being revived among the catalog set.

Those who lamented the loss of the general store in small towns now find they have been supplanted — at least in the food department — by convenience stores.

Still, a few of the old places hang on, and do business. At Smith Bros. General Store in Clinton, Iowa, you can buy a wash tub or a stove poker or a skate key.

In Elizabeth, Illinois, near Galena, visitors are pleasantly awed to enter Bishop's Dry Goods, certainly a genuine general store, where you can purchase shoes or cigars or peruse a bolt of calico cloth.

"We like to keep it this way; we keep plugging on. Some people like it this way. I'm never going to change," says Irwin Bishop, the owner. He will guide you to your purchase, weigh up a peck of potatoes and offer to sell you a yo-yo, too.

It was slower the old way, the way we once shopped. But it was — and remains — fun, if you can find an old place, steeped in memory, and an essence of pipe smoke and sawdust and pig's feet. You won't need a road map to find the cornflakes, either, or to search for a clerk to lead you to the paper towels.

Long before the U.S. Department of Agriculture got into the act, grocery stores such as Crescent Market, 422 West Second Street, Davenport, gave customers fresh, fresh poultry — not long off the farm, apparently.

During a lunch break in 1925, Evelyn Gleason Mumford, a buyer for Petersen Harned Von Maur, appears ready to tip a toe into the Mississippi.

From brooms to buckets — the hardware area of Denger's, at 2901 Brady Street, Davenport. Groceries also were sold.

Smith Bros. General Store, Clinton, Iowa, one of the last of the buy-anything stores in the Quad-City region.

Five-pound boxes of licorice gum drops were a dollar at confectionary shops.

The way we shopped and promoted: A giant display of coffee at an A&P Store, 417 West Second Street, Davenport, which sold the most coffee in this Midwest district in 1945. Behind the bunker of coffee, Clarence Bracewell and Hazel Cox ... A 1931 newspaper ad for M.L. Parker Co ... Fred Rowley's Quad City Trading Center, in downtown Rock Island, offered most anything a customer might desire, including notary public service ... Omar Van Speybroeck promoted the family clothing store with a banner atop a car on the July 4, 1938, parade in East Moline.

PHONE 8-6115
1617 THIRD AVENUE

RES. 8-5513

NOTARY PUBLIC

QUAD CITY TRADING CENTER

FRED ROWLEY, PROP.

ANTIQUE GUNS & OLD IRON BANKS

WE BUY AND SELL
FURNITURE, TOOLS, MOTORS, ANTIQUES
AND ANY ARTICLE OF VALUE

ROCK ISLAND, ILLINOIS

M.L. Parker Co.
Davenport, Iowa

DOWNSTAIRS LUNCHEONETTE

LUNCHEON
45c

Spring Vegetable Soup

Choice of

Stuffed Pork Tenderloin
Indian Relish

or

Pot Roast of Beef
Brown Gravy

Whipped or Escalloped Potatoes
Hot Cornmeal Muffins and Butter

Choice of

Hickey Brothers Famous Home-made
Apricot Pie
Chocolate Ice Box Pudding

Coffee

Milk

Tea

The M. L. Parker Company Luncheonette Is
Operated by HICKEY BROTHERS.

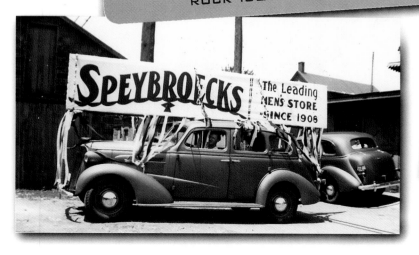

Hanssen's, a Davenport landmark, was one of the major hardware stores in the Midwest. Its money-or-receipt-carrying railroad "mouse" was an attraction unto itself.

The Mouse That Roared: Hardware Heaven for 135 Years

Bed knobs and broomsticks, horse collars and buggy whips shared shelf space with the 20th century in Louis Hanssen's Sons, a five-story hardware heaven and downtown Davenport fixture for 119 years.

Hanssen's had a coast-to-coast reputation for good service and square deals. And when the empire folded in 1970, brought down by competing retail chains, receipts for materials used in construction of the Rock Island Arsenal Clock Tower in 1865 were found in the mix of thousands of items to be disposed of or auctioned.

"The Arsenal was a big customer during all of the wars that occurred while we were in business. I imagine we also sold supplies to Union forces during the Civil War," recalled Robert Hanssen, great-grandson of the founder.

He was president of Hanssen's Village Shopping Center store, until it suffered the same fate as the downtown store in 1986. The Hanssens left a legacy of service nearly as old as Davenport, 135 years.

Likely there wasn't another store in the world quite like Hanssen's with its ceiling-high shelves, five stories and a basement, groaning with wooden barrels of finger-thick chains, catcher's mitts and flower seeds, millions of nails, nuts, bolts and screws, and so much more.

Inventory control? It was in the memories of the grayheads who could quickly scrounge up a Morse twist drill, a Flexible Flyer sled, ice tongs or a square-headed nail.

And if you wanted dynamite or blasting powder, Hanssen's could supply that, too, from its powder magazine in the then-sparsely populated area near Middle and Devil's Glen roads in Bettendorf.

If hardware store junkies breathed with satisfaction the proper aroma of coiled hemp and lubricating oil and metallic tang of nails, screws and rolled fencing, the big attraction for all ages was the "mouse" that soared.

Kids gaped and visiting dogs yelped as the "mouse" (or "mice") scrabbled up walls and across high ceilings at a whiz-bang 200 feet a minute. Each "mouse" was a little money-and-receipt-carrying "car" on a miniature railroad-like system, each powered by a half-horsepower motor.

The "mouse," twisting and turning, zipped along hundreds of feet of track to four floors, eventually stopping at the second floor office to be unloaded, reloaded, and sent scampering on it way back to the waiting customers.

How close Davenport came to not having Louis Hanssen as one of its leading entrepreneurs! Born in Itzenhoe, Holstein, Germany, he sailed for America in 1849 aboard a steamer that caught fire at sea. Miraculously, passengers were rescued by an English sailing ship. After 54 days at sea, Hanssen finally arrived in Davenport on December 31, 1849. (Davenport had been incorporated for only 13 years.)

Three succeedingly bigger stores were built on the same location, 213-215 West Second Street. Starting out, Hanssen worked 16-hour days, then walked home. Year by year, his business grew.

The firm entered the wholesale hardware business in 1910 and soon became one of the biggest houses in the West, serving as a distributor for many of the largest U.S. manufacturers.

At the time of its closing, Louis Hanssen's Sons was the oldest hardware store in Iowa, and one of the largest west of the Mississippi. Its products were shipped to all of the lower 48 states.

Proudly the firm proclaimed its motto: "If you can't find it at Hanssen's there's no use to look around."

There were tears in president John Hanssen's eyes in June 1970 when he announced that under-selling stores, high labor costs, government buying practices, and a depressed economy had sounded the firm's death knell.

"I can't sleep and my stomach keeps churning. This is a terrible time, but we can't go on," he said. The 76-year-old man, who lovingly tended a small flower garden right in the store, had worked there a half-century.

The 28,800 square-foot building first was sold to the Fashion, a woman's clothing store, and then was occupied

The old store building in the 1930s. The company sold material to build the Rock Island Arsenal Clock Tower in 1865, and likely was a supplier to Union forces during the Civil War.

by Rhomberg Furriers. Still on the east face of the building is the Louis Hanssen's Sons Hardware sign.

Broken-hearted, John Hanssen still was sorting through the mountain of merchandise four months after the closing date when he accidentally

stepped into the store's open elevator shaft, fell 15 feet, and was killed.

Robert Hanssen, 40, presently 69th president of the Davenport Jaycees, remembered working in the downtown store after school when he was 14.

"I swept floors, took out garbage, and began to learn how to find the thousands of item we carried. It's not as difficult as it seems when you spend some time around it."

He was at the Village Center's Hanssen's store for 13 years, assuming the presidency after the death of his father, Frank.

"I remember at the old store, when I was little, the operator of the cage elevator used to let me sit by her and take it up and down. Later, I helped Helen Pott in the seed department, and Grace Priborski in housewares."

The wrought iron from the hoary hardware elevator lives on in grillwork at busy Riefe's Restaurant, 1417 West Locust Street, Davenport. The owners bought it at auction and dismantled it.

It fell to Bob Hanssen to write the final chapter of Louis Hanssen's Sons' 135 years in 1986. It was a wrenching choice.

"I decided that rather than try to go on and face bankruptcy, we would close with dignity with all our debts paid and our history secure.

"Sure, there were some days that I miss it," he said wistfully, "but then, remembering the headaches, there are other days I'm glad to be out of it."

—Jim Arpy

Bobbin lace making, brought by immigrants from Belgium, is a craft that their descendants still learn with pride.

Strong hearts, willing hands

"The first requisite of a good citizen in this republic of ours is that he shall be able and willing to pull his weight."
— Theodore Roosevelt

....

chapter seventeen

Our New Americans

The train conductors would call, "Next stop, Moline." The immigrant Swedes — stoic and nervous, understanding no English — stayed as erect as statues in their coach seats. No one moved until the conductors would cup hands and shout, "Next stop, Deere."

Deere was synonymous with Moline. They had arrived in the promised land of Deere & Co.

Immigrants trundled off trains in Moline or Rock Island or Davenport, bewildered in a world that was as mystical to them as a Shangri La.

So proud of their success in America, the Nagel brothers of East Moline — newly arrived immigrants — posed as cigar smoking big shots in this studio photograph that was sent home to Eede, Holland. They are Henry, Alphonse and Frank. All prospered in later years.

They were the blue-collar workers of the early 1900s, lured to this puzzle of prosperity and strangers.

Immigrants expanded the heart of the burgeoning Tri-Cities, all from far-away cities with strange-sounding names, but with a common emotion: They were happy to be here!

The sleepy hamlet of Gilbert was renamed Bettendorf for the brothers who moved their factory to the city, and an import of immigrants was needed to help Bettendorf Co. turn out railroad car frames and wheel trucks. Skilled molders from Austria — grim from unpromising drudgery in their homeland — were enticed by good wages and a new beginning.

All ages carry on the Belgian lace-making tradition at the Center for Belgian Culture in Moline. From left, Frances Bollaert, Celie Donohoe and Kathy Knobloch, all of Moline.

A church made from two boxcars: Immigrants from Mexico in front of Our Lady of Guadalupe Church, Silvis, in 1929. Many Mexican workers in the Silvis Shops of the Rock Island Lines lived for years in boxcars.

Andy Haber came from Austria to settle in what now is Deer Run, a subdivision of elegant homes. Cows grazed by the house, and Andy hauled water to his home from a well near what became Lincoln School. After his first long day's work at Bettendorf Co., Andy couldn't find his home in the darkness of the wilderness. His wife, Katerina, had remedied that by the next night. She hung a kerosene lantern on fence post.

In those long-ago days, the able Bettendorf volunteer fire chief Art Voelliger remembered a mucky clay road slicing through farmland where wagons became tangled and mired to the hubs, and even walkers would get stuck. Today, it's a land of people, houses and businesses, but the road name has, appropriately, remained nearly the same — Tanglefoot Lane.

Rafael Arguello, of Holy City, with his new bride, Angela, in an early 1940s wedding picture at Cook's Point, a Mexican settlement at the western edge of Davenport.

While the Swedes and the Belgians came to build John Deere farm equipment and Velie automobiles in Moline, the Mexican population settled in Bettendorf to build railcar frames. William Bettendorf traveled to Juarez, Mexico, to recruit 150 workers for his foundry. They brought families with them, and built a small community of apartments and cottages that came to be known as Holy City.

Al Stafne, longtime city attorney, recalled that Bettendorf once had more children named Jesus than any other community in MidAmerica.

"It wasn't much, but to us, Holy City in 1934 was like living in a country club," says Tony Navarro who grew up there. "When I was little, my family lived in the middle of Irish and Italian immigrants along Davenport's East Sixth Street, but when the Depression came along,

A second generation from Italy: Little did Tom Lagomarcino Sr. know what the gift from his godparents would be after his First Communion at St. Mary's Church, Moline. He received two live chickens that, he remembers, did not stay alive very long.

Perched and posing in Cook's Point.

we moved to Bettendorf where dad took work with Bettendorf Co. Holy City had about 150 people, in side-by-side little homes and some in flats, with $1 a month rent. It was a happy time, not far from the river, and we'd go swimming. The river was clean, then.

"Sure, we were poor, our parents from Mexico. We'd knock coal off the train gondolas to keep our potbelly stoves warm. I like to tell the story that my wife, Rita, married me because she thought I was rich, living in Holy City. That is because Cook's Point, where she lived in the west end of Davenport, wasn't much."

Tony's wife was Rita Quijas, and she remembers Cook's Point, at the foot of Howell Street, as mostly shacks.

"We'd put cardboard over the windows to keep out the cold. We were young, and didn't know the difference."

The Mexicans in Bettendorf generally dispersed, but those who came to work in the Rock Island Lines Silvis Shops remained together to form a thriving ethnic community. In the beginning, the railroad housed its Mexican workers and their families in abandoned boxcars.

Even a church, Our Lady of Guadalupe, thrived from 1927 to 1930 in two boxcars.

Where would our Quad-City region be without its immigrants? Davenport would not be Davenport without the immense influx from Schleswig Holstein Germany. In the early 1900s, one-third of the community's population was German. The language was taught, along with English, in the schools. There were German singing societies, Strasser's German symphonic band, the German Theater, three Turnvereins, or Turner Halls, where physical fitness was Teutonic. The Turner movement expanded to Moline, where a Turnverein prospered for years.

The thrifty Germans — who brought funds with them from the homeland

A love of music arrived on the boat with German immigrants. Members of the Davenport Zither Quartette, from left, Louis Ockerschausen, William Wagner, A.K. Fahrner and Hugo Ranzow. Zither music, still heard in the Amana Colonies, was popularized in the 1939 film classic, "The Third Man."

Below, Turners held "turnfests" to demonstrate fitness. The credo: "A free mind in a healthy body."

German Turner societies were among the most notable groups in the Tri-Cities. In their flashy white uniforms and leather boots, the Davenport Turngemeinde women's drum and bugle corps in front of the old Scott County Courthouse in 1926 or 1927. Above, the corps leader, Marie Kai.

A weekly Belgian newspaper was published for decades in Moline. The newspaper continued publication here until the early 1930s, when it was transferred to Detroit, Michigan. It remains in business, one of the largest ethnic-language newspapers in America.

Pigeon racing came to the Tri-Cities with Belgians. It is a mystery how the birds know the way home when they are placed in coops and sent to places such as Kansas City. By uncanny sense, they return to the home coop. Pigeon racing remains a pastime, though not as popular as 50 years ago. This was the LaVerne Schumann coop in Davenport.

— created the vast lumbering industries. Families like the Muellers and Beiderbeckes built mansions along what became Davenport's Gold Coast. Germans brought us butcher shops and banks and a cigar-making empire; 250,000 Brown Beauties, the working-man's cigar, were turned out each week in the mid-1920s in Davenport at Peter N. Jacobsen's factory at West Fourth and Harrison streets. The smoke never settled. Thirty Davenport cigar factories made 18 million cigars in 1918.

Germans brought a potpourri of trades. Carol Skahill of Davenport remembers that "Grandpa John" Bergbauer was one of the finest barbers in Davenport. He was apprenticed in Germany, where he was required to learn the craft of wig-making. He opened his Davenport shop, in the early 1900s, in his parlor.

The Germans had their taste for beer. Davenport Malting Company prospered and breweries like Zoller's flourished. The Swiss, too, had a special taste for brew and the Yegge family — of German/Swiss heritage — had a brewery of stout ale in DeWitt, Iowa. The sweet smell of hops flushed down the gutters from the hilltop breweries in Davenport. Along the way, friendly street-corner bands oom-pahed, and portly Max Moeller — with his parrot Polly shrieking from his shoulder — peddled mustard to west Davenport stores and housewives from a bushel basket, while a gentle-voiced Swede named Knute made the rounds of Tri-City grocery stores selling a delicacy favored by all our European immigrants ... long, stiff, smoked sturgeon.

The Belgians left the Old Country in search of the same opportunities sought by every other immigrant. And, within a generation or so of arriving in Moline, the names of their children were showing up on the lists of Tri-City bankers, lawyers, physicians and merchants.

At the center of the Belgian community in Moline was the church. The Rev. J.B. Culemans organized Sacred Heart Catholic

Fingers carefully move with thread and bobbins as Celie Donohoe practices her craft.

Rev. J.B. Culemans: His influence was so great in Moline's Belgian community that when his Sacred Heart Church was built, a cardinal traveled from Belgium to dedicate the cornerstone.

Parish in 1906, and remained as its pastor until his death in 1943. His influence was such that when the present church was built, Cardinal Mercier came from Belgium to dedicate the cornerstone.

Culemans realized that the fortunes of the Belgian community were tied to the prosperity of the Tri-City community, and he labored in the secular world to make both strong. He is credited as one of four men responsible for establishment of the Moline airport.

Keeping up on news of their adopted land as well as the land they left behind always has been important to our newest citizens. Quad-City Hispanics read *Voces*, published in Rock Island. Newcomers from Southeast Asia receive newspapers in their native languages. And Belgians throughout the United States subscribe to a newspaper, now published in Detroit, that got its start in 1906 in Moline as the *Gazette van Moline*. Culemans was the "father" of the Flemish newspaper, and many Tri-City merchants had their advertisements translated to reach the Belgian audience.

They may not have entirely cut ties to their homelands, but for immigrants from every corner of the world, this was the promised land. Most prospered as the Tri-Cities prospered. And, along with their trunks, they brought Old-Country ways of having fun — from Belgium, rolle bolle and pigeon racing; from Mexico,

Photographs were important. They were a sign of status, to be mailed back to the Old Country by immigrants. Peter and Stephanie DeKezel immigrated to America from the border of Belgium and Holland in 1905. The ship's manifest showed he had only $15 in his pocket. They reared their family near Kewanee, Illinois, where they farmed. A thrifty European, Mrs. DeKezel made the clothes for all the children in this photo.

Rolle bolle, a Belgian game, is played on indoor and outdoor dirt courts in Moline and East Moline. The idea is to get the heavy disc (once wood, now plastic) to roll and lean against the peg at the opposite end. The opponent tries to knock it over. International tournaments have been held in the Quad-City region, and the game is popular among Belgians in communities such as Atkinson, Annawan and Kewanee, Illinois.

Target shooting was the favored sport of many Germans in the Davenport area. Here, the Davenport Schuetzen at a match in Dubuque, Iowa. One shooting society had its own cigars, with an imprint of the group on its cigar bands and boxes. In the upper right, badges from German schuetzen (shooting matches).

whirlwind dancing and plaintive songs; from Germany, the shooting societies.

Schuetzen Park in west Davenport was the German center not only for tournament ranges, but also an amusement park with roller coaster and a zoo. It was the Disney World of its day, with a special trolley running up the hillside to its wooded plateau.

"I remember my father and grandfather telling about the popularity of what the Germans called 'birdshoots,' a contest that was especially popular with the Northwest Davenport Turners," says Alan Jansen, Bettendorf, who comes from a long line of German marksmen.

"An air rifle would be fired by kids at a mechanical-type bird, high on a pole. If a wing was knocked off, a certain prize would be earned; to shoot off the head meant another award. Should a certain hidden part of the bird be hit, it would totally fall apart. That meant a grand prize, and the shooting game would begin all over again with the bird reassembled."

The Belgians also enjoyed shooting — but with bows and arrows. Trophies and photographs from early competitions fill the shelves at the Center for Belgian Culture in Moline. Pigeon racing, another Old-Country sport, made its way to the New World, and for decades elaborate coops were common in backyards in Belgian neighborhoods. The Belgian equivalent of bowling — rolle bolle — still is played in some parks. But there's one big change in the way the game is played over the century: now women are out there, too.

Swedish immigrants to Bishop Hill, Illinois, in the early 1900s. Men and women smoked pipes.

Olof Forse, enjoying a cup of coffee.

The Charles Falk family on a Bishop Hill porch.

The heroes from Billy Goat Bluff

Few neighborhoods have made a greater sacrifice to our nation than Hero Street U.S.A. The predominantly Mexican-American section of Silvis produced 120 veterans who fought in World War II, Korea, Vietnam and the Persian Gulf.

Eight, all sons of Mexican immigrants, were killed in action during World War II and Korea.

Hero Street, formerly Second Street, was little more than a muddy, rutty lane until former Silvis alderman and mayor Joseph Terronez led a movement in the late 1960s to create a monument recognizing the neighborhood's distinction.

In 1968, Hero Street Memorial Park was created out of the old Billy Goat Bluff, a grassy hillside where children once romped. Since then, the neighborhood and its famous sons have been the subject of numerous stories by national media, a PBS documentary narrated by actor Martin Sheen, and a proposed feature film.

October Red Field

"The people who know the place only by driving through it know the flatness.
They skim along a grade of least resistance. The interstate defeats their best intentions.
I see them starting out, big-hearted and romantic, from the density and variety of the East,
to see just how big ... the Midwest ... and how big this country is ... the vista opens up,
a true vision so vast that at night as they drive, there are only the farmyard lights ... "

— Michael Martone, *A Place of Sense*, a collection of essays in search of the Midwest

chapter eighteen

From the Land to the Machine

M y name is John A. Schnekloth and I'm a fifth-generation Scott County farmer. My name is not really that important. You could plug in a lot of names from Scott County who are long-time multi-generation farmers... Moellers, Keppys, Meiers, Golinghorsts, Sievers, Holsts, Storjohanns. While their stories might

Making hay on the Hugo Schnekloth farm in the 1930s.

be different than mine, you would find them similar in scope of hardy stock, with ancestors who immigrated to America and have successfully farmed here all these generations.

In 1851, Heinrich Schnekloth, my great-great-grandfather, put his family on a ship and made the three-month voyage to America, landing in New Orleans.

They came to America with nothing more than the promise of opportunity and the ability to work, loading cotton bales on ships in New Orleans until they had enough money saved to come north in 1860 and buy 80 acres in Scott County ... the very 80 acres that I farm today and the house I live in, Sunny View Farm.

John Schnekloth and son, Hans. He hopes Hans someday will take over Sunny View Farm, the Scott County farm that John's ancestors bought in 1860. This generation lives in the farmhouse built then, modernized and updated over the years.

T ry to imagine what this farm would have been like in 1860. The road to it would have been nothing more than a dirt track. Only stoves for heat. Maybe no well, just a nearby creek for water. There probably was a barn, some kind of crib to store a little grain, a chicken house of some sort, and a wide bunch of animals. All work was done by hand

or by horses for clearing, planting and harvesting, and it would take a large part of the production from the farm just to feed the horses that worked it. There probably was a large garden, because life at this time was about surviving on what you could produce.

Move ahead to today, a farming enterprise my great-great grandfather probably would not believe. Well-heated homes, electricity, plumbing, gravel and paved roads, cars, trucks, pickups, tractors, combines, no livestock, computer screens, market screens, telephones, cellular phones, two-way radios, no gardens (except sweet corn for occasional sweet corn boils). We have become consumers just like the rest of society.

Other generations of Schnekloths followed Heinrich on our farm — Hans and a couple of Hugos. They worked hard, expanded our land, and prospered.

Cindee Schnekloth is a partner in the operation of Sunny View Farm. Her husband, John, gives honor to farm wives ... "The women who married these men in our family helped on the farm and reared the children."

My father, Hugo A. Schnekloth, took over Sunny View in 1947, and no generation had seen as much change on the farm as his. Tractors had been introduced, but it still was a mix of horses and tractors when my dad began farming.

The debate in those days was whether steel wheels or rubber tires were better on tractors, and we can see which side of that argument won. Dad's generation saw the change

Between the chinch bugs and the drought, there was singing

As if the Great Depression were not enough, farming was near-failure in many places because of drought and chinch bugs. Art Olson stands in a field of corn stripped by chinch bugs on the family farm, located between Andover and Cambridge, Illinois.

A story of farming, the hard way ...

"I was born in 1922, the 11th of 12 children, on our farm between Andover and Cambridge, Illinois. There were seven girls and five boys.

"Times were severe. There was 1935, when we had a corn crop failure due to the chinch bugs. The fields were stripped bare, with only the stalks showing. The chinch bugs didn't have an appetite to eat the stalks and tassels. The next year was just as bad — the great drought of 1936. It was terrible!

"Still, we were a happy family with never a lack of things going on. We had races and played games like pom-pom-pullaway and andy-over and lots of baseball.

"Since we lived on a farm, we were able to survive on a diet of milk, eggs, meat, fruits and vegetables — all grown on our farm. Mother spent hours canning fruits and vegetables in the hot kitchen. Mother was a remarkable woman. Her name was Esther, and she came from Sweden, by herself, at the age of 16, on the boat. In America she met Swan Olson, my dad, another Swede.

"Money was not plentiful. An uncle owned a shoe store and he furnished shoes for all the kids. Music was an important part of family life. With no money for lessons or to go to things like the movies, our entertainment was to sit on the big porch at night and sing.

"They say 'Cheaper by the Dozen' ... but surely not at the time of the Great Depression."

— Marjorie Gustafson, Cambridge, Illinois

"Picking Corn" — a mural painted by John Bloom, and hung in the DeWitt, Iowa, post office.

from labor-intensive agriculture to almost complete mechanization. They went from driving work horses in the field to driving 350- to 400-horsepower air-conditioned, four-wheel drive tractors. They saw the advent of commercial fertilizers, hybrid seed corn and beans, herbicides and insecticides which dramatically increased production and reduced labor requirements.

I became a full operating partner with my dad in 1970 when I married. I had the privilege of working with him for close to 30 years before his death in 1996; we not only worked well together and complemented each other's weaknesses, but we liked each other. Working together was easy because we had a common goal, success of Sunny View, which by now had become Schnekloth Farms Inc. We survived the farm crisis of the 1980s, and we were able to expand afterwards.

Our family has always been blessed with someone who has wanted to stay on and run the farm business. That doesn't always happen. The earliest recorded history of our family is in 1662 in Krummbek, Germany, and they were farm laborers. It's in our blood, it seems. As the one in charge at this time, my concern goes to the future. Who will follow me? How can I help it happen? This is a good place to farm; my ancestors knew it. It has proven to be so ever since, and still is today. Scott County, Iowa, is known far and wide as a good place to farm.

The barnyard of the Schnekloth family's Sunny View Farm, as it appeared about a century ago.

We have another Hans in the family, my youngest son. He shows interest in wanting to farm some day. The opportunity is here. We'll nurture that interest and enthusiasm. We'll help him grow, and then we'll find out if he has the heart for the business. That's what this is really all about. Having the heart and mind to succeed ... at Sunny View Farm.

Vegetable and flower seeds for the farm were sold from colorful D.M. Ferry & Co. wooden boxes. A lid is shown.

"So Simple a Child Can Operate It," said the literature proclaiming the wonders of the American Tractor, 1919. At the wheel is John Vize Sr.

177

Planted firmly in the soil

Bliedorn, Iowa — Twinight in the country. Early, almost-autumn, and a steamy gray haze hangs over the corn in tassel, but I cannot hear it grow as the old farmers will insist that you can. Fall is nearly an onset, but out here — 45 minutes from the Quad-Cities — the air feels like a season's fresh start.

Nowhere in Iowa or Illinois is the land so table-flat. The wind has blown so far to reach the land of Bliedorn and as I head my car north on Y-54 near Grand Mound I stare to imagine the awe of the early settlers, with teams straining wagons through the head-high prairie grass carrying the hopeful to homestead the rich black land.

To reach Bliedorn is something of a misnomer, because there is no Bliedorn anymore, save for the church which I am told is somewhere out there. I look for a tall steeple, but see none on the landscape that is so senior. Just ahead, a slow-moving car stops. The driver gets out.

"I am Maurice Rogers of Clinton," he says. "I am to play trombone tonight at church services in Bliedorn, but I can't find any trace of a town."

I am heading for the same place, directed to head north on Y-54 off the good old Lincoln Highway until coming to a gravel road. Both of us shrug and drive to the first farmhouse for directions. No one is home (perhaps they have gone to Bliedorn?) but a farm dog barks and wags his tail — but that tail is not the end he bites with.

Through the haze we spot a single building, a frame chalk-white Lutheran church. The lawn, in the twilight, is a half-tunnel of shade trees. Children laugh and play tag or take turns for rides in a varnished wagon, pulled by a team of Carroll Flather's beige ponies.

Grownups stand to visit, the farmers red-faced from the summer's hot sun in the fields.

Carroll, whose grandfather Matthias was one of the first settlers, points here and there to where the store once stood, where there was a blacksmith shop and a school and a railroad stop. Now, of Bliedorn (named for its founder William Bliedorn) nothing is left but Bliedorn Church, which says something for the unbending dedication of Lutherans. The rest is a ghost town, the foundations at rest in the corn and bean fields.

This is a Sunday night of celebration, a blessing of the hopeful harvest and those who work the fields, and yet another fete for the 100th anniversary of St. John's Bliedorn Lutheran Church. In the church basement, eyeglasses steam from all that hot food — platters of pork and beef and hot German potato salad. Verla Wulf, who made about a half-dozen gallons, laughs: "It's all in the bacon and the onions."

"It's a night for joy," says Diane Claeys, the organizer and cheerleader of sorts for the church. Before the evening is up, there will be 250 people elbow-to-elbow in the place. "We're devoted out here. If someone doesn't show up for Sunday ser-

Top photo: The rush of spring: Under a blossoming fruit tree, one farmer holds the reins while another struggles with a single-row plow in a Western Illinois field.

Middle photo: Henry Keppy, proudly showing off his F20 Farmall in 1942. He bought it used.

"Cousin Ralph" on Vernon Brooks' first tractor, a McCormick Deering, on the family place north of Welton, Iowa.

In 1939, Charley Grayson, an enterprising young newspaperman, posed these women with a 23 foot, 10⅜ inch stalk of corn, raised by Don Radda on his farm near Washington, Iowa.

vices, they get a get-well card the next day in the mail." The Rev. Daniel Olson, from Wartburg College seminary, has been Bliedorn's minister for a dozen years. He is in a sports shirt, and though his sermon touches on the serious, he emphasizes it will be a night of delight and informality. He repeats, "There is no compassion burnout here."

The Pastors Polka Band (made up mostly of Clinton ministers) is playing. The greeting song is "We Welcome You, Alle-Alle-lu-ia," sung to "In Heaven There Is No Beer." There is good, Lutheran traditional music, too, but "The Lord's Prayer" is sung to the music of "Tennessee Waltz" while the congregation sways and "The Lamb of God" is sung to "Liechtensteiner Polka."

It is pitch dark, with a light mist, when everyone leaves, chatting about crops and kids and quilts for the upcoming bazaar. Life is good, and God is happy in his heaven in a town like Bliedorn, even though it is no longer a town — only a church.

Tooting the gospel in the Pastors Polka Band are, from left, Robert Negehoft, Cal Michaelsen, Maurice Rogers, Bill Flikkema and Pete Hagglund. (And no, not all are pastors.)

24 tons of horsepower

Roy Curtis tugged hard on the reins. His wrists ached, for in his hands were six lines — 480 feet of reins to handle.

Roy, a McCausland, Iowa, patriarch of horses and stables, was king of the oatburners one September day in 1937 when he did the unheard of: assembled a 24-horse multiple hitch for the Farm Progress Show at the Mississippi Valley Fairgrounds in Davenport.

Earlier, he had thrilled a Farmers Union Picnic crowd by cutting figure eights and showing driving skills with six- and eight-horse teams.

"But hitching and driving 24 horses was something else," Roy told Herb Plambeck in a story written for Wallaces Farmer.

Roy accepted the 24-horse challenge. First, he had to line up 14 horses to add to his own 10.

"It took more than an hour to get them hooked up in six columns of four abreast to make a checkerboard pattern," Roy recalled.

He wanted it to be an eye-catcher. By checkerboard, he meant to alternate dark and light horses.

"When we got through, I had 480 feet of reins to handle, six lines in each hand."

Then came the big moment. All eyes were on him when the 24 horses and wagon moved onto the track.

"A few tense moments when the horses — most of them had never before performed — heard the thunderous applause and started to bolt," Plambeck wrote. But cool and experienced, Roy Curtis (he died at age 97) knew his way around horses. He quickly gained control.

"Not only did Curtis take the 24 tons of spirited horse flesh down the track at full gallop, but he maneuvered every turn successfully, stopped the hitch on command, backed the show wagon into a marked spot, and closed out by cutting large figure eights in front of the grandstand to the crowd's delight."

A decade later, the thrill of a 24-horse hitch was passe.

A new generation was getting its thrills on the same track from stock car racing.

"It took more than an hour to get them hooked up in six columns of four abreast to make a checkerboard pattern."

— Roy Curtis

Elsie's calf: Beulah, the million-dollar baby

"Has anyone sung the song of the patient, calf-bearing, milk-flowing, cud-chewing, tail-switching cow?"

— *Frank Lloyd Wright*

Fawn-colored, she was a million-dollar beauty. That she was, said the farmers of Western Illinois, admiring the world's most famous calf — Beulah!

No wonder. Beulah was the calf of the world's most famous cow, Borden's dew-eyed Elsie.

Elsie the Cow was the star of ads, screen and stage. She even moo-o-o-ed once on Red Skelton's radio show.

Elsie's baby, Beulah, ended up on the farm of Russell and Gladys Lindquist near Lynn Center, Illinois.

Their son, Bob Lindquist, who grew up to live in Andover, Illinois, was a lad of 16 when he was picked as the perfect farm boy to assume ownership of this famous million-dollar calf.

Before Beulah came to live with Bob Lindquist, her first bid to fame came one week in 1944 when she had a stall in a Chicago department store. Twenty-thousand people paid admission to see or pet her by buying war bonds or war stamps. The calf starred at a Chicago Cubs patriotic rally, where Quaker Oats bought $525,000 in war bonds to purchase Beulah. Before the cheering ended, Beulah had raised a million dollars in war bond sales.

Quaker Oats sought the help of *Prairie Farmer* magazine and Chicago radio station WLS to find an owner for the prize calf. Bob Lindquist was chosen, after a Midwest search, as being the typical farm youth — active in 4-H and involved in running the family farm.

A special white shed was built for Beulah on the Lindquist farm, and when she came home, Kewanee, Illinois, had a special Beulah Day parade with three bands and a drum and bugle corps. The event was broadcast live by WLS to Midwest audiences.

"She was 6 months old when I got her. She was a fine calf, and grew up to have two calves of her own," Lindquist says. "She lived to be 5 years old. Really, a fine animal."

Top photo: The Beulah Day parade in Kewanee, Illinois, with the Orion, Illinois, High School band rounding the corner by the Leader store.

Bob Lindquist attaches a sign to the new barn built for Beulah, the million-dollar calf presented to him after a search for the most typical farm boy.

Reprinted by permission, Bob Artley.

The Rembrandt of the milking barn

"The cow is the foster mother of the human race ... the thoughts have turned to this kindly and beneficent creature as one of the chief forces of human life."
— *William Dempster Hoard*

An Iowan, Bob Artley of Hampton, has put his hand to the task many times — meaning, he is an old hand at milking cows. He has assembled his reminiscences of farming and milking into a syndicated cartoon series, and his drawings and essays have been collected into several books, the latest, *Living With Cows* (Iowa State University Press).

Artley has done a number of books, *Memories of a Former Kid* and *A Book of Chores As Remembered by a Former Kid*.

"My heart is really in Iowa, but in the winter it's in Florida," he says.

Artley has a love-hate relationship with the bovine species. He told *The Complete Cow Book* (Voyageur Press): "Cows are high on the list of our fellow creatures for which I feel a genuine affection."

These four drawings depict the trials and tribulations — and the pleasures — of living with cows, as recounted by a former kid.

Heavy snows in February 1960 closed U.S. 6 in Davenport, with Harlan's Truckport becoming a haven for stranded truckers and motorists. U.S. 6 was the main east-west route through the Quad-Cities. Interstate 80 was a few years away.

Weather woes and wonders

"We are weather junkies. We monitor it the way a hypochondriac listens to his own breathing and heartbeat in the middle of the night."

— Lance Morrow, *"The Art of Weathercasting"*

chapter nineteen

Mother Nature's Vengeance

Thumbing through the past shows how close to the edge we have skated. But we are survivors. We have survived the Winter of '36, the Summer of '36, the Winter of '79, the Flood of '65, the Flood of '93 and other meteorological menaces and miseries in between, such as the treacherous Duck Creek flood of 1990.

Our weather woes have attracted a U.S. president, cabinet officials, governors — even a stripper, whose hot gyrations in a publicity stunt of the late 1960s failed to melt Mississippi River ice jams in Buffalo, Iowa.

For weather extremes, nothing could match 1936. One season seemed to want to live up to the other's awful reputation. If suffering through the Great Depression weren't enough, we were hit by a double whammy of winter cold and summer heat.

In that summer of 1936, *Newsweek* wrote: "Withering heat, rushing out of the furnace of the prairie dust bowl, blasted crops, sucked up rivers and lakes, and transformed the nation — from the Rockies to the Atlantic — into a vast simmering cauldron."

In July 1936, the mercury stood at 100 degrees or higher for 11 consecutive days. People keeled over in the streets and heat victims were delirious. The Davenport *Democrat & Leader* described "a crazed farmer coming in from the fields and saying it was too hot to live." He ended his life by jumping into a well.

Bishop's Cafeteria in Davenport offered daily cold plate specials, advertised to take diners' minds off the heat — 20 cents for a "fancy cold meat plate."

The winter before was as miserable. On February 4, 1936, high winds battered the Tri-Cities, whipping the seven inches of existing snow and three inches of new snow into impassable drifts. Four days later, the 30-40 mph winds roared again. For days, the temperatures failed to rise above zero.

Each winter seems colder than those past to those who shiver through them, but it was more than four decades before we would be hit again with such vengeance. The Quad-Cities was shivering and shoveling snow in mountainous proportions as the Winter of '79 struck. The average daily temperature for January 1979 was 6.3

For 11 consecutive days in 1936, the temperature was 100 degrees or higher.

degrees above zero, with the coldest reading dropping to 27 degrees below — that before wind chills were factored in. On January 13, a blizzard buried the Quad-Cities under 14.8 inches of new snow and brought the total accumulation on the ground to 28 inches!

Floods go hand in hand with blizzards and heat waves in the Quad-Cities. The Mississippi River, running through the region like a spine, can be — as Mark Twain sagely observed — "a lawless stream" that cannot be tamed.

By far, the most ravaging and destructive were the Mississippi River floods of 1965 and 1993. The '65 flood crested at 22.48 feet in the Quad-Cities, a figure that river watchers thought would stand forever. But in 1993, the Mississippi unleashed its full fury, first cracking the '65 mark, then swamping it with a crest of 22.63 feet on July 9.

Down on Davenport's South Concord Street, Will VanFossen, who had lived 70 years on the Mississippi's banks, watched the river rise a foot a day around his house. He said, "It's as bad as it can be."

The flood's magnitude moved President Clinton to visit the Quad-Cities on July 4. When his motorcade stopped on the Centennial Bridge, he surveyed the cocoa-colored water below. What the president said was a confirming echo of the comment of old Will Van-Fossen.

Said President Clinton: " ... This is about as bad as it gets."

— **John Willard**

... By contrast in that era, sweltering families found cooling breezes in camps on Davenport's Credit Island before it became a public park.

... Cold and hot: On an icy February night in 1923, the First National Building at Second and Main streets, Davenport, burned, turning it into a towering icicle ...

Bobsleds and wooden sleighs came out in heavy snowfall. Jiggs, the pony, pulled Nancy and Virginia Traver on the family farm near Elvira, Iowa.

Three chugging locomotives in a row could not buck their way through heavy drifts in the winter of 1936.

The Plainview-Dixon road in Scott County was a single-lane tunnel in the wind-whipped zero days of February 1936.

Train crews were trapped by drifts in cabooses in 1936.

Workmen cut ice at Locks and Dam 15 to allow passage through the gates as spring approached in 1936. The ice was so thick that they were able to stand on it as they worked.

In his *Life on the Mississippi,* Mark Twain prophesied: "One who knows the Mississippi will promptly aver — not aloud but to himself — that 10,000 river commissions, with the minds of the world at their back, cannot tame that lawless stream, cannot curb it or confine it, cannot say to it, 'Go here or go there' and make it obey; cannot save a shore which it has sentenced."

Photos here show how floods have been a regular threat over the century. The flood of 1951 covered Davenport's Harbor Road (now Concord Street) and allowed Arleta and Darwin Livington to fish from their backyard.

Nuns from Marycrest College filled sandbags during the 1965 flood.

The Rock Island levee, awash in the 1965 flood, now is protected by a floodwall. The area was filled in and Modern Woodmen of America built its headquarters there.

Levee Inn, on Davenport's riverfront, has provided an everyman's gauge of how high floodwaters have crept through many rampages.

The curious gathered at the foot of Main Street, Davenport, to watch the flood of 1922 go by.

Hard, heavy work dragged on into the night in the Great Flood of 1993 as National Guardsmen sandbagged in the Village of East Davenport.

Working side by side, residents and National Guard troops filled sandbags in Oquawka, Illinois, as the crest moved downstream.

Davenport's John O'Donnell Stadium became a lagoon in 1993 as the Mississippi crept out of its banks to 500-year flood levels. A tractor parked on the pitcher's mound was nearly submerged by the time the river crested.

Kathy Webster grabbed for a sand-bag moments before the sodden wall collapsed, flooding two businesses on West River Drive, Davenport, during the 1993 flood.

The front page from July 9, 1993, the day the Mississippi crested at 22.63 feet — making the flood the worst in recorded river history.

RIVER RISES INTO HISTORY

Record crest in Q-C

Usually a sedate stream, Duck Creek became a river on June 16, 1990. At far left, Kimberly Road, Davenport; center, El Rancho Inn.

Don Whitemore of the Scott County sheriff's posse was a rescuer who wound up being rescued.

In a flash, a quiet creek went mad

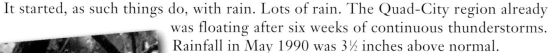

Even those not inclined to profanity were hard-pressed, once it was over, not to declare the 1990 Father's Day Weekend flood one of the damndest things ever seen.

It started, as such things do, with rain. Lots of rain. The Quad-City region already was floating after six weeks of continuous thunderstorms. Rainfall in May 1990 was 3½ inches above normal.

June brought scant relief — and on Saturday, June 16, the heavens truly opened. Rain. Thunder. More rain. Police scanners crackled as low spots in thoroughfares like Davenport's River Drive filled with backwash that had nowhere to go; swamped sewer basins couldn't hold all that water.

Duck Creek, normally a placid thread running through Davenport and Bettendorf, is meant to catch rainfall runoff and funnel it into the Mississippi. As John Freund, a hydraulic expert who spent most of his life along the creek, explained: "The rains came too fast and too hard, and with all the grading and paving around Duck Creek, the water had nothing to slow it down."

With nowhere else to go, the rainwater clogged the creek, overran the banks — and just kept raging.

Areas of Davenport and Bettendorf crosscut by Duck Creek were hardest hit. More than 8,000 homes and businesses were swamped. Damage was estimated at more than $25 million.

Residents of Davenport's Garden Addition are veteran floodfighters. But flash floods give no warning, and the Garden Addition was awash, too.

Worst of all was the loss of life. An 11-year-old LeClaire, Iowa, girl drowned when she was swept away by rushing water. A railroad bridge near Morrison, Illinois, washed out, and a Burlington-Northern crew member died when his train was derailed. And two motorists died in a head-on collision near Alpha, Illinois.

One of the most dramatic rescues of the Duck Creek flood was when a Davenport man, his blind wife and their two children were pulled from their car minutes before it sank at Hickory Grove and Hillandale roads, Davenport. Carlos Rush pulled Thomas Burl to safety as Mark Houk, whose black hat is just visible, helped Burl's wife, Denise. A third rescuer, Gary York, waded at left.

They found salvation in a bar

Anxious moments during a June-noon of 1990 for passengers on a big Tennessee Southern Revival Baptist Church bus:

Their driver had stopped at a Harrison Street service station the day that Duck Creek was on a rampage.

Before he had finished refueling, creek water was at the wheels of the bus, and so he drove to the nearby dry driveway of Pat McGuire's Irish-American Grill.

The bus passengers were all women, all very worried women, says Mike Shouse, who runs the restaurant-bar with his wife, Pat.

"They were agitated, not just because of the water, but most of them had to use a restroom," Mike said.

"At that moment, all refused to enter our bar. Some called it a den of iniquity — really. By now, Thirty-fifth Street was under eight inches of water and those church folks were a very, very concerned bunch.

"There was no alternative. They had to enter our bar — which was still high and dry — and use our facilities. Some held their eyes closed. Some were saying, 'Forgive me, Jesus' and 'Praise the Lord.' Some claimed it was the first time they had ever been inside a bar. Anyway, they were thankful, and may I say, relieved.

"There was no chance of returning to the bus, which I recall was painted on the side, 'And God shall save the world.'

"All the passengers were loaded into little boats, which was quite a scene. They waved goodbye to us. By then, we had ladders and were safe on the roof of our place."

In the midst of a cheering mass, presidential candidate John F. Kennedy spoke at Second and Main streets, Davenport, on an October night in 1960. An equally great audience was waiting to greet him at Rock Island High School.

Always the best show in town

"The President cannot make clouds to rain and cannot make the corn to grow. He cannot make business good, although when these things occur, political parties do claim some credit for the good things that have happened in this way."

— William Howard Taft

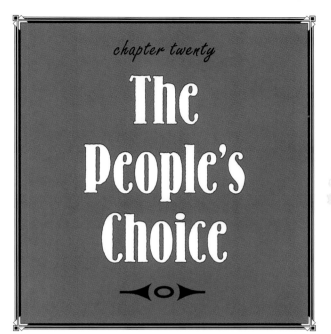

chapter twenty

The People's Choice

Politics can be like the theater. The candidates must be savvy enough to know when to enter the stage, and when to leave. The role of a presidential candidate is to shake hands and to take credit for all the cheers that are roaring toward the bandstand.

Just about every presidential candidate in modern times has found his way to this corner of the nation, by train or plane or car. Bill Clinton arrived by bus. All have found this fertile ground for courting voters.

Their words always have been well-rounded, but few have had anything new to reveal. It is best to simply report that they were here, to smile and to shine and to be seen and to show. Will Rogers said that politicking is the best show in America.

In the years before anyone still able to walk can remember, Teddy Roosevelt ranted amid the greenery of Vander Veer Park, Davenport. By contrast, Richard Nixon spoke in the dark from the back of a pickup truck.

Jimmy Carter arrived by steamboat and jogged. George Bush changed shirts in the back of a limo. Herbert Hoover came back home to Iowa and spent a sparse seven minutes in Davenport. Clinton had to roll up a sleeve and get a shot for his allergies when he visited in the waning moments of Campaign '92 as the mold and spores that cause sneezes hung heavy in the late-October air.

They all drew uproarious crowds. Dwight Eisenhower, a war hero, had immense audiences, but the most tumultuous was for John Fitzgerald Kennedy, whose visit was one of clamor and color.

Here, and on the following pages, we touch upon a few visits of presidential candidates, all seeking to be the people's choice.

After campaigning in Rock Island and Davenport, President Hoover and his wife, Lou Henry, visited his home town of West Branch, Iowa. He recounted his days in West Branch: "No food will ever taste so good as the family supper of those days; no sport will ever equal the mud-lined swimming hole."

"There are only two occasions when Americans respect privacy, especially in presidents. Those are prayer and fishing."
— Herbert Hoover, 1947

HERBERT HOOVER
The passing president

O n midday of October 4, 1932, Herbert Hoover and his wife, Lou Henry, were about a half-hour late for their visits to Rock Island and Davenport. Still, there was a cheery — perhaps curious — welcome for a president whose popularity was barely registering in the throes of the Great Depression.

In a whistle-stop tour, when candidates pleaded for votes from the rear platform of trains, Hoover made a seven-minute stop in Davenport after spending about 15 minutes in Rock Is-

land. It was a quest to retain a presidency which overwhelmingly went to Franklin D. Roosevelt.

"Back in their native Iowa, President and Mrs. Hoover were the guests of Davenport at noon today," wrote the *Democrat & Leader.* "The boy from West Branch and the girl from Waterloo were given an enthusiastic welcome."

Security was casual. Charley Witt, a burly Davenport police officer, muscled his way through the crowd and ordered the president to shake hands with Iowa Governor Dan Turner ... "so the boys can get a good picture."

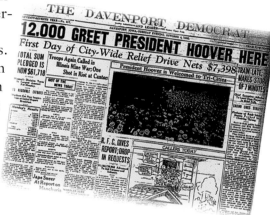

The autograph-seeker

Children released from school made up about half the crowds greeting President Hoover in Rock Island and Davenport.

Early that morning, Billy Baltzer, a Rock Island school kid, swiped a pencil from his brother and stuffed a piece of tablet paper in his pocket.

"I really intended to get an autograph of Mr. Hoover, and I did," says William Baltzer, now 83 and living in Bettendorf.

"I was a student at St. Mary's in Rock Island and met the Hoover train in Rock Island. It was pulling out and I ran up to the back platform, yelling, 'I want your autograph, please, please.' The nuns were running after me, because the train was moving. But I got the autograph. I lost the pencil he used, and I don't know whatever happened to the autograph."

Billy Baltzer

W earing a gray suit and a silver and black necktie with a stiff collar, the president made a few off-the-cuff remarks: "I was in Davenport before perhaps half the people in this crowd were born. Today, I would probably scarcely recognize anything that was here at the time of my first visit, some 40-odd years ago ... "

While crossing the Mississippi River to Davenport, he observed the multi-million-dollar locks and dam system being built, a project that was one of the positive efforts of his administration. From the train, he looked, too, upon the Rock Island Arsenal.

It was intended that a double presidential salute would be fired as the train passed the Arsenal. But the commandant received word at the last minute that the fusillades could not be fired unless Hoover actually stopped and set foot on Arsenal Island.

Bob Feeney, whose column, "Home Made Hooch," appeared in the *Democrat*, wrote: "We all join hands in extending a welcome to his excellency, the President of the United States. We have expressed more or less displeasure with his official and political activities. Today, however, Mr. Hoover is a guest in our house. We are glad to be able to give him the best room, the best piece of steak for dinner and best wishes."

"Last night the moon, the stars and all the planets fell on me. If you fellows pray, pray for me."

— Harry Truman, to reporters on the day after becoming president, April 13, 1945

HARRY TRUMAN

The tide turned in Davenport

For "Give 'em hell," Harry, Davenport was the city of hope. Harry Truman always claimed that Davenport gave him his first solid chance of winning the presidency on his own after Franklin Roosevelt's death.

First in 1948, again in 1952, he was in the Tri-Cities to warn what kind of hell the nation would be in if a Republican took possession of the White House.

On a bright September morning in 1948, plain-speaking Harry had his first look at the Tri-Cities. His Truman Special train eased to a slow stop at the depot in Rock Island, where he was cheered by 4,000 people. Next stop was Davenport, where 6,000 jammed the Rock Island Lines station.

Beaming from the platform on the back of his train, he cracked:

"I'm not surprised to see this many in Iowa — Iowans get up early — but I was surprised over in Illinois."

Truman was said to be pursuing futility. Suave Tom Dewey, the darling of wealthy conservatives, was expected to be a shoo-in. Harry showed 'em. He won.

After his victory, he credited Davenport as a turning point. In interviews with the *New York Times* and *Time* magazine, Truman said:

"If 6,000 people would turn out in a place called Davenport at 6 in the morning to see me, I knew there was hope of winning."

It was that way all across Iowa that hot and dusty day as the Truman Special whistle-stopped across the state to an event that is uniquely MidAmerica — the National Plowing Match. He stopped at every tank town on the railroad right-of-way, accepting ears of corn and jars of strawberry jam. That night he spoke in Des Moines, and it was estimated that 600,000 people saw Harry Truman in Iowa in a single day.

Four years later, in 1952, he returned to the Quad-Cities, politicking in Davenport and Moline. Truman was at a feisty, "Give 'em hell, Harry" peak.

"Harry Truman has lost none of his touch," wrote Forrest Kilmer, a reporter who went on to become editor of the *Quad-City Times*. "Not a candidate himself this year, Truman was in

Studying his hands, President Truman in a caravan from Moline to Davenport. This was 1952, his second visit to the Quad-Cities.

'He's not a Republican ... '

Fred Schwengel, an eight-term congressman from Davenport whose name now adorns the Interstate 80 bridge between Port Byron, Illinois, and LeClaire, Iowa, once was at a Masonic meeting in Missouri where Harry Truman was the speaker.

Schwengel recalled their first meeting:

The chairman said to President Truman, "Here's a fellow you should meet. He's in the House of Representatives, and both of you have something in common — you both were school teachers. The only thing you don't have in common is that you're a Democrat and he's a Republican."

Always outspoken, Truman looked sternly at Schwengel: "He's not a Republican, he's a goddamned Republican."

They shook hands.

"I was taken aback, felt intimidated," Schwengel said, "but Harry smiled, and we both laughed. We became friends. He was a great president, something I could not say about Nixon."

the Quad-Cities to boost the candidacy of Adlai Stevenson for president. He has the same old zip that characterized his whistle-stop campaign here in 1948."

Truman aimed his guns at Stevenson's opponent, Dwight Eisenhower. "Anyone who poses and talks like a superman is a fraud," Harry railed.

At Davenport Municipal Stadium (now John O'Donnell) 7,000 jammed the stands. Police estimated at least 3,000 lined the streets for a glimpse of Truman as he cruised from the depot to the stadium in an open, canary-yellow Lincoln convertible.

He clasped his hands together and beamed at signs urging "Give 'em hell, Harry." But his ire was stirred when — during a 15-minute speech lambasting Republicans — a bunch of students began to chant, "We want Ike, we want Ike."

President Truman glared over his glasses at the students in the stands, scolding them like the school teacher he once was:

"After you young men over there have had your fun being discourteous to the president of the United States, I hope you'll listen to this. It will be a lesson to you."

Secret Service agents flank President Truman's car in a caravan through the Quad-Cities on October 29, 1952. He was campaigning for Adlai Stevenson, who lost to Dwight Eisenhower.

With his daughter, Margaret, beside him, President Truman made a whistle-stop speech in Moline in 1952.

'A keen poker player, too'

In the days that Harry Truman trod the campaign trail, one of the reporters who covered him was Bill Bakrow, who in later years became president of St. Ambrose University.

Bakrow was a young reporter for United Press International and was on the Truman train when the president whistle-stopped through the Midwest.

"He was a keen poker player," Bakrow recalled of those days of being in the press pool that traveled with the president. "I'd come up with three of a kind, and invariably he'd slyly have a full house."

Bakrow, now retired and living in Massachusetts, often wondered if modern presidents would have the same rapport with the working media.

"No one should ever sit in this office over 70 years old, and that I know."

— Dwight Eisenhower, 1987

DWIGHT EISENHOWER
A hero in search of another victory

Beaming, smiling, waving, Ike was here. The HERO of World War II was in our towns. The cities were jittery, tittery, the crowds not knowing whether to stand up and salute or to cheer and shout, "We like Ike."

When his plane landed at the Moline airport on a September evening in 1952, a surprise awaited the Republican candidate. His wife. Climbing down the stairs, above the cheers of the waiting crowd, he shouted:

"Why, Mamie! I didn't dream you'd be here at the airport."

Ike had flown in from New York after an American Federation of Labor convention. Mamie was due in the Quad-Cities, but the time was uncertain. She beat Ike here

by several hours, traveling aboard a special train that had fast-trackage right-of-way from St. Paul, Minnesota.

Here was the storied couple everyone wanted to see, and they were met by a tumultuous welcome. Eisenhower, by himself, was the image of our victory in World War II. There was little question in anyone's mind that the hero would defeat Adlai Stevenson, the articulate candidate from Illinois.

That night, Eisenhower filled the Rock Island Armory with all the place could hold, 3,700. The maximum crowd, jammed in chairs on the armory floor meant for National Guard close-order drill, was in one of the most uncomfortable of all settings for any kind of event.

Eisenhower offered a four-point program for the basic needs of America, about the same that he had been touting at rallies in other cities. But when he outstretched his arms in that famous victory salute, newspaper reporters said, "The crowds went wild, Republicans in particular, but Democrats in grudging admiration."

Draped with bunting, Scott County's old courthouse was a backdrop for Republican candidate Dwight Eisenhower's pitch for the presidency in 1952. Crowds stood shoulder to shoulder on the courthouse lawn and filled Davenport's Fourth Street.

Next day, Ike was the center of a packed scene on the old Scott County Courthouse lawn. The sagging sandstone building had never looked more festive. Flags and bunting draped the gray building until it actually became presentable. He spoke from a platform on the courthouse steps. It was so red-white-and-blue patriotic that one of the bystanders, Roger "Gabby" Crow, said it made a person want to rush out and re-enlist.

While the national press said that Ike was showing the strain of the campaign, in Davenport he had the enthusiasm of a general marching into battle, certain of victory.

Everyone, everywhere, from the GIs who fought for him in Europe to the governor of Iowa, wanted to grasp Eisenhower's hand. He tried not to disappoint anyone within a handshake.

Speaking at the Rock Island Armory during his only Quad-City visit, Dwight Eisenhower in the familiar outstretched arms salute.

'May I take your picture, general?'

After the melee of his stump speechifying on the clogged lawn of the Scott County Courthouse, Dwight Eisenhower adjourned for a breather to the inside of the sagging old building. There, Sheriff C.H. "Pete" Wildman said someone was in his office and wanted to take his picture. The general affably agreed.

Wilson Shorey, a Davenport attorney, had set up a mini-studio in the sheriff's office, lights, backdrop, the works.

Ike was a cooperative subject, smiling or stern, as Shorey directed. The attorney took a half-dozen poses with his 4x5 Speed Graphic camera and made many 11x14 matte-finish prints for his friends. Several hung for years in the courthouse.

The general, after receiving copies of the photos, wrote Shorey a note: "You made some of the best pictures ever taken of me."

195

Handsome John Fitzgerald Kennedy fascinated immense audiences. He worked his way through crowds at Rock Island High School Fieldhouse. A reporter wrote: "Hands everywhere tugged the dull-blue trouser legs of the candidate and shook his hands. To touch him was enough."

"I had plenty of problems when I came into office. But wait until the fellow who follows me sees what he will inherit."

— John F. Kennedy, 1963

JOHN F. KENNEDY
Hollywood charisma, MidAmerican frenzy

Mammy's little baby loves Kennedy, Kennedy, Kennedy." Twanging that peppy parody, the Five Tune Rockets steamed up a wild reception for Sen. John Fitzgerald Kennedy at Rock Island High School Fieldhouse on an October night in 1960.

It was one of Kennedy's wildest, most raucous nights in the memorable slugfest between the Massachusetts senator and Vice President Richard Nixon.

Crowd estimates are largely illusory, dependent on who is doing the counting. There was a claim of 10,000 at Second and Main in Davenport to cheer Kennedy, and more than that were shoehorned into the big, new gym at Rocky.

The Kennedys thumped the Quad-Cities hard in a warmup that was a typical family frolic. Eunice Kennedy Shriver, the senator's sister, was at Moline's LeClaire Hotel to visit with well-wishers. Earlier in the day, Rose Kennedy, the senator's mother, had hosted a reception in the crystal-chandeliered Gold Room of the Blackhawk Hotel in Davenport.

Jack Kennedy had a magnetism unlike any candidate ever to chant, "If I am elected..." to a Quad-City crowd.

Campaigning was long past the whistle-stopping railroad platform pleas of the Hoover-Truman era. The handsome senator arrived at the Quad-City Airport in his plane, the Caroline, named for his little daughter. Five thousand surged onto the field to see him, cheering, "Jack, Jack," as he emerged from his DC-3.

Jerry Szumski, a colorful writer for the *Morning Democrat*, wrote: "Hands everywhere tugged the dull-blue trouser legs of the candidate and shook his hands. To touch him was enough." He was a handsome deity.

As nightfall darkened downtown Davenport, Second and Main streets became a blinding maze of TV lights and flashbulbs and shouting partisans. It was claimed that 10,000 people fanned out in all directions from Dime Store Corner to wave banners and hear the young senator — his hair mussed by the breeze of an early autumn night — shout his New England-accented rhetoric, "I've come to ask your help."

At Rock Island High School, Kennedy-ites had been waiting 2½ hours for his arrival. "They couldn't have packed another sardine into the gymnasium," the *Morning Democrat* wrote. Before Kennedy's arrival, 1,200 Juniors for Kennedy whooped it up in a rally of their own in Rocky's smaller girls' gym. "Jack, Jack, Jack," they clamored to a guitar's rhythm.

The moment of Kennedy's arrival — 9 p.m. — was timed almost to the nanosecond to allow TV cameras to catch the screaming greeting and speech.

Kennedy, in a fresh shirt and diagonal-striped tie, took the platform. It was the same old litany, but little did it matter. The crowds were there to be charmed by the Kennedy mystique.

"Will you help us win?" came the question from the ruddy face and Hollywood teeth.

"In many respects, Illinois may be the key to this election."

At 10:15 p.m., he returned to the Quad-City Airport to board the Caroline. "It's been a great visit," he yelled.

Then, the consummate politician backed down the steps of the plane to shake hands with Moline police officers and Illinois state troopers.

At 10:25 p.m., the Caroline was the lead plane to take off, followed by two planes of the press corps. It would be an hour's flight to Chicago, and a good night's sleep.

A tedious night of 1960 campaigning in Davenport for Republican presidential candidate Richard Nixon. Before going to bed, he ordered a small steak sandwich and a milk shake.

"Certainly in the next 50 years we shall see a woman president, perhaps sooner than you think."

— Richard Nixon, to League of Women Voters, 1969

RICHARD M. NIXON
From the back of a pickup truck

Husky-voiced, Vice President Richard M. Nixon overnighted in our towns in 1960 within a week of his opponent, John F. Kennedy. In the waning moments of the bitter presidential campaign, Nixon's plane touched down at Davenport's small municipal airport on a chill October night.

He launched tedious hours of hard Iowa campaigning, hand-pumping and hugging and speaking from the back of a pickup truck while an aide to his wife, Pat, handed out Nixon ballpoint pens.

"Smiling, looking only a shade tired and plagued with a throat soreness, Nixon told excited crowds that he never had seen a reception equal to this," wrote Art Nauman in the *Times-Democrat*.

Such comments were the common platitude of candidates wherever they visited, big town or burg.

Nixon threaded his way through a long line of admirers, Iowa GOP leaders, local Republican hot-shots and a chorus of Marycrest College singers. He paused to visit two Hungarian freedom fighters who had just adopted Davenport as a refuge, and his wife accepted a doll from them.

From the back of the pickup, Nixon shifted gears into his favorite campaign theme, an attack on Kennedy's claim that the country had lost its prestige and power.

The Friday night crowd was big, and there were curbsides of admirers and arches of signs along the streets as Nixon's motorcade headed to downtown Davenport and reception lines at the Blackhawk Hotel.

The vice president, whose face had the omnipresent look of needing a shave, was nearly outshone by Pat. "She wore a smile that never faded," wrote Alice Nauman, part of the husband-wife team covering the Nixons' arrival.

It was an exhausting finale to a long day of politicking. The Nixons retired to Suite 412, and he asked for room service. Bob Mulvihill, then assistant hotel manger, recalls that Nixon wanted only a small steak sandwich, a salad and a milk shake.

"He shook hands when I brought the meal, and said nothing else I remember. Pat Nixon was not visible, and did not order anything."

Suite 412 was renamed the Nixon Suite, with the name on the door. But it was painted over after he resigned the presidency.

Nixon returned in November 1968, speaking at Wharton Field House, Moline. In that campaign, against Hubert Humphrey and George Wallace, he won the prize that had eluded him for so long.

A perspiring Jimmy Carter shook hands, as expected of a candidate, after doing the unexpected — he left the steamboat Delta Queen at the LeClaire locks to jog with Secret Service agents.

"If I'm elected ... I hope people will say, 'You know Jimmy Carter made a lot of mistakes, but he never told me a lie.'"
— Jimmy Carter, in an interview with Bill Moyers, 1976

JIMMY CARTER
Running on the river

Ho-o-o-o-t. Steamboat 'round the bend. President Carter was around the bend, too. It was an unlikely but nostalgic way to campaign. Carter paddle-wheeled along this part of the Mississippi aboard the sternwheeler Delta Queen. On a misty August morning in 1979, the Delta Queen stopped its big red paddlewheel and tied up before breakfast at Lock and Dam 14, LeClaire, Iowa.

Carter bounded off the old steamboat's landing stage in the company of a couple of athletic Secret Service agents. The president jogged on the lock's walkways and greens, waving to admirers.

Campaigning is no easy back-slapping trick. Jogging was the easiest part of his day in this bend of the river.

"It was an energy-draining day," commented the *Quad-City Times*. He worked the crowd waiting for him at Oneida Landing in Davenport, and Rosalynn Carter and daughter, Amy, made friends.

Later in the day, Amy had her picture taken on a John Deere garden tractor and Carter — the one-time peanut farmer — acted quite at home posing on a piece of farm equipment during a reception at the Deere Administrative Center in Moline.

One of Carter's biggest opportunities for pressing palms was a backyard reception for 130 folks at the Davenport home of Lynne and Mary Ellen Chamberlin. Mary Ellen, a card-carrying Democrat, had been a longtime friend of Carter.

Later, looking tired and sunburned from the five hours spent ashore, the president seemed content to lean on a railing and chat with crew members on the ship's bridge as the steamboat hooted the traditional two long shoving-off blasts and headed to mid-river. Carter obliged that the weather looked good downstream, but he found himself getting soaked while addressing a riverfront crowd in Muscatine at 9:15 that night.

It was the first time, and perhaps the last, that a U.S. president has campaigned in our towns from the decks of a steamboat.

"I've often wondered how some people in positions of this kind ... manage without having had any acting experience."

— Ronald Reagan, in an interview with Barbara Walters, 1986

RONALD REAGAN
You CAN return home again

It was a red, white and blue opportunity for Ronald Reagan to come back home for the first time since becoming president. The trip was brief — just two hours and 15 minutes — on a blazing hot July day in 1988, and Reagan was, as always, the witty charmer.

"I can't tell you what this day means to me," he said, speaking for 20 minutes at Davenport's Palmer Auditorium, mixing anecdotes, jokes, one-liners and, in a serious mood, promising drought aid to farmers.

Coming home meant coming back to the community that gave him his start in show business, as an announcer on WOC radio.

Reagan looked so young, though 77 at the time, on this sentimental journey. Riefe's Restaurant served only right wings of chicken, and the right-side of the breasts at the luncheon. The red, white and blue tablecloths were borrowed from the Rock Island Arsenal, and Reagan stood to applaud when the U.S. Army Band from Fort Sheridan, Illinois, played, "This Is My Country."

It was a democratic event, with all the heavy-hitters from the Republican Party standing and sweating in line with common folks to get inside the door. It was a long wait, because Secret Service agents were working the crowd, warning that luncheon-goers would be checked for things like scissors or knives or worse.

Mark Minnick, on the air with President Reagan. Minnick had 10 minutes with Reagan at the station where the president began his career. Minnick said he was a good broadcaster, "very delightful to talk with."

President Reagan with a picture of himself as a broadcaster on WOC. He said it must be trick photography, that he never looked that young.

The event was so tightly orchestrated that Bob Mast, in charge of Palmer Auditorium, said he had reset the chairs at least a dozen times in the few days preceding Reagan's visit.

Everyone was up and down to get a good look at Reagan. He wore a light tan suit, and never stopped beaming.

"If I stretch anymore to see him, I'll need a chiropractor," said Bernie Goldstein, chief of Alter Co.

Reagan's speech was interrupted four times by applause from the 1,400 Quad-Citians who jammed the auditorium. The luncheon attracted 270 international, national, regional and local reporters and photographers.

"It was one of the biggest press turnouts in recent years," a White House staff member said.

During all the folderol, Reagan returned to face the microphones of his old employer, WOC. It was not in the old digs atop Davenport's Brady Hill, but in the new building that housed Signal Hill Communications. Reagan officially dedicated the building, surrounded by old props as he went down radio's memory lane, recalling when he was paid $5 to cover a game in the 1930s.

He was shown a photo of himself in a topcoat and fedora, behind a vintage WOC microphone.

"It's a photographic trick. I was never that young," he cracked.

Reagan had been in and out of the Quad-City region in the years between his radio days and his residency at 1600 Pennsylvania Avenue. There are photos of him from his acting stint in the '50s on TV's "Death Valley Days," as he stumped for the program's sponsor, General Electric, at places like the company's Morrison, Illinois, plant.

As president, though, the delight genuinely beamed in his ruddy face to be back in Davenport.

Repeatedly, he kept saying, "God bless you all."

George Bush during one of his Quad-City visits. This, in 1986, at Davenport Rotary.

"If you really want to make a difference, whether it's in helping other people, or whether it's in fighting for your country, or whether it's in the political arena, or journalism, or physics, you've got to persevere … you've got to be guided by certain principles and stay the course."

— George Bush, 1995

GEORGE BUSH
Campaigning for others and self

The first time George Bush came to the Quad-Cities, it was to help others win votes. After that, it was to win them for himself. In 1986, then-Vice President Bush was in town to tout fellow members of the GOP tribe. He paused that October afternoon, after a chock-full day of glad-handing, for a change to running shorts in his limo, then relaxed by doing a fast eight around

Davenport's Brady Street athletic field.

Earlier in the day, when Bush was speaking at a Davenport Rotary Club luncheon, U.S. Sen. Robert Dole, the Kansas Republican, stopped by, too, to throw his political weight around.

All the big politicos were out and about that day. U.S. Sen. Edward Kennedy was in Davenport for his compatriots. In Illinois, U.S. Rep. Bill Gray, a Pennsylvania Democrat, was in the 17th District to boost Lane Evans, seeking his third term in the U.S. House. Iowa Gov. Terry Branstad was visiting a Davenport food pantry, politicking amid the cans of tomatoes and packages of Kraft Dinner.

Bush admitted to the listening Rotarians, who were of a Republican bent, that he knew some people were hurting, and hurting bad in that year of 1986. "But a lot is right in America, and the economic woes in such states as Iowa just make us all the more committed to finishing the job that we were elected to do."

In 1987, a couple of days before he tossed his hat into the presidential ring, Bush strolled the streets of Bettendorf, promising to out-hustle other Republican candidates in the Iowa caucuses of February 1988. He began on Holmes Street, and was greeted by William Glynn, the mayor, who happened to be a Democrat but wore a "Bush '88" button.

His pre-caucus visit to the *Quad-City Times* in January 1988 is remembered by reporters and photographers who found themselves in an unusual position — on the other side of the story. While Bush was being cornered by the newspaper's editorial board, staffers were not allowed to visit the rest rooms, for security reasons.

As vice president, Bush worked the Quad-Cities a number of times, boosting Republican Congressional candidates in 1986 and on his own behalf in 1988 for the presidency. In 1988, when he spoke at Assumption High School, Davenport, students gave him a school sweatshirt.

"America's greatness can be found not only in its large centers of wealth and culture and power, but also in its small towns, where children learn from their families and neighbors the rhythms and rituals of daily life. They learn about home and work, about love and loss, about success and failure, about endurance and the power and dignity of their dreams."

— Bill Clinton, 1999

BILL CLINTON
On the road, again and again

First time: On a hot and hectic night in August 1992, candidate Bill Clinton kicks the wheels of a big bus and with a Clinton-esque grin says, "We're on the road again."

Second time: Still roaming the hustings, Clinton returns to the Quad-Cities on Halloween 1992, nibbles on treats in the Village of East Davenport and stumps to win.

Third time: As president, he is on a mercy mission of sorts to see firsthand the devastation of the Great Flood of 1993.

"Forward with Clinton." He won the backing of many ethnic groups during campaign rallies in the Quad-Cities.

That first visit was a hootenanny. He'd been busing and campaigning all day with his vice presidential candidate, Al Gore, and Hillary and Tipper, rolling toward the Quad-Cities. Fifteen-thousand heard him in Burlington, Iowa, and clusters of supporters stood along dark U.S. 61 to see the Clinton caravan as it threaded its way north. Bus lights blinked to show appreciation.

Final stop was Bettendorf, but the caravan didn't arrive until after midnight at Jumer's Castle Lodge. Up to 2,000 were waiting, some perched in trees around the lodge. He was shocked that so many were on hand so late. He launched into a 40-minute rally on the spot.

"Shoot, folks," he laughed. "I didn't want to have a rally this late at night, so we showed up late enough to start it in the morning. I feel right at home here. That crowd in Washington, they think they own the White House. Their deal doesn't work. Let's try our put-people-first approach."

That next visit, on Halloween 1992, candidate Clinton was alone. "No Gore, no Tipper, no Hillary," a Secret Service agent said.

Clinton spent more than an hour in the Village of East Davenport. "There's no secret why he's here," said John Gianulus, Rock Island County Democratic Party chairman.

"This is a major media market. He's out to win. That's why he's here."

Clinton was sniffling during that October visit, bothered by seasonal spores that irritated his autumn allergies, and Barbara Lykam, a nurse, was rushed to the airport to give him an allergy shot. She was active in the Democratic Party, and it made sense they'd call a Democrat, not a Republican.

She said, "When I give you the shot, don't say ouch." He didn't.

By July 4, 1993, Bill Clinton was comfortable in the presidency but the Quad-City region was miserably awash in floodwaters. The president was so deeply concerned about the renegade flood that he spent four hours and 15 minutes of a drizzly day in city and country. Along rural roads, he saw swamped fields and low pastures that had turned into lakes big enough to stock with crappies. At the farm of Don and Elaine Schneckloth, he sat on bales of hay in a tent and visited with farmers and their families. They had a good chance to get a lot of things off their chest.

The Iowans were appreciative. Glen Keppy stood and said, "Thanks, Mr. President, for caring."

In 1992, Clinton was alone, campaigning in the Village of East Davenport. A Secret Service agent said, "No Gore, no Tipper, no Hillary."

3 times we mourned

Americans never have elected a president by acclamation. And no president ever has been universally popular. When he acts, when he speaks, for every cheering citizen, there are others who curse what he has done.

But one tragic moment unites all of us — when a president dies in office. Partisanship gives way to shock, then grief, then prayers for the vice presidents who, without warning, are handed the reins of the most important corporation in the world: leadership of the United States of America.

That has happened three times since the century turned. Two presidents — William McKinley and John F. Kennedy — died at the hands of assassins. Franklin Delano Roosevelt was worn out by shepherding the nation through the end of the Depression and, although he did not live to see the final act, the tragedies and triumphs of World War II.

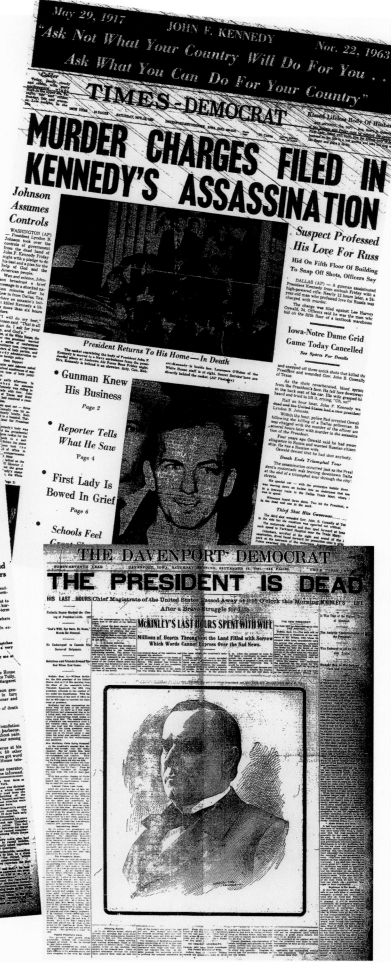

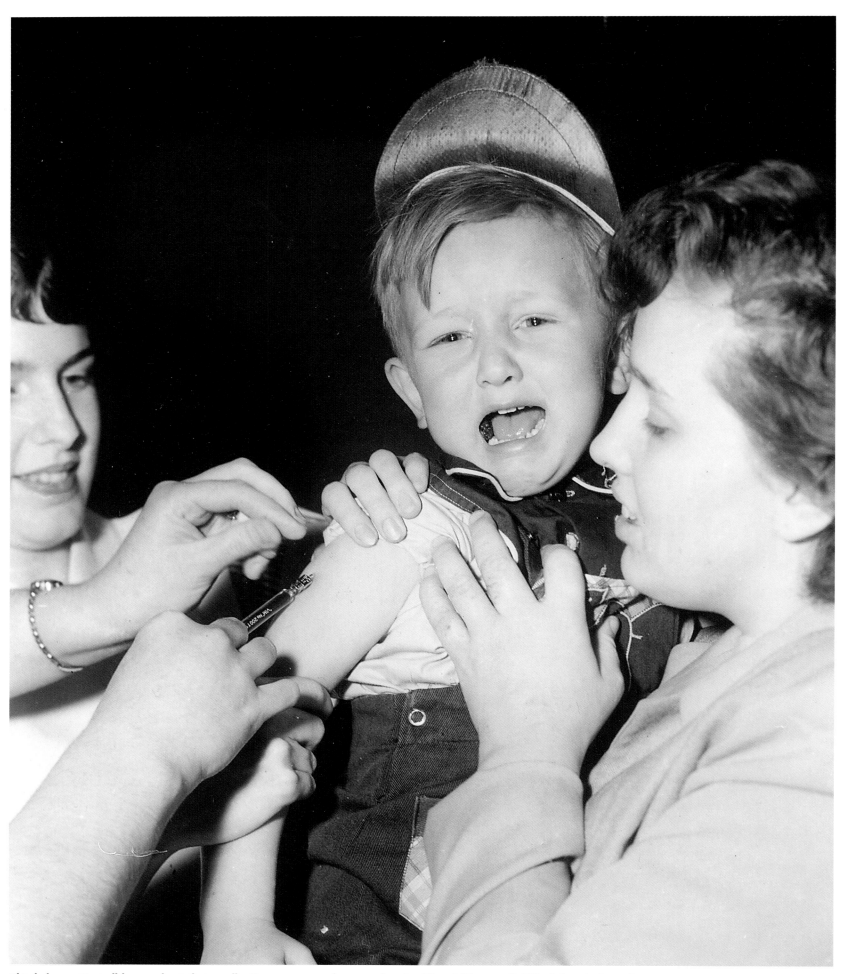

This lad wasn't at all happy about that needle. He was among the more than 1 million children — 3,400 of them in Scott County alone — who took part in nationwide tests of the Salk polio vaccine. Polio was the worst scourge of the 1950s. The Salk vaccine was approved for use April 12, 1955; ultimately, polio shots were replaced by an oral vaccine.

Say ah-h-h-h

"All interest in disease and death is only another expression of interest in life."
— Thomas Mann

chapter twenty-one

In Sickness and In Health

We're lucky. We bellyache today about HMOs and short hospital stays, but we've conquered — or at least quieted — some pretty major bugs in the past century.

Not so long ago, the flu could be so deadly that you didn't go to a movie without wearing a 2-cent gauze mask. Tuberculosis forced people to spend years in sanitariums. Those who survived polio were encapsulated in iron lungs or leg braces.

Del Riefe, a Davenport restaurateur, agonized with polio in Isolation Hospital before his full recovery. "My kids stood outside on the sidewalk and waved at me, and then I would cry like hell."

Today, we have antibiotics and an arsenal of over-the-counter drugs at our disposal — something that wasn't the case in 1918, when influenza virtually closed down the Tri-Cities, infected 7,500 people and resulted in at least 2,000 flu-related deaths.

It was the most virulent epidemic ever to hit the area.

"All theaters, moving picture houses, churches and dance halls will be closed at once," a city-wide quarantine order for Davenport read. "There shall be no social gatherings, conventions or lodge meetings." Attendance at funerals was restricted to members of the family.

In Davenport, no beds were left at Mercy and St. Luke's hospitals so a flu hospital for 300 patients was formed in the vast Central Turner Hall. The less-afflicted were propped into blanketed seats of the adjoining Grand Opera House theater.

In the days before sneezing-coughing-aching-stuffy-head-fever medicines, Davenport's Dr. John Sunderbruch remembers how his Grandma Kelly had him swallow a turpentine rag to clear his throat passages. (A string was attached so the rag could be pulled back up.)

Later, the most dreaded scourge of its time — polio — would strike fear in Tri-Citians. Those who were nurses in the late 1940s and early 1950s recall the Kenny hot packs and muscle re-education treatments.

"We had 2½ floors of polio patients. Most were in high iron lungs, which made terrible swooshing noises," remembered Joyce Pease Taylor, who graduated from Moline Public Hospital's nursing school in 1947.

"For patients with paralysis of the limbs, we spent the mornings packing them in hot packs — boiling large cloths in huge tubes of water, putting them through wringers, wrapping them in rubber and getting them to the patient as quickly as possible. By

Grim headlines before Christmas told the panic of the flu epidemic of 1918.

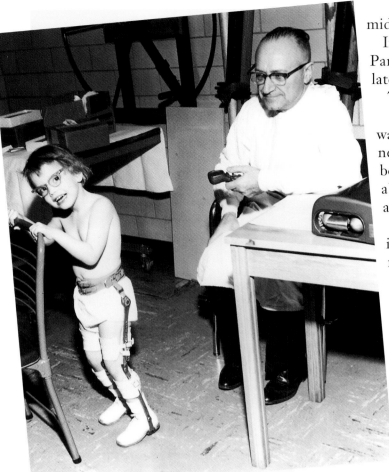

Dr. Leo Miltner, Bettendorf, with a young patient at the Visiting Nurse Association in the early 1950s.

mid-morning, your nurse's cap was limp and corners were dangling."

In 1955, a vaccine created by Dr. Jonas Salk was licensed for general use. Parents lined up at clinics and doctors' offices to get their children inoculated.

There have been other improvements, too.

Before the days of sophisticated anesthesia and disposable needles, ether was administered through a cloth-covered cone and nurses had to re-sharpen needles and remove burrs from them. In the 1930s, mothers with newborns stayed in the hospital 10 days after delivery, forced to wear breast and abdominal binders. Today, some mothers leave the hospital only hours after giving birth.

These days, there is open-heart surgery that has us out of the hospital in just three days. Cancer no longer is an automatic death sentence. And more often than not, there is outpatient surgery that does not even necessitate an overnight stay in the hospital.

Even something as simple as air conditioning helps cool our illnesses.

Nurse Leota Belford DeGreve of Moline recalled the impact of the summer of 1936, when the Tri-Cities saw 11 straight days with temperatures reaching 100 degrees or more.

"Overheated patients came to us, their temperatures at the top of the thermometer. We rubbed them down with ice cakes, placed them in bath tubs with ice water and even put one man on the front porch and turned the hose on him. We lost about 50 percent of them."

Yes, we've come a long way.

— Linda Barlow

No relief in sight

"My son was born in the heat wave of 1936 at old St. Luke's Hospital, Davenport. It was HOT. No air conditioning, even in the nursery. Every day, the paper boy went up and down the hall shouting, 'No relief in sight.' In those days, we had to stay in bed 10 days after delivery, and in spite of the terrible heat, we were on rubber sheets. I begged the nurse to remove the rubber sheet; after enough begging, she finally did. What a relief. Can you imagine rubber sheets."

— Lilah Bell, Bettendorf

When we feared to walk the streets

Before the mid-1940s, folks with contagious diseases had two equally miserable options. They could go to a place like the three-story Davenport Pest House or stay locked up in their homes with a big "quarantine" sign tacked on the door.

Dr. John Sunderbruch was a young physician, outraged that Scott County provided such primitive care for the contagious. He lobbied to build an isolation hospital. "Anyone could see we needed such a hospital," he says. "In 1939, we had 92 smallpox cases."

Isolation Hospital opened on Marquette Street none too soon. In one post-war year, when Jonas Salk still was working on a polio vaccine, Scott County had 54 polio cases. Rock Island County had 30.

A consultation between nurse, patient and physician at the former Moline Public Hospital.

Mabel Walker was one of a troop of Visiting Nurses who delivered health care to Davenport homes in the 1920s.

"There was such a fear of contagion that the wading pool at Vander Veer Park was closed," says Beth Fox, whose polio case was so severe that she was given last rites by a young priest, the Rev. James Conroy. It was the first such rite he had ever performed, and returning to the rectory, it was feared he would spread polio germs.

"I was so paralyzed that I could not even swallow Jell-O," Fox says.

"They took me to Iowa City in a McGinnis Funeral Home hearse; they must have been pretty sure I wasn't going to make it."

Laughter: The best medicine

Most of the Tri-Cities was shuttered in a hush of panic during the influenza epidemic of 1918 when the daily flu tally was grimly listed, like ball scores, in the newspapers. Almost everything was locked up.

But there still was room for humor ...

George Sheets, a reporter for the old *Democrat & Leader*, wrote: "Pool halls are to be closed during the epidemic, but one in Davenport secretly opened last night. A few fellows were lounging around when one of them sneezed. There was quick action. Those chaps who did not succeed in diving under the billiard tables to get out of the line of germs catapulted themselves out the door. One chap ran all the way to Rock Island."

Nursing memories

"Three-bed rooms were $2 a day and private rooms were $7.50. We wondered how anyone could afford that."

— **Joyce Pease Taylor, a nurse at the former Moline Public Hospital, Class of '47**

Moline Public Hospital School of Nursing: Class of 1902.

The Rock Island County Tuberculosis Sanitarium, in Rock Island, provided residential care for patients.

As the Tri-Cities grew, so did the demand for health care providers. This classroom at the former Mercy Hospital, Davenport, was a sea of starched white in the 1950s.

At one of the premier community events of summer, the starting gun sounded July 31, 1999, for the 25th annual *Quad-City Times Bix 7.* The seven-mile trek through the streets and neighborhoods of Davenport has grown 20,000 times the dreams of those who took the first Bix challenge in 1975. There was no starting gun for the first Bix — and no official race T-shirt.

chapter twenty-two

Our Age of Sports Heroes

"Outlined against a blue-gray October sky, the Four Horsemen rode again. In dramatic lore they were known as Famine, Pestilence, Destruction and Death. These are only aliases. Their real names are Stuhldreher, Miller, Crowley and Layden."
— Grantland Rice, writing about Notre Dame's football victory over Army, in the *New York Tribune*, October 18, 1924
(One of the fabled "horsemen" was Elmer Layden of Davenport)

This was the heroic age of sports in the Quad-Cities. Headline a legendary sports figure of the 20th century, and chances are he or she passed through here at one time or another.

Michael Jordan played in an NBA preseason game at The Mark of the Quad-Cities, 10 years after playing golf in the Quad-City Classic pro-am.

Babe Ruth came here a number of times during his barnstorming tours of the 1920s and '30s, hammering home runs into the Mississippi River from the Davenport stadium (now John O'Donnell) and banging them atop Wharton Field House, Moline.

Red Grange played for the New York Yankees football team against the Rock Island Independents in a 1926 American

Babe Ruth remained a hero after retirement, barnstorming many times in the Tri-Cities.

Football League game at Moline's Browning Field.

George Halas brought the Chicago Bears to Rock Island's Douglas Park to play the Independents on seven occasions. His brother, Walter, was basketball coach at Davenport High School.

Jack Nicklaus gave a golf clinic at Oakwood Country Club in 1985 and Sam Snead, Ben Hogan, Arnold Palmer, Greg Norman and Tiger Woods all have played here, either in the Quad-City Open or the Western Open, which was held at Davenport Country Club in 1936 and 1951.

Walter Payton, Pete Rose, Julius Erving, Ernie Banks and Bobby Hull all have made multiple personal appearances in the area.

Some of the legends have stayed a little longer than others.

Jim Thorpe, voted the premier athlete of the first half of the 20th century, spent an entire football season here, playing for the Independents in 1924. He was 37 years old and far past his prime, but reports of his first workout with the Indees at Douglas Park described how he punted the ball 65 yards and drop-kicked a few 50-yard field goals that landed in the yard of a nearby fire station.

Before Red Auerbach built the Boston Celtics into the greatest dynasty in pro basketball history, he spent the 1949-50 season coaching the Tri-City Blackhawks, an early entry in the National Basketball Association.

Red Grange played against the Rock Island Independents in a 1926 NFL game.

Bill Rodgers and Joan Benoit Samuelson, generally regarded as the greatest male and female distance runners in American history, ran the *Quad-City Times Bix* 7 so often and became so popular here that a statue was erected of them.

Heisman Trophy winner John Lujack settled in the Quad-Cities in the middle 1950s after becoming a national hero as a quarterback at Notre Dame and with the Chicago Bears.

The area has given birth to some fairly legendary figures of its own.

Rock Island native Iron Man Joe McGinnity became famous for pitching — and winning both ends of double-headers — in helping the New York Giants to the 1903 National League pennant. He won 31 games in 1903, 35 in 1904, and 247 over a 10-year career.

Davenport's Elmer Layden was one of the famed Four Horsemen of Notre Dame and scored three touchdowns in the 1925 Rose Bowl, two of them on interception returns of more than 70 yards. He later succeeded Knute Rockne as the head coach at Notre Dame and eventually became

The greatest distance runners of all times, Bill Rodgers and Joan Benoit Samuelson, became Bix 7 regulars.

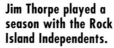

Jim Thorpe played a season with the Rock Island Independents.

Davenport's Roger Craig went on to play college football at Nebraska and professionally for the San Francisco 49ers.

commissioner of the National Football League.

Roger Craig of Davenport scored three touchdowns in the 1985 Super Bowl and the following season became the only man in NFL history to gain more than 1,000 yards rushing and receiving in the same season.

Don Nelson, Rock Island, and Steve Kuberski, Moline, were part of the Boston Celtics dynasty of the 1950s, '60s and '70s.

Michael Nunn, Davenport, won two middleweight boxing world championships.

Davenport's Jack Fleck out-Hoganed Ben Hogan in an 18-hole playoff to win the 1955 U.S. Open golf title.

Muscatine's Mike Berlin won the Pro Bowlers Association title in 1976.

Moline's George Magerkurth was the home plate umpire the day Ruth hit his

George Halas brought his Chicago Bears to play in Rock Island seven times.

Ken Anderson: Pride of Augustana

Roger Craig is not the only modern-day candidate for the Pro Football Hall of Fame spawned by the Quad-Cities.

In 1967, the freshman class at Augustana College included one Ken Anderson, who came to Rock Island from Batavia, Illinois, unsure whether his best sport was basketball or football.

And although Anderson scored more than 1,000 points in three seasons as a varsity basketball player, it quickly became apparent that his future was in football.

He led the Vikings to the College Conference of Illinois and Wisconsin championship in his sophomore year (1968) and ended up setting 15 school records. He passed for 6,131 yards in four years, nearly twice the number of any other quarterback in Augie history.

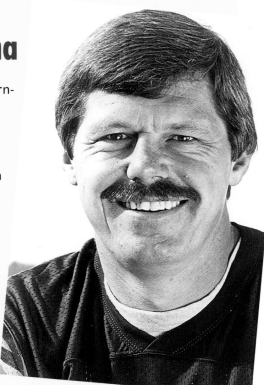

Ken Anderson arrived at Augustana College planning to play both basketball and football. He left for a job in the National Football League as quarterback of the Cincinnati Bengals.

Although players from Division III schools seldom attract any attention from pro scouts, he was a third-round draft choice of the Cincinnati Bengals in 1971. Within a year he was the team's starting QB. He held the job for 13 years, finally retiring after the 1986 season.

He was the NFL's Most Valuable Player in 1981, when he set the Bengals' record for passing efficiency and led the team to the Super Bowl for the first time. He completed an amazing 70.6 percent of his passes the following season. He played in the Pro Bowl four times and remains Cincinnati's career leader in passing yardage (32,838) and touchdowns (197).

Since 1993, he has served as a member of the Bengals' coaching staff.

Anderson is one of several pro football players to come out of Quad-City colleges.

A few St. Ambrose and Augustana players, including powerful center Louie Kolls, played for the Rock Island Independents in the early days of the NFL. Forrest Cotton served as the head coach at St. Ambrose while also playing for the Independents.

St. Ambrose lineman Art Michalik played for the San Francisco 49ers and Pittsburgh Steelers for five years in the 1950s before going into professional wrestling.

Another St. Ambrose alum, Bob Webb, played briefly with the Oakland Raiders in the early 1960s and an Augustana star of the mid 1930s, George "Chili" Lenc, spent one season with the Chicago Bears.

Heisman Trophy winner John Lujack became a Quad-City businessman.

The Four Horsemen of Notre Dame: Davenport's Elmer Layden is second from left.

Red Auerbach coached the 1949-1950 season of the Tri-City Blackhawks, an early entry in the National Basketball Association.

"Iron Man" Joe McGinnity, Rock Island, won both ends of a double-header to help the New York Giants win a National League pennant.

famous "called shot" home run at Wrigley Field.

Warren Giles of Moline became president of baseball's National League.

Pro baseball player (Cubs and Pirates) Gene Baker and wrestler Simon Roberts of Davenport and football great Duke Slater of Clinton all helped blaze paths for African-American athletes in their respective sports.

Throughout the 20th century, the Quad-Cities has been marked by team success at all levels.

Davenport High School — now Davenport Central — has won 40 state high school championships in various sports. Boy teams once made it to the basketball state championship game six years in a row.

Our area high schools have won nearly 300 state team championships in more than two dozen sports in two states.

Augustana College in Rock Island won four consecutive Division III national championships in football from 1983 through 1986.

More recently, the Quad-Cities has become a minor league sports hub. The hockey Mallards, basketball Thunder and baseball River Bandits all won multiple championships in the final decade of the century.

— **Don Doxsie**

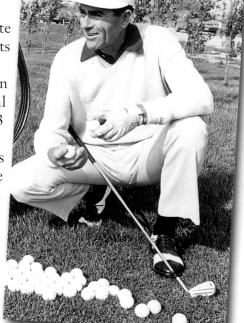

Jack Fleck, Davenport, out-Hoganed Ben Hogan to win the 1955 U.S. Open.

When Iowa and Northwestern met on the gridiron in Rock Island

Large sporting events attracting thousands of spectators have become commonplace in the Quad-Cities.

But at the dawn of the 20th century, they were something new.

So when the football teams from the University of Iowa and Northwestern University played one another on Thanksgiving Day 1900 in Rock Island, it sent ripples of excitement through the Tri-Cities.

There were front-page stories in all the newspapers for several days beforehand. New bleachers to accommodate 3,300 people were constructed at what now is known as Douglas Park, giving the place a seating capacity of 4,628.

Special trains were set up to bring fans from Iowa City for the game. Extra streetcars were arranged along the Watchtower line in Rock Island since carriages were not allowed on the grounds. Members of the Rock Island, Moline and Davenport high school teams were recruited to serve as ushers. Reserved seat tickets for $1.50 and general admission tickets for $1 were sold at W.H. Fluke's wallpaper store in Davenport.

"There is every indication that the contest will attract one of the largest crowds that either team has played before thus far this season," the *Davenport Daily Times* reported.

It was no idle boast. An overflow crowd of between 5,000 and 6,000 turned out for the game, which was played in unseasonably warm conditions. Precisely why the game was played in Rock Island never was explained in the newspaper or in the program.

The rules of football were slightly different then. The field was the same size, but each half was 35 minutes in length and teams were required to gain only five yards to get a first down. Touchdowns were worth five points. So were field goals, whether they were booted off the ground or with a drop kick.

There was almost no passing, lots of punting, and very little scoring.

The big game was to take place at 2:30 p.m. sharp — newspaper stories on the days leading up to the game emphasized this — but the Iowa team didn't even arrive until 2:40. The *Times* reported the players took the field with a dog serving as their mascot "and the crowd cheered vociferously."

Iowa, which was 7-0 entering the game, was expected to win easily but struggled to hold off a Northwestern club that finished with a 6-2-3 record.

Iowa took a 5-0 lead late in the first half when right end Morey Eby scooped up a fumble by Northwestern captain C.E. Dietz and ran 45 yards for a touchdown.

"The crowd then broke loose with yells of every description and immediately Northwestern seemed to put more 'ginger' in the playing," the *Times* reported.

Northwestern tied the score in the middle of the second half on a field goal by halfback Alton Johnson.

And that's the way it ended, in a 5-5 tie.

A rare program from the game survives to this day, owned by Don Challed, Davenport. It is in the shape of a football with a heavy leather-type cover. The pages have become jaundiced with time, but still are very readable.

Included are photos of the Iowa squad, the starting line-ups, profiles of the Iowa players, Iowa yells and "a description of football ... for persons unacquainted with the game."

— **Don Doxsie**

A time-worn souvenir of the 1900 Thanksgiving Day football matchup between the University of Iowa and Northwestern, played at Douglas Park in Rock Island: the official leatherbound program.

Monkey Island

Monkey me, monkey you, monkey see, monkey do.
Monkey on the left, monkey on the right.
Monkey in the middle, monkey out of sight.
Monkey up a tree, monkey on the ground,
Monkeys in a bunch, monkeying around.

— From *Monkey See, Monkey Do,* by Marc Chase,
a beginning-to-read picture book for children

Pictures from our past

Time it was and what a time it was
It was …
A time of innocence
A time of confidences
Long ago it must be
I have a photograph; Preserve your memories
They're all that's left you

— "Old Friends," Paul Simon and Art Garfunkel

chapter twenty-three

When We Were Young

Memory compresses time. The Great Flood of '65 seems but a blink ago. In truth, it has been nearly 35 springs since the Mississippi River came creeping into our then-thriving downtowns.

Ah, downtowns … what a rush of memories that word uncorks. Genevieve Rafferty, Rock Island, still savors the taste of the chocolate Cokes she drank on Saturday afternoons at Walgreens in downtown Davenport. Wayne Fields, St. Louis, recalls the sense of adventure he felt riding the city bus to downtown Rock Island for Saturday movie matinees at the Fort or Rocket.

Downtowns trip the memory trigger. So do thoughts of the old neighborhood.

It has been decades since John Bloomberg left the neighborhood of his childhood. But from his home in Ohio, his memory wanders back to summer afternoons spent playing baseball on a makeshift diamond at Rock Island High School. Chris Neely, now living in Texas, still sniffs the aroma of licorice being made at Brach's mingling with the yeasty bouquet of the Wonder Bread bakery as he and his mom ran errands around Davenport.

Memories are made of such moments, mundane at the time and sweet in retrospect. A special pet, a precious doll. A summer night, a Christmas morning. A baseball smacked out of the infield, a boat ride on the river.

Roving photographers would walk from house to house with a pony, offering to take photos of children sitting on the little Shetland. The price was minimal, maybe 50 cents. This, in 1923, of Charlotte and Jean Krick; now Charlotte Shear of Arlington, Virginia, and Jean Franck, of Rock Island. The photo was taken outside the Krick home, 2019 Ninth Avenue, Rock Island.

Ask Kristine Jensen what she recalls of her long-ago girlhood, and it's not the big milestones of a young life. It's the springs and summers and autumns spent playing with friends in a tree-filled, lush-lawned, safe Rock Island neighborhood. "I'll never be able to let my children have the freedom I had," the suburban Chicago mother of two toddlers laments.

When we were young, no matter how old we are now, the corner of the world we call, alternately, the Tri-City or Quad-City region was a wonderous place. That's what the photographs and words on the pages that follow tell us.

Saturday night at the movies

I was born and raised in Rock Island on Ninth Street between Sixth and Seventh avenues, which was a small business district. In 1921, my parents bought out a meat market at 616 Ninth Street from a man known as Pete the Hollander. It became Van Puyvelde's Market. We lived next door in an old brick house at 618 that was attached to the store, which must have been built when Ninth Street was called Commerce Street.

I was born in that house in 1922. Five years later, my parents bought the building next door, at 620, from the local rabbi. It had larger store space and a nice apartment upstairs. West of Ninth Street was a large Belgian settlement that had four Belgian taverns and the Belgian American Brotherhood. They were Saturday-night gathering places. I remember going to dances with my parents at the Brotherhood and watching them dance to the Belgian accordion band.

On Sunday morning after mass let out at St. Paul's Church, the Belgian church, many Belgians would stop at the store, and all you would hear spoken would be Flemish. Next door was the Rialto Theater. Whenever someone would visit to play cards, I would get a dime to go to the movie. I also was there every Saturday night when the stores were open until 10 o'clock. The Rialto was my sitter. On hot summer nights, the side exit doors were opened to let in the cool air. There was someone watching each exit, but somehow my dog, Merit, got by and walked

Pride in a new home and family, a Gothic scene near Maysville, in rural Scott County. Gustav and Amanda Schnoor Meyer, holding babies Alice and Grace. The house was built in 1868 and today is occupied by the fifth generation of the Meyer family.

When the Klan came to Davenport

When I was probably 8 to 10 years of age and my brother was a year or so younger, we went out one evening in Rockingham Township (Scott County) to attend a large gathering, a meeting of the Ku Klux Klan.

It was dark, of course. In the middle of the farm field was a boxing ring which was used as the stage. On the stage were a number of individuals wearing large white garments typical of the Klan of those days. My brother and I stood at the bottom of the ring and looked up. I recognized one individual and called up to him by name. He turned and saw me. It wasn't long thereafter that a couple of burly individuals ushered my brother and me off of the property.

I went home and told my folks about this. The individual happened to be in an organization of sales people with my father, and he visited our home quite regularly. After that night, he never visited our home again — period!

— Dr. John H. (Jack) Sunderbruch, Davenport

Grim reminders of racial discrimination: At left, an East Moline page from a 1921 city directory. The (c) following a name noted that the resident was colored. "Citizen 2nd Class" was a booklet about segregation, printed in the early 1950s. It noted that blacks living in Davenport had to go to Rock Island to get their hair cut and that racial segregation extended even to the grave. Only two of the five Davenport cemeteries would bury blacks, with restrictions; two refused black burials entirely.

across the stage during the movie and caused quite a stir. I can still see Barney Brotman chasing him off the stage.

I still like to drive by the old neighborhood on Ninth Street, now Martin Luther King Drive, and remember how it was with the neighborhood shopping community, and then past the old Belgian American Brotherhood. Looking back, it was a great time.

— **Albert Van Puyvelde, Moline**

Germans not welcome

During World War I, my 11-year-old brother, 6-year-old sister and I (age 9) attended a one-room country school. A Christmas program was being planned, which made the students happy.

Word got out and one parent complained that our family was of German descent. Consequently, we were not allowed to participate in the program.

The teacher was upset and the program was cancelled.

— **Gladys K. Bondi, Davenport**

The night the Coliseum burned down

On October 24, 1913 — a clear, cold evening — someone noticed the red glare straight east of us, toward downtown. My father and I and several neighbors began walking toward the fire, wondering which building could cause such a blaze. As we approached Fillmore Street, we realized it was the original Coliseum at Fourth and Myrtle streets. It was two stories tall, with a woodworking shop on the ground floor and a dance floor surrounded by seats reaching to the ceiling on the second floor.

The whole structure was wood, and there was a lot of wood dust and shavings from the shop on the ground floor. The second floor usually was decorated with tissue paper festoons and streamers. It made a tremendous blaze. Flames were shooting hundreds of feet into the air. It was impossible to save the building, so firemen were busy wetting down nearby buildings to save them.

By about 10 or 11 p.m., the whole building was a mass of embers. We arrived home about midnight and, as there was no radio or TV, my mother was worried about our delay.

It was not long thereafter when plans were announced for erection of the present Coliseum, across Fourth Street from the old building.

— **Arthur Buesing wrote this in 1963, on the 50th anniversary of the Coliseum fire**

Faith shared by mother, child

In the memories of my childhood, what comes to mind most often are the times when I was making novenas with my mother. A novena is a nine-day series of special prayers offered to God, Christ, Mary the mother of Jesus, or a particular saint for a cause of special favors.

Top photo: To lift the shantytown population of Rock Island, Susanne Denkmann Hauberg created what she called the West End Settlement, a vigorous program of housing and aid for the needy. It operated from 1909 to 1922.

Whispers, 1914: A charming old snapshot of Elvera and Louella Korthaus on the front porch of the Korthaus homestead east of Walcott, Iowa.

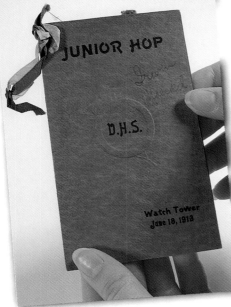

In the 1900s, "the girls" kept track of their dancing partners in little dance programs worn around the wrist. This is for the Davenport High Junior Hop at Watch Tower Inn. Among the songs played, "Yoo-Hoo, That's Me" and "You're My Blue-Eyed Baby."

Grace McDonald Elliott (in the big hat) and her sister, Harriett McDonald Jackson, dressed up and primped for a studio photograph when they lived in Davenport. "I never had curls like that," Harriett says. Where did they come from? Rags, used to twist and curl the hair.

When we were really young, modesty prevailed — even on a sultry summer afternoon on Credit Island beach. These bathers were covered from shoulder to knee, and note the not-too-becoming swim caps.

In the 1920s, my mother was a pretty, young widow, grieving over the sudden loss of her beloved, young husband — my father — who had died of a ruptured appendix. She had three children, and her goal in life was to take of her family, support her children, educate them so they would be prepared to take care of themselves. She wanted to be able to handle the heartbreak she had suffered, and was having a hard time understanding why it had happened. She didn't know that she had the Depression ahead.

My brother and sister were older than I and had other activities to keep them busy. I was her pal and companion until I was 16. She died when I was 17. In those 16 years, we went to novenas together all over the city of New Orleans, where we then lived.

Besides the novenas, which I still pray from time to time (and always think of my mother when I do), I had a companionship with her I might not have had.

— **Betty Rhomberg, Davenport**

Bernie and the home brew

I grew up in the 1930s on a farm just outside of Davenport, the baby in a family of 16. Mom and Dad went to town every Saturday for groceries and supplies, and left those of us who still were home on our own. We could almost set a clock by our parents' departure and return: they left at 9 a.m. and were always home at noon.

Dad was famous for his home brew. It was strong stuff! The delicious and forbidden brew was in the shed out in back, and off-limits to the children. But my brother Bernie was the daredevil of the bunch, good at getting all of us into trouble — and getting himself out of trouble.

One April morning Mom and Dad were in Davenport and my sisters and I were busy

Lois Moeller wears the polka-dot shorts in this photograph of a gymnastics routine learned at the Central Turner Hall.

An emphasis on physical training

My heritage was German on both my mother's and father's sides. I was born at 621 West Second Street, Davenport, above the grocery store only three blocks from the Central Turner Hall.

In a German family, when the children started school, they started gym classes. The Germans liked to get the children young and condition them to adulthood. Ages 6 to 9 took gymnastics classes — separately — each Saturday morning. Older groups had more classes.

I vividly remember, after school, walking down Harrison Street from J.B. Young Intermediate, then from Davenport High School to attend gym classes. Classes lasted 1½ to two hours and had a set routine:

1. We all lined up by height and came to attention (very important!).
2. Then we marched, toes down first.
3. Running.
4. Calisthentics or dance routine, dumbbells, Indian clubs or wands.
5. Apparatus, track and field, or tumbling.
6. A game (volleyball, basketball, baseball, etc.).

The charge for gym classes in the 1920s and '30s was $3 a year per child.

I graduated from high school in June 1932 — the height of the Depression — and a group of us would go to the Central Turner gymnasium two or three afternoons a week, before classes began, and work out on apparatus or practice field work, like high jumping. This was a good, healthy thing to do. It kept us out of trouble.

I kept going to gymnastics classes at the Central Turner Hall until I entered public accounting at age 29, and we worked many a night.

A routine such as this — shoulder stands on the parallel — was not an exception. It was expected of us in our teens, through gradual conditioning.

— **Lois Moeller Holzinger, Davenport**

A Christmas parade in downtown Davenport, and sisters Jacqueline, left, and Janet Murphy were curbside to await Santa's arrival. The year was 1937, and Janet Willetts of Aledo, Illinois, smiles to recall the matching outfits — from caps to leggings to muffs — that she and her sister wore that day.

with housework. We didn't know that Bernie had made a bee-line for the shed. I was outside beating a rug on the line when I looked up and there he was, staggering from the shed. It was close to 11 a.m.; Mom and Dad would be home within the hour. What to do?

Our property had creeks to the north and south. We grabbed Bernie and hustled him to the north creek, which has more water. We pushed and — plop! — Bernie was in the water. He got up about three times, and back we pushed. Finally, he yelled that he was OK and we started back to the house. We got him into dry clothes before Mom and Dad pulled up.

It wasn't often that they could afford to buy treats, but that day they came back with a bag of the candy suckers we all loved. Bernie knew the price of our silence: We got his share of the suckers.

— Vera Guy, Davenport

The place to be

Downtown Davenport in the '30s and early '40s was THE place to be. I came to Davenport for a month each summer to visit my father's family. It was a magic time for me.

I worked at Scharff's for two weeks during my freshman year at Marycrest College. I was a member of the "college board," working in the dress department. I was fired because I told a young woman that the dress on which she was planning to spend $8 of her savings was not the only one like it in her size.

At Second and Main streets was a big Walgreens with a soda fountain and several large, round tables. Many a Saturday I spent all afternoon at one of those tables, with other students from Marycrest and St. Ambrose, nursing a chocolate Coke while securing a date for Saturday night.

Davenport was a small, intimate town, as I saw it then, in the '20s,

Youngsters read books such as "The Red Runners" by a fictitious character named "Seckatary Hawkins." The character starred in a comic strip in the Daily Times, and books such as this were offered as prizes in newspaper contests.

The Nelson Five on their way to a performance.

The Nelson Five — a family of singers

There was little money to spare in the years of the Great Depression, but my mother and father, who were from Sweden, both were musical and they wanted their five children to share that pleasure. So every week, we traveled from our farm near Cambridge, Illinois, to Moline, where we took music lessons from Albert Bellson, father of the great drummer Louis Bellson. I don't know where the money came from for the instruments. But our family group became known as the Nelson Five, and we had quite a following. We played at churches, schools, everywhere we were invited; hymns, popular songs — a full hour of entertainment. We got so well-known that we were on the radio quite often, even on the WLS "National Barn Dance." We were about to get our big opportunity — performing on "Major Bowes Amateur Hour," but World War II broke out, and there were more important matters to attend to.

— Glenn Nelson, Davenport

Snapshot reminiscences of happy days in 1920 with the Noens family of Rock Island. A boat with a motor would pull the one without power down the Mississippi River to Andalusia Slough. A farmer would pick them up, drive all 11 of them to his house, feed them a Sunday dinner. They would return upriver to Rock Island by dark. What a wonderful way to spend a Sunday afternoon.

'30s and into the '40s. My aunt (who worked for attorney Clark Hall in the Union Arcade building) called me one evening in the '60s to report on her day, and she lamented that when she had gone out for lunch and walked around downtown, she hadn't seen one person she knew. Times were changing.

— **Genevieve Rafferty, Rock Island**

Sunday afternoon at the farm

In the mid 1940s, after World War II, our family would drive out to rural Belle Plain, Iowa, to visit our grandparents, Julius and Urbanie DeBrower-Cornelis. There was a Sunday kermis at the farm with relatives and friends bringing food. The men played rolle bolle on two courts by the garden and the women played hoop bolle. One of the main Belgian foods was knoedals (Belgian dumplings), which is yeast bread dough with raisins that is dropped in boiling water. They were served in soup bowls with syrup or a homemade sweetened milk sauce.

— **Art Holevoet, Atkinson, Illinois**

Top photo: That old gang of mine, outside Larson's confectionary and ice cream parlor, Rock Island. Carl Larson is in the apron.

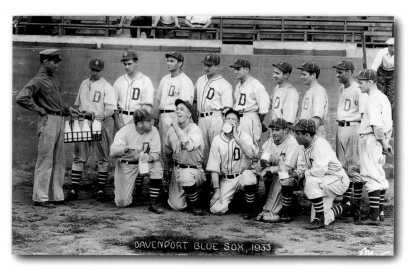

Young in business in 1939: House-to-house, kids peddle fruit in Clinton, Iowa. In the wagon are Carol Parker Dettner and Darrell Parker. Elaine Parker Shannon is selling to a little customer. The horse is Patches.

Customers came first

It was World War II, and any boy who looked old enough and strong enough could get a job. Harry's Army Store on Davenport's West Second Street was looking for help. I was in ninth grade, and it was just a month or so before Christmas. I was hired as a clerk and paid between 25 and 50 cents an hour.

Harry's taught that when anyone came into the store, you greeted them and offered to help them find what they wanted. You learned to sell everything in the store. You stayed with customers at all times, showing merchandise. When a sale was made, you carried the item for the customer until he or she quit buying, then you led the customer to the counter at the back of the store where an adult clerk collected payment and bagged the purchases. You then helped carry the purchases out the door, thanked the customer for their business and told them to come back again.

This experience served me well. I learned to talk to and listen well to all types of people from all walks of life. When Christmas arrived, I had money to buy some really nice gifts for the family, and some of them came from Harry's

You betcha these members of the 1933 Davenport Blue Sox baseball team were Iowana Milk drinkers. Or could they have been hoisting those bottles simply for the publicity photo?

All dressed and ready to go to work in the early 1940s; Kenneth Davis, who delivered telegrams for Western Union in Davenport.

DAVENPORT BLUE SOX, 1933

Army Store, using my employee discount.

The experience I had at Harry's opened the door for me to work at Radmachers Appliance and Music Store on East Second Street. I was a salesman in the record department, working from after school until close. Then I became the janitor, gathering trash, sweeping and mopping floors, and cleaning the restroom. My last act of the day was to roll up the awning and bring in the RCA Victor dog.

Saturday was a full day — I washed the store windows inside and out, no matter what the weather. I swept the sidewalk in front of the store and cleaned the gutter of debris. I put down the awning and set out the dog.

My wages were $5 a week, and I worked about three hours after school and all day Saturday. When summer came, the owner had me go to the Moline store to work. Every day, I rode my bike from West First and Pine streets over the Arsenal to Moline. The owner paid me an hourly rate of 50 cents — not bad for a kid. I was treated well, never like a kid, but as an important part of the workforce.

— **Robert G. Swanson, Davenport**

1932: a kite-flying contest at Credit Island Park, Davenport

Water fights in the stock tanks

When we were young, we always had a good time on the farm of my grandparents, Joe and Leonie Holevoet, who lived south of Atkinson, Illinois. During the Belgian Sunday get-togethers with relatives, the adults played rolle bolle and the children had a great time having water fights in the stock tanks. My grandmother taught me to write a letter in Flemish in 1940, when my sister was born.

— **Helen Foote-Holevoet, Geneseo, Illinois**

There were no sleepyheads at this 1948 Tri-Y slumber party attended by girls from Davenport High School.

The tragic night we grew up

I entered nurses training in 1948 at Mercy Hospital, Davenport. We were the first class to be affiliated with St. Ambrose and Marycrest colleges, and we received college credit while becoming nurses. There were only 12 girls in my class among a whole college of boys at St. Ambrose. It was great.

One night we were awakened by smoke and screaming. St. Elizabeth's, a mental health facility behind Mercy, was on fire. Many of the patients were trapped by bars on windows and locked doors.

We cared for the burned and transported the dead. Our classrooms became a morgue. I think we grew up that tragic night, for to this day I'll never forget that horrible scene.

— Pat Early, Davenport

A top-hatted young man roamed the streets of Rock Island in 1940 to advertise the film, "It's a Date" starring Deanna Durbin.

Student nurses at Mercy Hospital await a call to duty at the St. Elizabeth's disaster.

"Born on a mountain top in Tennessee, greenest state in the land of the free." Kids wore coonskin caps in the 1950s, popularized by the TV series "Davy Crockett" starring Fess Parker, one of the first television shows to spawn a movie.

Happy summers and 'Hit Parade'

We lived a big stucco house on Eastern Avenue and Locust Street in Davenport, behind Holy Cross Lutheran Church. We raised chickens and had cherry, apple, peach and walnut trees, grapevines and wild flowers. Our yard was big enough for a baseball diamond plus a croquet set, so it was always full of kids.

One of my favorite things to do was to rent a bicycle from the Standard service station at Locust and Bridge Avenue. For 25 cents, I could have the bicycle for exactly one hour. I made sure I got it back right on time.

During the hot summers, we would walk barefoot to Vander Veer Park carrying our swimsuits wrapped in a towel. We would spend the entire day at the pool. In the evenings, the family took a ride in our 1934 Plymouth, ending up at the levee where we cooled off by putting our bare feet in the river. Before heading home, we all got ice cream cones from the tiny concession stand.

Saturday evenings were spent playing jacks or board games with my older brother and younger sister. Mother would shampoo

Founded during the Great Depression, Bussell's Beauty School was in the Security Building, downtown Davenport. A sign on the wall says, "We Accept No Responsibility for Error In Student Work."

Everyone was snapping pictures when they were young. In 1930, Inez Jane Beckmann of Rock Island with her new box camera.

Leading cheers in 1953 for St. Vincent Laboratory School, Davenport, were, from left, Josephine Miszkiewicz, Judy Korte, JoAnn McGrath, Lynne Shields and Phyllis Deters. The squad won a blue ribbon for their cheers, judged best among Quad-City parochial schools at the Mississippi Valley Junior Tournament.

our hair and set our curls in rags to be ready for church on Sunday. She then would go to the cupboard and bring down a large bag of chocolate candy she had purchased at Woolworth's. We listened to the "Hit Parade" on the radio, tried to pick the Number One tune of the week, then went to bed.

One of the happiest days was when World War II ended and everyone got in their cars to go downtown where horns were blaring and confetti was dropping from the sky. The saddest day was when President Roosevelt passed away, and my mother cried as if he were a member of our family.

— **Joy Andrews, Davenport**

Aunt Lola's paper dolls

My Dad and Mom used to say, "You are just like Lola Mae." I always wondered in what way I was like her. Aunt Lola was my Mom's sister; she lived in Louisiana with my grandmother. My mother said that Lola would always be a child.

I watched Lola from across the room one summer as she rocked from front to back. She was about 40 years old, and had thick, black hair in two matching corn row braids.

As I sat with Lola, I decided an investigation was in order. I watched as she smacked her lips

Like paper dolls, turkey notes were kid-fun, but the boys got involved, too. Turkey notes were indigenous to Davenport.

Rosie the Riveters, all roommates during World War II. They've caught live chickens (which they were allowed to keep) in a contest on Labor Day, 1943, Mississippi Valley Fairgrounds, Davenport. From left, Wanda Henning Rathje, Alice Elam and Amy Peckinschneider Bahns.

The "in kids" had their own skates and cases in the mid-1950s. Carolyn Wiese of Eldridge, Iowa, lined her skate case with names of tunes of the day — "Jailhouse Rock" and "White Sport Coat."

Charley Witt, a Davenport police officer and official Santa Claus for Davenport, arriving from the North Pole by seaplane.

The police officer who played Santa

With a ho-ho-ho, Charley Witt, a Davenport police officer, was the ultimate Santa Claus. The portly Witt looked the part. All he needed was a beard, carefully made of combed yak hair. Once, he arrived by seaplane on the Davenport levee; another time, he packed Davenport Municipal Stadium (now John O'Donnell) with thousands of kids and parents. This Santa was everywhere during the holiday season, from pediatrics wards to nursing homes.

tight together, then protruded them out from her caramel face. She was a medium-sized woman, with average features and small, delicate hands.

I looked at my hands, then took the mirror off the table and held it to my face. I saw no resemblance between Lola and me. I said aloud, knowing she would not answer, "How am I like you?"

I looked at Lola's hands. She was tearing strips of folded pages of newspaper. She hummed, her face opened up, and a huge body-shaking laugh came from deep down inside. She appeared not to be watching what she was doing; she didn't seem to know I was present. She kept humming, rocking and occasionally laughing and tearing randomly at the paper. I looked at her face and saw pure joy. She rose to her feet and came toward me. In her hands, she held a chorus line of perfect paper dolls, clothed in newspaper print. She smiled at me, and pushed the dolls into my hand. I looked at the dancing dolls and knew that not one tear to create them had been done at random.

I would like to think that Lola was sending a message that my love of art and creativity had, somehow, been passed from her to me. Somewhere deep inside me, a laugh shook my body from my head to my toes, and my eyes left Aunt Lola's face as I accepted a simple gift of pleasure given by a woman who always would be a child. In her laughing face and simple gift, I found the answer to my long unanswered question. In her deep laugh, I found myself.

— Johnnie M. Colvin, Rock Island

Girls of every generation enjoy playing with dolls, and in 1933 that certainly was true as Nancy Traver and her kewpie doll received a stroller ride from Jean Gailbraith. Nancy Schmidt recalls that her family's rural Clinton County farmyard was a wonderful place to play.

Land of opportunity

I came to Rock Island in 1949. Like many other veterans, I was looking for work in the Quad-Cities. John Deere, Farmall, Case, Caterpillar and the many shops and foundries that served the area provided a great opportunity for a young man.

One of my earliest and fondest memories was the beautiful Belgian neighborhoods of the West End. The area around Ninth Street and Seventh Avenue was like a little downtown. The Rialto Theater was a nice family theater.

The thing I remember the most was how neat and clean the Belgians kept the neighborhood. The little rows of

Cupid's day: Old Valentines from the 1930s; most could be contemporary in the year 2000.

The annual parade of student-made Easter hats at Johnson School, Davenport, was quite an extravaganza. In 1965, winners included Teresa Nelson, fourth from left, and Vicki Nelson, sixth from left, daughters of Doris and Robert Nelson.

houses with white picket fences all had flowers planted along the sidewalks. The Belgian ladies would hose down the sidewalks in the late afternoon and sweep them clean with straw brooms.

— **Paul D. Booker, Rock Island**

Where things were

I am not at all sure how much of my recollections of growing up in Rock Island are reliable, but as I've tried to sort through the various events and people all these years later, I've returned again and again to matters of geography, to the shape of things, the territorial boundaries that seem to have defined my life in those days.

More even than the rivers, Eleventh Street seems to be the definitive line in my past. Prior to 1963, my family lived at three different locations below Eleventh — the first two below Ninth Street — and from the very start I recognized that Eleventh Street marked a boundary of incalculable significance, one to be crossed only with more years and experience and, even then, cautiously. My elementary and junior high schools were on our side of Eleventh; Ninth Street, with less traffic and mom and pop stores, provided my early training.

In fourth grade (my first in Rock Island) and new to life in anything larger than a small town, I found Ninth exciting enough to cross. We lived on Twenty-fifth Avenue, just a few doors away from where the houses ended and the flood plain began. Buildings were scattered and traffic was light. By contrast, Ninth Street separated two unbroken lines of homes facing each other across the bricks. This was my early notion of a city street. Eleventh was still far away and unthinkable.

But every year brought Eleventh closer. As I grew in size and confidence, Ninth shrank to something closer to its actual proportions, became a quiet side street, a back-

A potpourri from one young life: Charm bracelets and spirit buttons, junior high letters and class rings and "Jonathan Livingston Seagull."

Bob Balzer's ID card when he ran the Davenport Draught House, a place for fun for the young from 1965 to 1970. Draught House took over after Pronger's Restaurant closed the lower level of the building, which now is The Dock.

water, and I forgot that it had ever been sufficiently frightening to require a crossing guard to get me over it. By the time I left Frances Willard School to enter Franklin Junior High — now biking back and forth — Ninth was child's play. But I still did not often or comfortably cross Eleventh. This reluctance had much to do with the fact that things got bigger and busier on that street. It had more lanes, more cars and trucks, and everything moved faster there. If Ninth was a kind of creek, Eleventh was a river, one with a swifter, less predictable current.

In those earliest years, streets had been barriers, but later I became more interested in their length and the larger world to which they might connect me. Eleventh went downtown in one direction and out of town in the other. It represented a way in and a way out. By the time I got to junior high, these possibilities were increasingly on my mind as I rode city buses to the Fort and Rocket for movies and began to consider where beyond Rock Island things might lead.

When I started high school, I crossed Eleventh and came to take it, too, for granted. Still I never lost a sense that there was something different on the other side, a Rock Island not really mine. The neighborhoods that rose above ours on the uphill side of that street, in my thinking, stood apart from ours, and those who lived over there were

It Takes a Village

We took sunshine showers during the summers
in my neighborhood
skipping and jumping
twirling round and round until we dropped
and hugged ourselves,
getting lost in all that laughter
and carefree day tripping,
feeling lucky to be alive in a place
where everyone knew our names.

The ice cream man peddled his product
from a bicycle with a freezer
in the front,
We bought popsicles to cool us down
if we had the nickels,
sucking and savoring until the drops
of colored sugar ran down between our fingers
mingling with the dirt there
and we licked that too.

The rag man pushed an old cart
slowly through the street
calling for scraps of cloth.
Though we mocked him secretly,
he was a major player,
an entrepreneur known by our parents
who waved and called him by name
as they stood behind the screen door
or worked from the clothes line.

Old Mrs. Robinson stood spying
from her window,

ready to check us when we dared to
climb her tree or run through her yard,
but she forgave us and often shared ice water,
cookies, and stories of herself
as a young woman, still in love
with her husband who had passed.
We ran errands for her and shared
our precious moments
when her loneliness slowed us down
every now and then.

We chased grasshoppers as a ritual,
stacked them in jars and punched holes
in the lids so they could live
until we placed them in garbage cans
and fried them.
The tobacco juice they left amazed us.
At night, lightning bugs supplied homemade rings
for our fingers full of dust now and ready
for a bath.

We sold popcorn and Kool-Aid for pennies,
played hand games,
Red Rover, kick ball, baseball,
hide go seek,
practiced the latest dance steps
as we sang
the latest songs,
and took sunshine showers all day
beneath the familiar eyes of our sky,
surrounded by love in a place
where everyone knew our names.

— **Shellie Moore Guy, Rock Island**

separated from us by more than four lanes of traffic.

In the '60s, my family moved across town, nearly to Moline — a long way from Eleventh Street as I remember it.

— **Wayne D. Fields, St. Louis**

What I learned from my friend, Chris

"The present is the past rolled up for action, and the past is the present unrolled for understanding."

— Will and Ariel Durant

Often we look back to see what brought us to the present, or where we are heading in the future. Other times we remember in order to commemorate people who have taught us lifelong lessons, immersing ourselves in memories that have molded us like potter's clay. For me that means reminiscing about the experiences I've had and the people I've met while growing up in the Quad-Cities:

My neighbor, Chris Berg, would run with me to the bus stop. We had to get there early enough to meet our friends. Kent was the zaniest of the bunch. He once climbed a tree and wouldn't get down because he had allowed a goal to be scored against us in a soccer game. We'd also meet Jeff, Brian, Kerri, Jay and Ryan and others to squeeze in a game of touch football before catching that dreaded bus to Mark Twain School.

Not that school was bad, but a 21-21 tie was a shame to everyone. No one wanted to leave a tie game forever etched in the Tanglefoot Terrace/Denniston Avenue annals. Chris was an especially serious competitor, as we all were. Last-second touchdowns would cause the strongest among us to burst into immediate frustration or jubilation.

As we got older and middle school became our new stomping ground, Chris no longer could play football. He developed a rare disease called Franconi's Anemia which left him short of breath and bedridden. His mother asked me to help. Ironically, she couldn't take care of Chris all the

Rock Island's annual Lantern Parade wrapped up the parks department's summer program and filled the high school stadium as families and friends crowded in on a sultry evening to watch children carry their colorful, candle-lit lanterns onto the infield. These were the winners in 1969. The parade took a hiatus until 1997 when it was revived and moved to Longview Park.

When the band began to play

Sissy Bloomberg, summer of '73

There are many moments that I recall fondly from growing up in the Quad-Cities. Some of my earliest memories lead me to the backyard of my home, right down the street from Rock Island High School.

I don't know if the tradition continues, but the high school band used to practice during the summer and fall by marching through the streets of my neighborhood.

Too young to be in school myself, I often would play outside on sunny days in the green grass of my backyard. I'll never forget the excitement I felt as I heard the whistle blow and the band begin to play. The excitement would mount as the band came closer. I could hardly keep my feet from following the band as it passed by and continued down the street.

As I got a few years older and was able to flee my backyard, my neighborhood pals and I would grab our batons, toy instruments or kitchen gadgets at the sound of the whistle and join the band. Marching alongside the horn and flute players and the drummers, I can remember twirling my baton and spinning cartwheels. We would continue through the streets with the band until the marchers turned off onto the high school grounds.

I giggle when I think of it now, but at the time I thought that if any talent scout could see me he surely would sign me up for something. What, exactly, I don't know.

We were always doing such goofy things. But what fun we had! Lots and lots of fun. The '70s was a fantastic, carefree time to grow up, especially in the streets of my beautiful Rock Island neighborhood.

I wish that my daughter and son could experience the freedom that our gang — my brother, John, our friends and I — had running through the streets and alleys of our awesome neighborhood and hear the joyous sounds of that marching band.

— **Kristine A. Jensen, Buffalo Grove, Illinois**

While Vicki Gray is high on most things connected to the '70s, even she admits the style of the dresses worn by her wedding attendants hasn't aged well. Vicki and her husband, DG, won the "honor" of having KSTT deejay Spike O'Dell, above, broadcast his morning radio show from their dining room.

The '70s get a bad rap

Retrospectives always focus on the very best and very worst of times, and when it comes to the '70s, it's the worst that grab the headlines. Public scandal — then a novelty — created a backlash of cynicism that pollutes our memories, making things seem even more hideous than they were: Pet rocks, WIN buttons, gas shortages, Watergate, pop psychology, earth shoes, "Gong Show," mood rings, platform shoes, Moonies, hot pants, shag carpet and the ubiquitous leisure suit.

Normally sensible women flocked to hair salons, hoping to be transformed into Farrah with odd bits of permed and streaked hair protruding here and there. Otherwise sane men, some pillars of the community, opted for porkchop sideburns and over-the-collar hair. Every guy, from your meter reader to your preacher, wanted to be big-haired like John Davidson or giant-haired like Richard Pryor.

Treasured wedding pictures from the '70s elicit giggles today. Take my own wedding album ... please. There we were, arrayed at the altar, looking for all the world like a casting call for "Love Boat." "Mom, how come nobody matches?" ask my teen-age daughters, eyeing the rainbow-hued ruffles of the groomsmen's shirts, carefully matched to the gingham pinafores worn by the bridesmaids. (Don't tell my kids, but our wedding invitations were purple.)

There was an unforgettable breakfast in 1978, when Spike O'Dell broadcast his morning radio show from our home as a "prize" for winning a contest. Ah, the low-tech wonders of a jerry-rigged system of wires, antennas, extension cords, three microphones and early touch-tone phone that linked us to the KSTT station on "Twinkie Boulevard." Today I need my glasses to recognize myself in photographs as the young woman in plaid bellbottoms, attacking Spike with an egg beater.

I don't know how history will judge those years, but to me they seem pretty bizarre.

Still, there is something endearing about the way we were. Maybe it is because, as today's kids are discovering as they rummage through attics and thrift shops in search of disco shirts and gaucho pants, there was a lot of decent stuff in the '70s. And because polyester decomposes so slowly, it's still here to enjoy. Long live the '70s.

— **Vicki Gray, Davenport**

Red platform shoes, part of Vicki's treasure trove from the '70s.

time because she was single and working as a visiting nurse.

My help consisted of going to Chris' house after school, sleeping over, and waking at 7 a.m. to go to school again. This continued for a year and a half. And remarkably Chris never changed a bit. He continued to earn the title I gave him, "the biggest smart-mouth I know." A day didn't go by where I'd wake up off the couch and tell Chris I was going to school and he'd reply, "Yeah, well get some brains while you're there." And I'd respond, "No, I'm going to wait for you to catch up." He'd laugh.

Our neighbor buddy, Jeff Katz decided we should change our Friday night routine of movies and pizza. We would bring our new friends, Steve, Bill, Jared and Dave (another group of rowdies) to meet Chris, maybe hold a few parties. Mrs. Berg never said anything about it. And we always believed she gave us her silent approval.

On one night, I recall watching the Tyson/Douglas fight at his house. The room of people (all Chris' new friends) jumping to their feet, yelling, amid a fury of Buster's fast fists sending Tyson to the canvas. The living room was buzzing, the TV announcers were fast and frantic. Flashbulbs went off like fireflies among the Tokyo crowd. But most memorably, Chris was arguing with my friend David about how Tyson was a "sissy" and needed to lose. Like an epiphany, I thought I'd never seen anything so wonderful as those two guys arguing in that small room. I watched them and realized, at that moment, those parties made Chris feel just like everyone else. It made me proud to be there. Especially proud of how my friends were people I could truly admire.

Chris lived three years longer than expected and I'd like to think we played a small role. He taught us an enormous amount about responsibility, dignity, community and friendship. And he taught us to take advantage of everything the world has to offer. Our group of friends have become graduate students, city administrators, writers, bookstore managers, and much more. And I'd like to think Chris played a small role in that too. We learned what it meant to truly "grow up." I look back on those days in the Quad-Cities and smile, knowing we're taking the lessons learned then into the future with us.

— David Robbins, Bettendorf

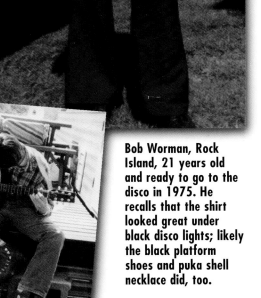

Bob Worman, Rock Island, 21 years old and ready to go to the disco in 1975. He recalls that the shirt looked great under black disco lights; likely the black platform shoes and puka shell necklace did, too.

When we were young in the '70s, everyone wanted to play the guitar, and Richard Brown moved his 1979 practice session into the great outdoors.

That's 8-year-old Joe Larson sitting among the performers at the 1972 Labor Day Indian Powwow at Black Hawk State Park, Rock Island. The annual shows brought descendants of Black Hawk back to the site where their village, Saukenauk, had stood. It also gave youngsters a look at the first residents of the area that became the Quad-Cities.

The scents of time

Science tells us the sense of smell is most closely linked to memory. It is for me, anyway. Having grown up where Davenport's breezes congregate, carrying the scents of a city's industry, my past dwells in scratch-n-sniff synapses.

From my bedroom at Sixth and Division streets I could, for instance, know what was cooking at the Ralston Purina plant. The damp, grain-laden clouds would billow in, conjuring pictures of mammoth freighters piled high with Puppy Chow. When the air seemed more primal, I imagined Monkey Chow was the kibble du jour. My brother, who is five years older, told me Ralston Purina made a Chow for every species and I believed him. Wildebeest Chow, Beluga Chow, Silverfish Chow; you name it, he said, they make it. Maybe they do, I don't know. But I do know you seldom see Dromedary Chow, even in the largest pet stores, so I suspect they were turning out more plain dog food than I was led to believe. It's that way with a lot of things my brother told me.

On other days the yeasty bouquet of the Wonder Bread bakery wound its way around town, cartoon-style, with a doughy, four-fingered hand at the end to tap us on the shoulder before swaddling us in its golden perfume. "Empty calories," my mom, who worked in a health food store, would warn us. But how could a calorie be empty that was steeped so full of gooey, bleached-white redolence?

The stabbing musk of death from the Oscar Mayer slaughterhouse brought everything back into harsh focus. My dad's uniform reeked of bloodletting days after his shift, and he was just a security guard a block away from the killing floor. The in-between smell — no longer hog, not yet bacon — was a stark reminder that all that lives dies and of the promise of redemption in the afterlife, even in the form of boiled ham.

My clearest memories, though, are of when these distinctively flavored winds would swirl together, mostly because of the unsettling pictures they painted. Like when the pungent front from Fejervary Park's Mother Goose Land accosted the syrupy tang from the Brach's candy factory, evoking bizarre confections: Giraffy Taffy, Llemon'n'Llama Drops and Goat Brittle.

Ah, the Brach's factory. Life is full of possibility for a kid whose neighborhood smells of licorice.

When I was 16, I would ride my bike toward the sweet promise of the candy plant to my girlfriend's house, where other fragrances took over: Love's Baby Soft, Aqua Velva and suntanned skin. I loved her first and best and thought we would be together forever, but she had another idea. (The fact that I love her today confirms that years of therapy await me.)

After an entire summer listening to a Roy Orbison album, I felt better, but never quite as trusting. Today, all I remember are the scents of a time — and a place — that won't be back. Most days that's enough.

— Chris Neely, Corpus Christi, Texas

As the first nephew in a family where six aunts and uncles were eager to fulfill his every wish, Doug Averill didn't need Santa Claus to deliver his most-favorite toy, a Stretch Armstrong doll, in 1976. Poor Stretch; the following summer, he was left out in the sun, sustained a puncture wound and bled red gel all over the driveway.

Max Collins of Muscatine, Iowa, authored these four comic books, "Wild Dog," based entirely on the Quad-Cities.

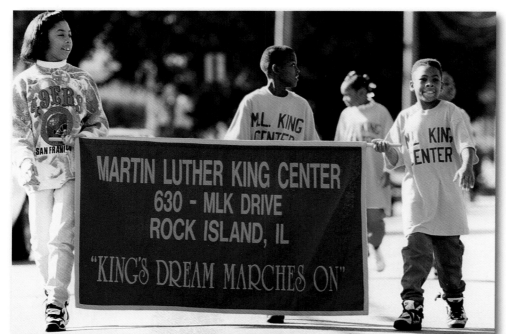

In 1993, young people from the Martin Luther King Center carried the banner during a parade that opened Family Fun Day at the neighborhood center in Rock Island.

Princess Iowana: Cult figure

Royalty reigned, with braids and boots and a feather in the headband. Long live the princess ... er, princesses. Because there was more than one Princess Iowana.

Princess Iowana was the clever promotional thought up by Iowana Dairy Farms, Bettendorf, one of the major Quad-City dairies. There were several Princesses Iowana, every one of them an instant success, greeted with hoops and hollers by kids from the late 1950s until 1972. Wearing Indian garb, she appeared at supermarkets, on television, anywhere that kids might gather with their Io-Wampum or to get free feathered headbands. She became such a cult figure that high school and college skits parodied her.

Io-Wampum was like scrip, or play money of sorts, something kids collected to redeem for toys or gimmicky things. Io-Wampum was printed on the sides of Iowana dairy product cartons, or on the cardboard top from glass bottles of Iowana milk, cream or half-and-half.

One of the first Princesses Iowana was Kay Duyvejonck Whan, Rock Island, who reigned in 1957 and 1958.

"I appeared at so many places as Princess Iowana," she remembers. "Supermarkets, everywhere. On Saturday mornings, I was on a half-hour children's show on WHBF-TV. Milt Boyd, 'Trader Milt,' did the auctioning of prizes for Io-Wampum and I did commercials for Iowana products and assisted Milt. We performed at childrens shows at the Fort and Capitol theaters, too. Kids brought huge boxes of Io-Wampum, which was carefully counted by Iowana employees."

Jerri Daebelliehn of Tipton, Iowa, was recruited as Princess Iowana in 1962, and still treasures her jet-colored real-human-hair wig and braids and her picture on milk cartons.

"I was 19, had lunch with four executives of Iowana at the old Plantation. I poured on the charm and they unanimously chose me to be the new Princess Iowana," Jerri says. "I worked grocery stores, parades, trade shows around the Midwest. They even made a TV commercial of me running through the woods at Prospect Park, Moline — after milk or ice cream, I suppose. They paid me extra for commercials, $125. One was shown during the Super Bowl."

Jerri took time off to have two children, and returned to the suede tunic as Princess Iowana in 1970.

"By then, the outfit had changed, updating my old image as the princess in a long white felt fringed Indian dress to a princess in a mini and knee-high suede boots."

Kay Duyvejonck Whan as Princess Iowana with "Trader Milt" Boyd.

Jerri Daebelliehn, another Princess Iowana.

Timeline, 1966: Arrival of the miniskirt

Hemlines have gone up and down, down and up over the past 100 years, but never was there a stir like the day the miniskirt arrived in the Quad-Cities.

These photos are from a May 8, 1966, page in what was then the *Times-Democrat*. The premise was simple. A local model was gussied up in a dress with a short, short hemline and sent to stand and walk along a downtown Davenport street. Oh, one other instruction: She was told not to speak to anyone, to let her dress do the talking.

As the newspaper story explained it: "Just how is the average Quad-Citian going to take to the new four-inch-above-the-knee skirts? When they begin to appear on the streets, will they attract much attention? To find out, the *Sunday Times-Democrat* had a young woman model in an outfit (taken from stock at Arnold's) stand on a busy downtown Davenport street corner. She strolled back and forth, while a newspaper photographer photographed the results with a telephoto lens from a vantage point a half-block away. Did the short skirt stop traffic? Judge for yourself as you study expressions on the faces of the people who passed."

(The model, Nancy Owen Fabricius Moore, now lives in Phoenix, Arizona. And yes, she has held on to these photos for 33 years.)

"Time flies, we say, ah no. Time stays, we go."

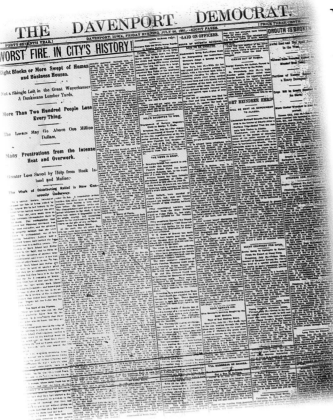

July 2, 1901

When Davenport went up in flames

By a narrow margin Davenport escaped the fate of being visited by the largest fire in her history in the midst of the hottest weather she ever saw. That she owes many lives to this fortunate circumstance there is no doubt. The conflagration that visited her Thursday afternoon was the most extensive, and the greatest in property damage, that she ever knew. It extinguished one of her leading industries, burned half a hundred homes, and carried the loss figures close to a million dollars. The firemen of Rock Island and Moline joined in the fight, and to them directly the salvation of another large establishment, and scores, if not hundreds of other homes, is due.

There are none who can say they know positively how the fire started. It is very likely that there are some who do know, but they are not telling.

The initial point was on the edge of the rattlings revetment on which the Rock Island Fuel company carried a large stock of dry kindling wood on the south side of East River street between the foot of Fourth street and the Riverside mill, and nearer the latter.

March 27, 1912

Riot in Rock Island's Market Square

The streets of Rock Island were reeking with bloodshed last night. One of the worst mob riots in the history of that turbulent city took place. As a result, Frank H. Kellogg, aged 36 years, Davenport, was killed outright and Raymond Swingle, Rock Island, lies in St. Anthony's hospital in critical condition. It is reported he will die. A dozen others were more or less seriously injured.

It was a clash between the police and the lawless element of that city. The police were driven off the streets, assaulted and mobbed and sought refuge in the police station. Here the mob followed them and after firing brickbats and other missiles with a number of shots into the station, the police opened fire and repulsed the mob.

The disorder developed much as it did Monday night as a sequel to a so-called political meeting on Market Square.

Aroused by the excitement of the night before, some crowds gathered to hear the talks and witness the events of the evening. Few of those in the crowd, it is safe to say, anticipated that bloodshed would be the outcome of the evening. Few probably looked for the ugly attack made upon the city hall or the attempted raid upon the Rock Island Hardware company's stock of weapons and ammunition. Few could have foreseen the development of a situation so grave that armed troops were deemed necessary to preserve order and protect property.

Newspapers have a great advantage over television. They have headlines, a sense of permancy that cannot be erased by a flick of the remote control button. Behold our past, brought to you daily in a neat package of triumphs and tragedies. In this, "A Time We Remember," a sampling of some of the memorable Quad-City Times *and* Democrat & Leader *front pages of the past century, and the words of the lead stories that unfolded in print before your eyes ...*

chapter twenty-four

Pages From Our Past

November 20, 1928

When the Tri-Cities went dry

Some 4,185 pint bottles of home-brew beer were seized in a raid on the East Davenport Turner Hall at 11 o'clock this morning. Federal Prohibition Officer Roy E. Muhs and Police Officers William P. Hennelly, George Rogers and Reed Phillips conducted the raid. With the assistance of several other police officers they immediately set to work to dump the illicit liquor in the sewer.

In addition to the beer, which was stored away in a room in the basement adjacent to the bar, 90 gallons of mash, some 15 big crocks, 50 cans of malt, beer cases, cappers and other beer making equipment was seized by the officers.

It is reported that the beer has been sold at the East Davenport Turner Hall for 15 cents a bottle for several years. Sandwiches also were served and there were tables for cards. The basement, in fact, was a typical "rathskeller."

January 8, 1950

Tragedy — and mystery

City and state fire authorities admitted late Saturday they are stymied in determining the cause of the disastrous fire which snuffed out the lives of at least 38 women in a mental ward at Mercy hospital.

A total of 37 bodies had actually been recovered from the ruins by nightfall while the last known victim died of shock a short time later in a hospital bed.

Authorities said they believe the debris contains bodies of two listed as missing, but added that the intensity of the flames may have fully consumed them.

In the presence of two deputy state fire marshals, Chief Lester Schick said, following a joint, preliminary investigation of the blaze that "I doubt if we ever will learn the cause."

In their early probe, Schick and the deputies looked over the debris and sought all the information they could get. They said they planned to talk to surviving patients and hospital officials today but admitted the hopelessness of the task.

"Because we will be questioning mostly mental patients," Schick pointed out, "the validity of their testimony will be extremely doubtful."

The destroyed building, erected more than 70 years ago, was more commonly known as St. Elizabeth's and is one of two buildings on the hospital grounds housing mental patients.

December 17, 1950

After 107 days, a 15-cent pay hike

Deere & Co. and the United Auto Workers union (CIO) have reached a settlement in contract negotiations which started on September 1, when seven Iowa and Illinois Deere plants went out on strike.

"Deere & Co. and the UAW have agreed," F.L. Sheridan, U.S. conciliator, told newsmen shortly before 8 p.m. Saturday as he emerged from the conference table at the LeClaire Hotel in Moline.

The agreement, which calls for an immediate 15 cents an hour general wage increase, was signed by Pat Greathouse, UAW regional director, and Ralph Clifford, labor relations representative of Deere & Co.

Thus ended the 107 day strike.

May 23, 1975

Disaster on the riverfront

At least one person was killed, seven were injured and others feared trapped after an explosion shortly after noon today at the International Multifoods Corp. grain and flour mill complex at 803 East River Drive, Davenport.

At least three persons were unaccounted for, and officials said a second explosion was feared.

Rescue efforts and a search for more victims continued this afternoon.

Davenport fire fighters found that their ladders were not long enough to reach one blast victim on a roof at the complex, and a military helicopter was called in to assist in the rescue.

A second man also was reported trapped on the roof, but an aerial rescue reportedly was being delayed because of the feared second blast.

"It'll take us ages to get through the debris," Scott County Sheriff Kenneth Paulsen said of the search for other possible victims.

November 21, 1984

The most bizarre murder case in Quad-City history

SIOUX CITY, Iowa — Nineteen months after authorities fished a torso out of the Mississippi River, a jury convicted Davenport chiropractor James Klindt of second-degree murder in his wife's death and chain saw mutilation.

The verdict, which came after 15 hours of deliberation over two days by a Woodbury County District Court jury, added another chapter to this strange tale — surely the most bizarre murder case in Quad-City history.

Klindt faces a 50-year term.

But it certainly isn't the final chapter because there will be appeals and many other facets yet to be resolved in the case of Joyce Klindt's death.

When the verdict was announced Klindt quickly ducked his head low between his legs and just as quickly thrust it back up, a strained and almost quizzical look on his face. The judge dismissed the jury, but Klindt just sat there, perfectly erect as always, looking too large for the chair that he was sitting in, his brow slightly furrowed, his stare distant.

It was the same expression he wore throughout much of the testimony in the trial by witnesses who the prosecution said showed that Klindt had killed his wife on March 18, 1983, cut up her body with a chain saw, and then drove his air boat out on the Mississippi River in sloughs north of Princeton and dumped the pieces.

December 1, 1986

'Guys like Cary Grant are supposed to live forever'

Cary Grant's sudden death in Davenport brought tears from here to Hollywood and around the world Sunday, as fans and friends mourned the passing of the 82-year-old movie legend.

Grant was stricken before his scheduled performance at Davenport's Adler Theatre. He kept apologizing to his Quad-City hosts, and his last words may have been, "I'm sorry that I can't go on."

He was taken from the Blackhawk Hotel to St. Luke's Hospital about 9:15 p.m. Saturday, and was pronounced dead at 11:22 p.m. of a massive stroke.

Davenport cardiologist James Gilson, who tried to save the famous actor, summed up the mood: "Guys like Cary Grant are supposed to live forever."

Grant's death was the talk of the town, and Quad-Citians paid their respects in different ways: Preachers prayed for Grant from the pulpit Sunday morning, while fans of Grant's movies were renting them by the dozen during the afternoon.

Quad-Citians had been eagerly awaiting "A Conversation with Cary Grant," the gala centerpiece of the Festival of Trees celebration at Davenport's River Center.

And Grant had been eager to perform here. He had never appeared in Davenport, and he was especially looking forward to seeing the renovated Adler.

Grant was charming and witty during his last appearance on stage — a rehearsal at the Adler Saturday afternoon. He tested microphones and moved his stage stool, making sure everything was just right. But it soon was clear that things were terribly wrong.

April 2, 1991

'It's not Las Vegas. It's not Atlantic City. It's something ... better'

Riverboat gambling opened a new chapter in Quad-City history amid tumbling dice and the ching-ching-ching of slot machines. The two Quad-City floating casinos plied the mighty Mississippi eight times, carrying thousands of passengers and holding live celebrations on national television.

On shore, ceremonies included fireworks, horse-drawn carriages for the day's celebrities, marching bands and other live music, balloon launches, Mark Twains and more hoopla than the Quad-Cities has seen in ages.

Bernard Goldstein's Diamond Lady could be seen all day churning the waters between her Bettendorf port at Leach Park and Lock and Dam 15 in Davenport.

She made four cruises, beginning at a cool, crisp 7:30 a.m. and ending with a midnight cruise under a canopy of stars.

John Connelly's President Riverboat Casino was confined to the river between Davenport and Rock Island because high water kept it from going beneath the Centennial Bridge.

But the confinement didn't limit the passengers' fun as the big riverboat tooled around the pool on four cruises.

Longtime backers of the concept felt ecstatic, vindicated and hopeful that Monday was merely a harbinger of days to come. They were like kids in a candy store.

Bud Pike, chairman of the Iowa Racing and Gaming Commission, said the riverboat gambling license "may be as important to Davenport as the Bill of Rights and the Magna Carta."

Bernard Goldstein said: "It's not Las Vegas. It's not Atlantic City. It's something that is, I think, better."

Vince Lindstrom, executive director of the Quad-City Convention and Visitors Bureau, said: "Riverboat gambling is finally here. It's OK to open our presents."

May 29, 1993

A 20-year dream fulfilled

A collage of light, music and fulfilled dreams marked the premier performance at The Mark of the Quad-Cities. Neil Diamond — the Brooklyn dreamer — shared his tales of love lost and found and dreams fulfilled. But the thousands of Quad-Citians looking on watched a decades-old community dream realized.

After more than 20 years of political wrangling, years of construction, thousands of tons of concrete poured and tens of millions of dollars spent — the Quad-Cities has a civic center.

And it works. The night went off without any apparent glitches. Even the anticipated parking woes and traffic jams never materialized.

"It doesn't matter that this is in Moline or that this is Illinois. It's in the Quad-Cities. That's what matters," Scott County Attorney Bill Davis said as he and his wife ambled toward the 12,000-seat arena. "It's something for both Iowans and Illinoisians to be proud of."